D0930230

THE GOVERNANCE of COLLEGES and UNIVERSITIES

THE CARNEGIE SERIES
IN AMERICAN EDUCATION

The books in this series have resulted from studies made under grants from the Carnegie Corporation of New York and, occasionally, studies supported by The Carnegie Foundation for the Advancement of Teaching. These books are published by McGraw-Hill in recognition of their importance to the future of American education.

The Corporation, a philanthropic foundation established in 1911 by Andrew Carnegie for the advancement and diffusion of knowledge and understanding, has a continuing interest in the improvement of American education. It financed the studies in this series to provide facts and recommendations which would be useful to all those who make or influence the decisions which shape American educational policies and institutions.

The statements made and views expressed in these books are solely the responsibility of the authors.

LB2341
.C77
1975

THE GOVERNANCE of COLLEGES and UNIVERSITIES
MODERNIZING STRUCTURE AND PROCESSES

Revised Edition

John J. Corson

McGraw-Hill Book Company
New York   St. Louis   San Francisco
Düsseldorf   London   Mexico   Sydney   Toronto

LIBRARY
FLORIDA KEYS COMMUNITY COLLEGE
Stock Island
Key West; Florida 33040

24565

Copyright © 1960 and 1975 by McGraw-Hill, Inc.
All rights reserved. Printed in the United States of
America. No part of this publication may be reproduced,
stored in a retrieval system, or transmitted, in any form
or by any means, electronic, mechanical, photocopying,
recording or otherwise, without the prior written
permission of the publisher.

Library of Congress Cataloging in Publication Data
Corson, John Jay, 1905-
    The governance of colleges and universities.
    (The Carnegie series in American education)
    Includes index.
    1.   Universities and colleges—Administration.
I. Title. II. Series.
LB2341.C77 1975   378.1   75-1200
ISBN 0-07-013205-4

1234567890BPBP798765

The editors for this book were Thomas H. Quinn
and Cheryl Love, the designer was Elaine Gongora, and
the production supervisor was Milton Heiberg. It was
set in Life by Cherry Hill Composition.

Printed and bound by the Book Press.

TO MY WIFE
Who for over forty years has generously forgone
many pleasures and has spent many lonely
hours that I might complete one more article
or book that just had to be written.

CONTENTS

PREFACE

During the past decade, books and journal articles about higher education have literally flooded the presses. The Carnegie Commission on Higher Education has generated five score works since 1967 and has stimulated widespread discussion and a rash of articles in popular as well as professional journals. A new book publisher and two significant new journals—*Change* and *The Chronicle of Higher Education*—each specializing in higher education, have come into being.

In the face of this flood of publications, one who would impose on the higher education community still another book must justify the addition to his conscience (as well as to his publisher). He must point to a niche on the shelves that can be filled by one more book.

The niche that this book is to fill concerns the governance of the individual college or university as a whole institution. Numerous other books treat of the role and the financing of higher education in the American society, the environment in which the individual institution operates, particular functions it performs, and the changing roles and responsibilities of participants in the operation of institutions, e.g., alumni or trustees. This book is written to be of interest, and hopefully of value, to the trustee, the president, the dean, or the scholar who strives to understand the governance of the whole institution rather than its specific parts.

Before I became concerned with the governance of institutions of higher education, I had, of course, viewed one institution as both an undergraduate and a graduate student; I had served as a professor in four institutions, a department chairman in one, and a trustee of four; and I had been privileged to weigh complimentary invitations to serve as dean in two institutions and as president of others. But those experiences, spread over a quarter of a century, provided, at the most, a thin backdrop for assessing the problems of those who bear the responsibilities for the governance of this country's colleges and universities.

It was two good friends, John W. Gardner and James A. Perkins, then president and vice president of the Carnegie Corporation, who in 1958 challenged me to put what I had learned as a professional management consultant to work on the problems of colleges and universities. They stimulated me to study the functioning of a variety of institutions and to write the first edition of this book published in 1960. That their diagnosis of the need was apt, and that their counseling as to how to go about the study which resulted in this book was wise, is reflected by the generous acceptance this book has received from academic administrators, trustees, teachers and others, over the ensuing years.

In 1972, it was Alan Pifer, president of the Carnegie Corporation, who, recognizing clearly how changes in the educational scene had made the book produced in 1960 obsolete, encouraged me and provided generous financial support enabling me to attack the problems of academic governance again. My interest, whetted in 1958, had persisted and grown over the years. Between 1958 and 1974 I was privileged to serve forty institutions as a consultant on problems of governance, to serve as a professor for four years on one of this country's most distinguished university faculties, to serve continually for much of this time as a trustee of four institutions of quite diverse types, and to visit universities (and bother their administrators with questions about governance) in various sections of this country, in Mexico, in England, in Yugoslavia, and in East and West Africa. Thus, between 1972 and 1975, I drew on these experiences, on the flood of new books that had appeared, and on a continuing series of visits to institutions in this country to provide such understanding of governance in the changed context of the 1970s as this book now offers.

During the years 1972 and 1973, I was aided, in turn, by two able, enterprising, and consistently helpful ladies who have served me as research and editorial assistants. Mrs. Marta Erdman assembled a vast supply of materials on each successive aspect of the governance of higher education. When Mrs. Erdman moved from Washington upon her husband's retirement, I was exceedingly fortunate to obtain the assistance of Mrs. Thomas J. Shirhall, who like her predecessor, delved deeply into the research the writing of this book required.

In late 1973, the manuscript was subjected to the review and criticism of eight experienced academic administrators and scholars. Five educators read and criticized the whole manuscript: Howard R. Bowen, chancellor, Claremont University Center; Morris T. Keeton, provost, Antioch College; Lewis B. Mayhew professor of education, Stanford University; Kenneth Mortimer, associate professor of higher education, Pennsylvania State University; and Paul F. Sharp, president, University of Oklahoma. In addition, Fred Harcleroad, then president, the American College Testing Bureau; John Nason, a former president of two colleges; and Allen W. Ostar, executive director of the Association of State Colleges and Universities, each read and criticized one or more chapters. This book bears the imprint of the combined judgment of these informed men.

Some material presented in this revised edition appeared earlier in different form. I am, hence, indebted to James A. Perkins, who edited the volume entitled *The University as an Organization* (New York: McGraw-Hill Book Company, 1973), for permission to incorporate here in a revised form some material that appeared in Chapter 9 of that volume, and to the publisher of the *Educational Record* for permission to use material that appeared in its spring 1967 issue in an article entitled "If Not the University?" I hope the reader will find that this edition reflects a more considered treatment and expansion of ideas voiced earlier, and I accept full responsibility for any errors in fact or judgment that the reader might find in the pages that follow.

John J. Corson

THE
GOVERNANCE of
COLLEGES and
UNIVERSITIES

PART ONE

THE
CONTEXT

Change Demands Modernization

*No one knows how dinosaurs became extinct. We know
only that something changed, and dinosaurs did not.*

G. G. Simpson[1]

*There seems today to be a world-wide consensus that
the traditional system of higher education does not meet,
any longer, the educational needs of a more and more
rapidly changing society.*

Arnold Toynbee[2]

1 In 1957 it was written, "Our colleges and universities are expected
to perform something close to a miracle in the next ten to fifteen
years."[3] Looking back from 1974, it can be said that higher education performed several miracles: It provided enriched educational
opportunities for a rapidly increasing number of students, expanded
the body of organized knowledge, widened markedly the scope of its
services, and earned the dependence of various segments of the society.
Because of that dependence, it attracted greatly increased support, for,
over the years from 1957 to 1974, the funds made available for the
support of our colleges and universities grew from $6 billion to $22.5
billion annually.

During the more than two decades of growth and substantial accomplishment, this country's colleges and universities were generally
regarded as infallible, even sacrosanct. In the early 1970s, however, the
capabilities of the schools were being sharply challenged. From without,
some legislators, parents, employers, and the general public began to
notice higher education's decreasing ability to ensure employment,
upward mobility, and the prospect of better-than-average income.[4] The

---

[1] Cited in the preface to Alvin C. Eurich's *Campus 1980* (New York: Delacorte
Press, 1968).

[2] Ibid., p. xix.

[3] *Second Report to the President*, The President's Committee on Education
Beyond the High School, Washington, July 1957, p. 3.

[4] A central conclusion of a report by the Carnegie Commission on Higher Education, *Graduates and Jobs: Adjusting to a New Labor Market Situation*, was that
"the realistic problem for the 1970s will be the necessity for the absorption of
some college-educated persons into jobs which have not been filled by persons
with a college education. . . . Perhaps somewhere in the vicinity of 1 million
to 1½ million college-educated persons will face this frustrating experience"
(New York: McGraw-Hill Book Company, 1973, p. 4).

failure of enrollments in 1973–74 to match earlier predictions has been interpreted by some as skepticism about the purpose of higher education. Indeed some parents wondered whether "on balance, college education may be detrimental to the spiritual, mental and even physical well-being of their children."[5] Other critics—legislators and parents among them—questioned the ability of the college or university to manage its own affairs.

From within, faculty members voiced growing dissatisfaction with their status and in a small minority of all institutions (mostly community colleges) organized unions to enforce their demands for a greater voice in the governance of the institution, as well as for improved economic well-being. Simultaneously the students, after demonstrating their power to disrupt and even close a number of institutions during the years 1967–1970, were quiescent but remained aware of a new-found strength that could be exercised when circumstance stirred them. And a substantial proportion of all institutions, particularly some private colleges and universities, were confronted with declining enrollments and financial stringencies of varying degrees of gravity, and a few with surpluses of faculties and facilities.

CONSEQUENCES OF CHANGE

Perhaps this country's colleges and universities should have foreseen the major social changes that enveloped them,[6] but the problems they encountered in the early 1970s were largely not of their making. The four preceding decades had witnessed great change.[7] Demographic, social, economic, and technological change—continually accentuated by the threat or actuality of war—conditioned the evolution of the institutions of higher education, thrust new demands upon them, and wrought consequences that lessened the stature and the strength of many of these institutions.

The first consequence of this welter of change was the substantial

---

[5] John P. East, professor, East Carolina University, in *Universitas*, the newsletter of the University Professors for Academic Order, Inc., cited in *The Wall Street Journal*, Apr. 19, 1973.

[6] Morris Keeton, provost of Antioch College, contends that the colleges and universities were themselves so much of the culture that they did not on the whole want to make the needed changes in the priorities they accorded to activities and in the roles of participants. Personal letter to the author, Sept. 15, 1973.

[7] Oscar Handlin and Mary F. Handlin, *The American College and American Culture*, Carnegie Commission on Higher Education (New York: McGraw-Hill Book Company, 1970), p. 4. For a more graphic depiction of the magnitude and character of this change, see Alvin Toffler, *Future Shock* (New York: Random House, Inc., 1970), particularly Part I: "The Death of Permanence," pp. 10–44.

expansion and restructuring of the American system of higher education.

The root changes that gave rise to the substantial postwar expansion, and the structural changes it engendered, were the substantial increase in the youth population and in the economic well-being of this country and its families. Between 1939 and 1969, the population of college-going age, i.e., those from 16 to 24 years of age, grew by approximately 50 percent, and within the ensuing three years by another 10 percent. During these same years the aggregate of personal incomes in the United States increased thirteenfold. These factors, combined with a growing conviction, voiced as early as 1947, that all young people should be provided with an opportunity to continue their educations beyond high school, greatly increased the proportion of the upcoming population that enrolled.[8]

The substantiality of this increase is made precise by the following summary data:

	(in thousands)			
	1951–52	1961–62	1971–72	1973–74
Public and non-public school enrollment, grades 9–12*	6,596	10,769	15,000 (proj.)	15,276
Degree-credit enrollment†	2,116	3,891	8,188	8,520
Graduate enrollment‡	234	398	971 (est.)	1,123
Public institutions of higher education§ Enrollment	638	743	1,152	1,200
	719,440	2,352,000	6,060,000	6,389,000
Private institutions of higher Education Enrollment	1,221	1,357	1,474	1,520
	1,396,560	1,540,000	2,128,000	2,131,000

*Data for 1951–52 and 1961–62 from the National Center for Educational Statistics, *Digest of Educational Statistics,* 1970 (Washington: U.S. Office of Education, 1972, p. 27. Figure for 1973–74 from *Projections of Educational Statistics to 1983–84,* a manuscript to be published by the National Center for Educational Statistics in April 1975, Tables 3, 6, and 13.

† Op. cit., 1951–52 and 1961–62, 1st issue p. 73.9: 1973–74, Table 6, *Projections ... to 1983–84.*

‡ Op. cit., 1972, 1st issue, p. 73.34; 1973–74, *Projections ... to 1983–84,* Table 3.

§ Number of institutions (in actual figures rather than thousands) from ibid., 3d issue, 1972, p. 72.117. Data for 1961–62 are actually fall 1962 figures due to the change in U.S. Office of Education reporting methods; public and private enrollment figures for 1951–52 are derived from ibid., 3d issue, p. 72.117, and 1st issue, p. 73.9. Figures for 1961–62 and 1973–74 from *Projections ... to 1983–84,* manuscript, op. cit., and *Digest of Educational Statistics,* 1974.

---

[8] *Higher Education for American Democracy,* a report of the President's Commission on Higher Education (Washington: Government Printing Office, 1947).

These data as to gross enrollments do not reveal simultaneous changes in the makeup of student bodies. In the early 1970s significantly larger proportions of men and women twenty-one years of age and over, blacks and other minority-group members, and young people from relatively low-income families were enrolled than was the case prior to 1960–61. But by the fall of 1973 enrollments had become nearly static. As the following table indicates, the prospect was that during the 1970s and 1980s there would be little further increase in the number of students to be served—an overall increase of perhaps 3 million between 1970 and 1980 and a decline of about 1 million between 1980 and 1990.

OLD AND NEW ENROLLMENT PROJECTIONS, 1970–2000 (in thousands)

					Percentage Change		
Enrollment	1970*	1980	1990	2000	1970–80	1980–90	1990–2000
Projections made in 1971	8,649	13,015	12,654	16,559	+50.5%	−2.8%	+30.9%
Undergraduate	7,443	11,082	10,587	14,123	+48.9%	−4.5%	+33.4%
Graduate	1,206	1,933	2,068	2,436	+60.3%	+7.0%	+17.8%
Projections made in 1973	8,649	11,446	10,555	13,209	+32.3%	−7.8%	+25.1%
Graduate	1,206	1,726	1,673	1,988	+43.1%	−3.1%	+18.8%
Undergraduate	7,443	9,720	8,882	11,221	+30.6%	−8.6%	+26.3%

* Final figures.

SOURCE: Carnegie Commission on Higher Education.

This prospect of a declining demand came at a time when the number of institutions, their faculties, and their facilities had been increased to accommodate the large enrollments resulting from the growth of the 1950s and 1960s. The growth that had taken place is shown by the data in the table on page 7.

The most substantial increase in enrollments, and consequently in the number of institutions, was experienced in the two-year institutions, the area vocational schools in some states (Kansas, Minnesota, South Carolina), and more generally in the "community colleges." Many states have striven to create postsecondary institutions within commuting distance of most prospective students. The accessibility of these institutions and their varied college transfer, vocational, and technical curricula constituted additional factors spurring the growth in enrollments. Simultaneously, the newer and rapidly growing community colleges and the proprietary schools engaged in preparing students at

	1951–52	1961–62	1973–74
Number of universities, colleges, and community colleges[a]	1,889	2,100	2,720 est.
Number of faculty members[b]	184,826	312,687	620,000 est.
Average size of institutions in number of students[c]	1,120	1,855	3,500
Proportion of all institutions with more than 5,000 students (in percentages)[d]	5	9	18
Current fund expenditures (in billions of dollars)[e]	2.486	7.190	5,000
Capital outlay (in billions of dollars)[f]		1.714	30,000

[a] American Council on Education, *A Fact Book on Higher Education*, 3d issue, Washington, 1972, p. 72.117, and National Center for Educational Statistics, *Higher Education*, 1973–74.

[b] Figures for 1951–52 and 1961–62 from the National Center for Educational Statistics, *Digest of Educational Statistics, 1970* (Washington: U.S. Office of Education, 1972), p. 79; 1973–74 figures from *Projections . . . to 1983–84*, op. cit. Table 6.

[c] Derived from data as to degree credit enrollment and non-degree credit enrollment and number of institutions stated above.

[d] Ibid., 3d issue, 1972, p. 72.123.

[e] Alvin Renetsky, ed., *Yearbook of Higher Education, 1969* (Los Angeles, Calif., 1972); 1951–52 and 1961–62 data from p. 570; 1973–74 figure estimated, National Center for Educational Statistics.

[f] Ibid., p. 571 (1973–74 figure estimated, National Center for Educational Statistics).

the postsecondary level for positions in business and industry and in the semiprofessions forced some four-year colleges and universities, particularly those located in centers where the presence of several institutions made competition keen, to consider the necessity for substantial adjustments in curricula and educational approaches in order that institutions might better compete for what has become for many vitally needed tuition income.

The vast increase in the demand for higher education reflected by the foregoing data could not be met by the privately supported institutions that existed prior to World War II and the limited number that were established after 1945. Higher education, hence, became, in major part, a responsibility of the state governments. The watershed years were between 1940 and 1950. For the first time, in those years, half of all students enrolled in institutions of higher education in this country were enrolled in publicly supported colleges and universities. By 1970, 70 percent of all students were enrolled in public institutions; by 1980 it is forecast that they will enroll 77 percent. Moreover, as the number of public institutions and the annual cost borne by the state governments have grown, these schools have in most instances become units within statewide systems of higher education. As some private institutions (e.g., University of Buffalo, New York; University of Pittsburgh; and Temple University, Philadelphia) have found it difficult or impossible to meet expanding annual costs, these too have become units within statewide systems in varying fashion.

> *The second consequence for the college, and particularly the university, of the change that has transformed the American society was a magnification of the functions the institution was called upon to perform.*

Higher education is founded on the fundamental ideas that knowledge can be acquired through scholarly processes of inquiry; that knowledge, once acquired, can be expanded as it is organized and evolves as it is transmitted; and that knowledge acquired and transmitted attracts users and usage and thus benefits the society. Higher education, hence, and the institutions that transmit it, are instruments of the society that supports them.[9]

Such pragmatic, as well as fundamental, beliefs underlay the establishment of the land-grant college in 1862. They were clearly perceived by the founders of Cornell University, for example, when they strove to create an institution capable of not only instructing the young but also facilitating the application of knowledge to a variety of society's needs. Such tenets underlay the federal government's dependence during World War II and since (apparently declining in the 1970s) upon the universities to discover and apply the new knowledge needed to create more sophisticated weapons, to explore space, and to find the causes and cures for disease. These ideas, too, underlay demands by government and others that the faculties of these institutions seek the causes of and ways of eliminating poverty, racial discrimination, drug abuse, and urban blight.

Thus this country's colleges and universities had acquired, by the close of the decade following World War II, a wide range of activities. Alan Pifer has enumerated thirteen types:

1. Offering liberal education to some students

2. Providing professional and occupational training for other students

3. Sorting and selecting students for various types of employment

4. Discovering new knowledge

5. Serving as custodians of the cultural heritage

---

[9] An adaptation of reasoning presented by James A. Perkins in *The University in Transition* (Princeton, N.J.: Princeton University Press, 1966), p. 7.

6. Providing a protected environment for detached, impartial criticism of the larger society

7. Providing the administrative base for public service programs in such fields as health care, foreign assistance, agriculture and community service

8. Providing a logistical base for a pool of specialized talent which the university makes available to government and industry

9. Certifying the entry of the particularly ambitious and able person of middle or working class background into the socially elite

10. Providing a "way station on the trail of life" for young people for whom the society offers no jobs or other meaningful opportunities

11. Offering educational opportunities for adults

12. Offering "remedial education" of less than college level for able individuals whose early training was inadequate

13. Providing commercialized entertainment[10]

"Our instinct time and again," Pifer commented, "was to turn to higher education whenever there was a new job to be done, and as a consequence both the functions of higher education and the varied activities these functions tended to spawn steadily multiplied. . . ."[11] Effectively, Pifer agrees with those who contend that universities have been transformed from intellectual centers into gigantic service stations principally for the government and the larger corporations. Those who hold this view believe that "our society simply expects too much from our colleges and universities.[12]

A third consequence of change for the college and university was the threatened politicization of the institution.[13]

---

[10] "The Responsibility for Reform in Higher Education," annual report of the president of the Carnegie Corporation, 1971, pp. 6–12.

[11] Ibid., p. 10.

[12] G. Kerry Smith, ed., in preface to *Agony and Promise* (San Francisco: Jossey-Bass, Inc., Publishers, 1969), p. x.

[13] George J. Stigler, Charles Walgreen Distinguished Service Professor, University of Chicago, wrote in 1973: "In the last dozen years the freedom to express unpopular ideas—unpopular, that is, with the audiences—at American colleges and universities appears to have shrunk drastically." Stigler illustrated this loss of freedom of expression with these questions: "When last did a former secretary of state fail to receive a single invitation to lecture at a major university? What major university would have felt it safe, when bombing of Northern Vietnam resumed last December [1972], to offer a forum to Secretaries Laird or Rogers?" And he attributes this loss of freedom to the exercise of "coercive power" by faculty members on their colleagues; ". . . the academic community imposes sharp limits on the range of respectable opinion within its ranks" (*The Chronicle of Higher Education*, Aug. 13, 1973, p. 12).

As the college or university expanded the array of services it provided in response to the society's needs and demands, the issues and controversies of the time affected their functioning. The institution became involved with the professions for which it trained entrants. It became involved with the problems of military defense, space exploration, and health care because its faculty was carrying on contract research in these and numerous other fields. It became involved in the issue of war and peace because its students were being drafted and because some faculty members and students, as citizens, felt deeply about an unpopular war. It became involved in the issues of race discrimination and poverty because its faculty members were assisting governmental agencies to develop programs to cope with these problems and because faculty members and students, like other citizens, were concerned. Many institutions became involved in the problems of the burgeoning cities as more and more campuses were located in the midst of urban centers and were continually interacting with the environment about them and from which their students came. And those scholars who lived up to their obligation to probe current realities and to hold current cultural trends up to the light were inevitably involved.[14]

These involvements engendered conflict externally (as between the institution and the legislature, or between it and research sponsors, the press, or the alumni) and internally (as between faculty members and students, trustees and administrators). Such conflict revolved around fundamental values and posed basic questions as to the goals of the institution, its posture toward the society, and its capacity to maintain an environment in which dispassionate, rational instruction, learning, and research could go on.

The long-held view that a college or university must be value-neutral, hence, has been subjected to rigorous reexamination.[15] Few would contend that a college or university in its role as an instructor of students should take sides in the intellectual battles between doctrine and doctrine (e.g., Keynesian versus Friedmanesque economics), dogma and

---

14 Merle E. Curti in his notable volume *The Social Ideas of American Educators* (New York: Charles Scribner's Sons, 1935) describes the efforts of educators over the years to serve as evaluators of the society about them. He concludes that generally educators have contented themselves with the role of supplying the young with accurate information, by pointing to the ways in which further information can be gathered, and by developing habits of careful thinking and judgment" (New York: Pageant Books, Inc., 1959, rev. ed., p. xxxiv).

15 For excellent illustrations of such reexamination, see Richard H. Sullivan, "The Socially Involved University," and Walter P. Metzger, "Institutional Neutrality: For Appraisal," in *Neutrality or Partisanship: A Dilemma of Academic Institutions,* Bulletin No. 34 (New York: Carnegie Foundation for the Advancement of Teaching, 1972).

dogma (even if a substantial proportion do). Trustees, administrators, and faculty members may fairly be criticized if the inquiries and teaching being carried on do not deal with such large issues as racial justice, relief of poverty, inflation, pollution of the environment, and war and peace.[16] They may be criticized also if they fail to maintain intellectual balance in the selection of professors for departments[17] and in the determination of courses (e.g., black studies) to be offered.

But as property owners, as investors, as contractors for research, as providers of public services, and as admissions officers these institutions support one or another set of values by their actions. They stand for certain values in the way they treat slum dwellers and the slums that adjoin their campuses; consider, for example, the contrasting approaches to the problem of Columbia University, the University of Chicago, and the University of Pennsylvania. In their acceptance or rejection of defense contracts, in their decisions as to what business firms may recruit on the campus, and in their decisions as to the companies in which they invest their endowments, colleges and universities implicitly or explicitly support one or another set of values. And in the extent of the efforts they make to seek out and provide financial aid for young people of especial ability among families with low incomes and among ethnic groups that have been disadvantaged in the past—blacks, Puerto Ricans, Chicanos, American Indians, and others—they manifest the values to which they are committed.

The experience of the 1960s (perhaps an unusual period) demonstrated that on such actions, and others, members of the typical college or university community—trustees, students, faculty members, administrators, and alumni—often hold sharply differing values. This experience indicated that during those turbulent years the forms and processes of governance obtaining in some institutions were not effective in resolving conflict as to what policies should be followed and simultaneously maintaining an internal climate marked by freedom of expression and rationality.

A fourth consequence for the college or university of the change in the society about it was the erosion of institutional autonomy.

---

[16] For consideration of this issue, see *The Nature and Purposes of the University: A Discussion Memorandum,* interim report of the Committee on University Governors (Cambridge, Mass.: Harvard University, January 1971).

[17] The maintenance of a balanced faculty and a balanced offering of courses in those departments, particularly in the social sciences, is a task that those responsible for the leadership of many institutions have failed to achieve. Frequently departments are "taken over" by the proponents of a point of view and those belonging to opposing schools of thought gradually disappear. The result is a loss of the intellectual friction that contributes to learning.

The autonomy once regarded as essential to the functioning of a college or university has been substantially diminished. The significance of this loss will be treated more fully in Chapter 3. Here it will suffice to identify this additional consequence of change.

The administrative autonomy of the college and university was curtailed as rising costs of higher education forced state governments to extend their surveillance of what the growing number of institutions they subsidized were doing and why.[18] The freedom of those responsible for institutional direction was further limited by actions of the federal government to assure equal employment opportunities and by the prescriptions attached to the increasing amounts of federal money made available for higher education. Together these forms of intervention by government limited the freedom of trustees, presidents, and deans to make decisions as to the hiring of faculty, the revision of curricula, and even the definition of the institution's objectives.[19]

The gradual and seemingly irreversible diminution of institutional autonomy has created for those responsible for governance a difficult problem of maintaining the enterprise of faculty members in educational planning. Their intellectual interests have been circumscribed to the extent that state authorities have specified educational roles for individual institutions and have claimed authority over the introduction of new programs and in some instances courses. There is little evidence, however, that the increased governmental control over institutions has curtailed the right of individual faculty members to speak and write unpopular views. If anything, the campus disorders and the increasing involvement of the institution in current, and often controversial, issues of the society developed support for the free expression by both faculty members and students of a wider range of views than had been voiced.[20]

A fifth consequence was the betterment of the economic and social status in society in general of the professoriate and the development of cleavages between professors and their institution and among each other.

---

18 In 1959, fewer than half the states had formal mechanisms for statewide coordination of higher education; in 1973, 47 states had such mechanisms.

19 Wilbur J. Cohen and Philip S. Gartenberg have suggested: "The concepts of academic freedom and university autonomy, as traditionally defined, may be anomalies in a modern society. The University is too much a vital part of our culture and technology to be allowed *complete* freedom to do as it wishes" (a paper privately circulated entitled, "New Challenges in Higher Education: The Rule of Law in the Academy—Help or Hindrance?").

20 W. Allen Wallis, Chancellor, University of Rochester, expressed a contrary viewpoint in a memorandum to the university community, contending that "few, if any, universities today can honestly claim to have free speech and open discourse . . ." (*Wall Street Journal,* Jan. 30, 1971).

The enhanced demand from within the burgeoning institutions of higher education for the services of men and women with talent and with trained minds, coupled with an increased demand for specialists by industry and government, resulted in the improvement of faculty salaries and the enhancement of individual stature within the institutions. In some instances, it resulted in an individual's placing undue emphasis on the research and services at the expense of his teaching responsibilities. More generally, it resulted in some larger institutions in the delegation of much teaching to younger and less experienced instructors[21]—a factor alleged by some to have contributed to student unrest in a few of these institutions.

Increased emphasis throughout the society on specialization accentuated many professors' identification with their professional discipline. This identification limited the attachment of the specialist professors in many of the most prestigious universities to the employing institution. Coupled with the essential independence of the intellectual way of life, this tended to erode the "social cement"—the mutual trust that derives from a complementary relationship among colleagues in an enterprise— that is essential to organizational effectiveness.[22] In the less prestigious colleges and universities where faculty members less often had the opportunity to climb the career ladder of their profession to larger and more prestigious institutions the association of faculty member to institution tended to be more permanent.

The greater involvement of the university in the affairs of a society that was increasingly divided by an unpopular war and by pressures for racial equality and for the betterment of the quality of life tended to divide faculties as between the new activists and the traditional scholars. A substantial number held that the intellectual man should aggressively promote those ends he believes to be right; the more conventional men hold that the scholar's obligation is to maintain a position of detached objectivity.

After two decades in which the economic status of professors was markedly improved, the tide turned sharply in the early 1970s. The financial stringencies faced by many institutions limited or precluded the further raising of salaries and, in some institutions, forced the re-

---

[21] The most recent available data relative to the use of teaching assistants were presented by John L. Chase in his monograph, *Graduate Teaching Assistants in American Universities: A Review of Recent Trends and Recommendations* (Washington: U.S. Department of Health, Education and Welfare, Office of Education, May 1970), chap. 2.

[22] For thoughtful analyses of this concept of "social cement" and its significance in understanding university governance, see Rufus E. Miles, Jr., "The Pathology of Institutional Breakdown," *Journal of Higher Education,* May 1969, pp. 351–368, and Burton R. Clark, "Belief and Loyalty in College Organization," *Journal of Higher Education,* June 1971, pp. 499–515.

duction of staffs. In the longer run, the status of professors appears to be even less bright. With enrollments growing more modestly during the 1970s and likely to decline during the 1980s, the number of faculty members to be hired is expected to follow a parallel course.[23] Yet the number of Ph.D.'s to graduate over the 1970s will likely continue to grow.[24] Thus the younger individuals, women, and blacks entering the market for teaching positions in the colleges and universities will do so during the 1970s and 1980s when opportunities will likely be scarce. Already these (and other) developments have given rise to threats to the maintenance of the long-standing, treasured system of tenure for professors and to the unionization of faculties on more than 300 campuses, many of them the campuses of community colleges.

A sixth consequence was the emergence of a new youth culture and an unprecedented demand for a student voice in the governance of colleges and universities.

Until the 1960s, the student was generally a passive participant in the functioning of institutions of higher learning. The faculty looked upon students as immature and inexperienced wards, incapable of sharing in the governance of the institution. The role allowed the typical student government was limited and innocuous.

The conversion of the student to an active, and sometimes aggressive, cotenant demanding respect and the right to share in decisions that affect him must be attributed to a variety of causes. Foremost among these causes was the development of a new youth culture.[25] That cul-

---

23 Allan M. Cartter, "Scientific Manpower for 1970–1985," *Science*, Apr. 9, 1971, pp. 132–140.

24 The U.S. Office of Education's National Center for Educational Statistics projects that the number of Ph.D.'s will increase from 37,700 (1972–73) to 53,500 (1981–82) (reported in Scientific Manpower Commission, *Manpower Comments*, April 1973, p. 5).

25 If the governance of the university is to be reevaluated in light of the impact of this new culture, its makeup must be made explicit. "New youth culture" means the tendency of youth:
  1. To emphasize pure idealism, to argue for liberty, equality, honesty, and democracy in absolute terms
  2. To hold that human life is *all*, that personal regard for each human being and for equality among humans is imperative
  3. To be concerned with how one ought to live and what one ought to consider important in one's life
  4. To doubt that America has lived up to the ideals it has historically claimed, i.e., equality, democracy, and the dignity of the individual
  5. To oppose the professed values of older people, to challenge much of the accumulated lore of its elders, and to attack the form and practice of existing institutions
  6. To reject the traditional obligation of the young to accept the counsel and

ture was (and is) apparent, not on the campuses alone. Most important is the new status, new rights and respect that youth has gained throughout the American society. These developments brought to the colleges and universities young men and women who, as a consequence of life in an urban center and of exposure to highly developed media of communication and as a consequence of other unspecifiable social forces, possessed a more comprehensive, even though superficial, knowledge of the society and greater sophistication than their progenitors.

Underlying the development of this new youth culture was what Daniel P. Moynihan has described as "a profound demographic change . . . a one-time change, a growth in population faster than any that had ever occurred before . . . with respect to a particular sub-group in the population—namely those persons from 14 to 24 years of age."[26] That demographic change contributed to and helped to shape economic and social factors that extended the period of growing up, despite the accumulation of knowledge and sophistication, during which young people were held out of the labor market by encouraging their enrollment in higher education. And this change in student attitudes toward the college or university was precipitated largely by such happenings as rising racial tensions and the Vietnam war.

Despite the traditional authoritarian character of the teacher-student relationship, a growing proportion of faculty members and administrators came to recognize the students' greater maturity and capacity to make choices.[27] The tradition of *in loco parentis* control over students was substantially abandoned, and the role of students in the governance of the institutions was increased. But the new view of students and their enlarged role in governance did not come, unfortunately, until after a costly succession of sit-ins, confrontations, and riots had driven

---

to submit to the will of its elders—be they parents, teachers, or simply elders

7. To become alienated from the adult society and opposed to any kind of authority structure; that alienation is reflected in its long hair, its unkempt clothing, its preference for drugs over alcohol; its opposition is manifest in its aversion to large organizations, to the police, and to the discipline *formerely* imposed by the university.

[26] "Peace—Some Thoughts on the 1960's and 1970's," *Public Interest*, Summer 1973, p. 5.

[27] *Report of the Committee on the Student in Higher Education* (New Haven, Conn.: The Hazen Foundation, 1968), Chap. 2, "The New Students," pp. 16–27. Earl J. McGrath expressed a confirming point of view when he wrote: "What students may lack in maturity and judgment they make up for in direct knowledge and a serious interest in the educational needs of their times" ("Who Shall Share the Power?" in Harold Hodgkinson and L. Richard Meeth, eds., *Power and Authority*, San Francisco: Jossey-Bass, Inc., Publishers, 1971, p. 203).

home the students' changed attitudes and had forced modification of their relationships to and status within the institution. Their efforts loosened some rigidities of academic procedure and gained for them the opportunity to be heard on a much broader range of questions but, viewed from the perspective of 1975, have not greatly increased their influence in the governance of institutions.

A seventh consequence of change in the environment about the college and the university was the undermining of leadership within.

Generally it is agreed that the aforementioned consequences—particularly the impact of social and political issues that revolved about the institution, the erosion of its autonomy, the greater status of faculty members, and the insistence by students (at least for the years 1966–1970) that they have a voice in governance—diminished the power of both presidents and trustees.

The growth in enrollment, physical facilities, number of component units, variety of functions, and annual budgets imposed additional administrative and financial responsibilities on the president, which prevented his playing the role on which the power of the office was founded—that of educational leader. The president, if he is to hold the allegiance of the faculty, must "be sensitive to the educational and intellectual needs and missions of the academic community," but the demands of the job will not permit many presidents "to be both a member of the faculty and its leader" nor "to initiate major academic study and reform" in any literal meaning of those words.[28]

Moreover, the power of the president and his key lieutenants—the vice presidents, deans, and departmental chairman—was circumscribed by the evolution of legal and quasi-legal procedures. As higher education became an essential rather than a privilege for many more young people, the protection of the Fourteenth Amendment to the Constitution was extended to students. As the power of faculties grew, the processes of promotion, assignment, and dismissal similarly were subjected to increasing proceduralization. Administrative discretion was whittled down.[29]

---

28 Phrases quoted are from no. 55 of the 85 "theses" promulgated by the Assembly on University Goals and Governance, January 1971, prescribing the responsibilities that should be fulfilled by the president (Cohen and Gartenberg, op. cit.).

29 Earl J. McGrath, "Who Should Have the Power?" in Hodgkinson and Meeth, eds., *Power and Authority* (San Francisco: Jossey-Bass, Inc., Publishers, 1971), p. 189. "In principle the trustees have much. In actuality, in the setting of the policies which determine an institution's essential character, they either have little power, or choose not to exercise it."

In a legal sense, the most important policy-making powers are squarely fixed on the board of trustees; in fact, boards of trustees can or do exercise only a fraction of those powers—and usually those that have the least immediate effect on the character of the institutions. Why? Predominantly because the kinds of individuals chosen as trustees all too often cannot give sufficient time or are not vitally interested in the central problems of higher education. It is substantially accurate to say that, as the institutions grew larger and more complex as the role of higher education broadened and as faculties grew stronger, the trustees devoted little or no attention to basic *educational* decisions. They concentrated their attention on the problems of physical facilities, financing, and public affairs. They lost contact with faculties and with students. And the inability of the trustees of some institutions to provide institutional leadership became painfully apparent when student confrontations broke out in the late 1960s, and subsequently in the early 1970s when many institutions were confronted by financial crises.

THE STATUS OF GOVERNANCE

The institutions' responses—or failures to respond—to change wrought consequences in:

- The size and structure of the system of American higher education and of individual institutions

- The functions our colleges and universities are called upon to perform

- The involvement of many or most institutions in the national policy

- The erosion of institutional autonomy, i.e., the subordination of the individual college or university within a national or statewide system

- The economic and professional status of the faculty and its ideological unity

- The attitudes and posture of students

- The ability of institutional leaders to lead

It became apparent that the system of governance obtaining in many or most institutions required modernization.

The exigencies of the late 1960s and early 1970s marked a period when authority was so diffused and the several constituencies of the institution so loosely related to each other and so limited in their allegiance to the institution as to make impossible deliberate, purposeful cooperation among trustees, academic officers, administrative officers, faculty, and students in resolving such problems, and importantly in bringing about persistent educational advance.

The organizational structure and processes that prevail in most colleges and universities were historically patterned after the structure of the business corporation. The hierarchy of a lay board of trustees, with a president to carry out its bidding and to direct the affairs of the institution, was established in the American colleges of colonial times and has persisted over the years. In early times, the lay board held all authority, established all policy, and approved all decisions (as is still the case theoretically). In many institutions the president served as chief executive and directed operations through a staff of academic administrators (deans and department heads), academic facilitators (the registrar, director of admissions, and dean of students), and business administrators (such as of finance, housekeeping, and physical maintenance).

A few academicians always doubted the suitability of this hierarchical structure for the college or university. They questioned the applicability of the presumption, implicit in the hierarchical concept, that authority should be centralized in a strong and relatively authoritarian executive; they contended, as time passed, that this concept was inapplicable to governance of a large group of individuals whose highly specialized competence endowed them with independence.[30]

Many observers of higher education came to realize that the authority originally vested in the board and its chief executive simply was no longer in their hands; it had been claimed from above by governmental authorities and from below by the faculty and students. Thus, leadership capable of defining missions, setting objectives, allocating resources, and coordinating efforts for the institution had been dissipated.

Other observers pointed out that as these institutions expanded and introduced more and more specialization they became loose confederations of largely autonomous departments. And students of institutional management pointed out that few had developed mechanisms and processes adequate to permit collaborative planning, communication, and decision making in a large, disaggregated institution. By the 1970s the inadequacy of the conventional structure to govern the affairs of the expanded and complex institutions that had come into being was sorely

---

30 It is "inconceivable," Jacques Barzun has suggested, "that a huge confederation staffed by highly independent individuals can move like an army at the command of a chief" (*The American University*, New York: Harper & Row, Publishers, Incorporated, 1968, p. 136).

obvious. In the words of one wise observer, "higher education . . . must be one of the most backward or least progressive parts of our whole economy. In a world of scientific and technological change, the university is clearly a laggard."[31]

ASSESSMENT AND PRESCRIPTION

This country's colleges and universities are destined to grow less rapidly in the future, but they are nonetheless essential to this nation's well-being. Their effectiveness in supplying trained manpower, in discovering new knowledge, in ordering, transmitting, and conserving what is known, and in applying accumulated knowledge to society's problems is of crucial importance. To make these institutions fully effective, i.e., to harness the energies, talent, and imaginations of trustees and administrators, faculty members, and students in a dynamic learning effort, requires modernization of the processes of governance that typically now prevail. The assessment of the deficiencies in the existing processes of governance and the prescription of where and how modernization should take place are the tasks undertaken in this book.

Subsequent sections of this book are focused on the problems and needs of public and private four-year colleges and universities. This is not to deny the large importance of the rapidly growing segment of American higher education—the two-year community colleges and technical institutes; it is simply a recognition of the fact that their functions are distinguishable, their constituencies are substantially dissimilar, and their traditions of authority distribution are quite different from those of the four-year institutions.

Before presenting an assessment of the problems of governance that beset the four-year colleges and universities, I shall sketch, in Chapters 2 and 3, the setting in which these institutions operate. Neither the college nor the university has ever operated in isolation from the society it serves and that supports it. But during the post-World War II years in the United States, these institutions have become much more integrally related with other segments of the society. Hence in Chapter 2, the environment within which these institutions function and the impact of this environment on internal governance are depicted. In Chapter 3, the formal context established by an expanding network of relationships with government—both federal and state—is described and its effect evaluated.

In Part Two the focus of the book shifts to the internal functioning

---

31 Toynbee, op. cit., p. xxi.

of these institutions. As a preface to the consideration in successive chapters of the governance of each service rendered by the college or university, the unique organizational characteristics of the academic enterprise are analyzed in Chapter 4. Then, in turn, the processes by which these institutions govern their rendering of instructional, student-oriented activities, research and other services are considered.

Customarily, analysts of the functioning of business enterprises, governmental agencies, and military organizations use the terms "manage" and "management." Use of the terms "govern" and "governance" is generally reserved for consideration of the functioning of institutions of higher education. Those terms are used to describe the process of "deciding" and of seeing to it that the decisions made are executed. That process involves—in the college or university—students, teachers, administrators, trustees, and, increasingly, individuals and agencies outside the institution in establishing policies, rules, and regulations, and in collaborating to carry out those guides to action.[32] The extensive diffusion of authority and the consequent need for collaboration warrant the use of a distinctive term.

It is this process of governance—the ways in which decisions as to what shall be taught, who shall teach, what relationships with students shall be maintained, what services shall be provided for students, and what research shall be undertaken—that is dealt with in Chapters 5, 6, and 7.

Part Three (Chapters 8, 9, and 10) deals in similar fashion with essential support activities. It describes how and by whom decisions are made as to the hiring, compensation, promotion, and tenure of both faculty and other personnel, as to the acquisition, expenditure, and conservation of the funds needed to support the institution, and as to the interrelationship of these several activities, i.e., the interrelationship of educational, financial, and operating activities in an ongoing institution.

Finally Part Four offers a prescription. Chapter 11 forecasts change in the functions of the college and the university. It suggests how the mission of each type of postsecondary educational institution is being

---

[32] Alice in Wonderland said at one point in her travels through Wonderland that when she used a word it meant just what she intended it to mean. I cannot claim as great a command over the subtleties of language. But when I use the term "governance" I am talking about the processes by which decisions are arrived at, who participates in these processes, the structure that relates these individuals, and the effort that is made (or should be made) to see to it that decisions once made are carried out, and to assess the results that are achieved.

For further development of the meaning of the term "governance" see John J. Corson, *The Governance of Colleges and Universities* (New York: McGraw-Hill Book Company, 1960), pp. 12–13.

reshaped and it indicates the prospective mix of institutions that will exist in 1980. Chapter 12 suggests how the authority of each of the participants in the processes of governance should be redefined; Chapter 13 indicates how leadership in the college and university has been undermined and how it should be strengthened; and finally, in Chapter 14, key problems of organizational structure are identified, and a central structural change is proposed.

The suggestions presented in these concluding chapters are designed to enable those who bear the responsibility for the effectiveness of these institutions to make of a "loose confederation" of departments, schools, institutes, and other units an integral enterprise that holds the allegiance and stimulates the minds and the efforts of students, teachers, researchers, and the growing body of professionals and administrators who make up the staff of a college or university.

Many young Americans will go to college during the years ahead. Whether their time is invested fruitfully or wasted in whole or part will depend in considerable part on the effectiveness of the governance of these institutions. Simultaneously these institutions, faced with the prospect of "zero growth" after a period of rapid and persistent expansion, must resolve the most trying problems of adjustment. Designing methods of governance equal to their needs is, we recognize, of the utmost importance.

Environmental Pressures
on Governance

The university of the future will no longer be able to
ignore many of the swift changes taking place outside its
gates, because some of those outside its gates are prepared
to go inside the campus and demand attention and aid.

Samuel Gould[1]

2 American higher education was subjected, throughout its first century and a half, to the influence of "outsiders."[2] The church influenced the program and policies of most colleges and universities well into the 1900s.[3] Alumni, donors, agricultural and business interests, government, and still other groups exercised influence on some campuses in the past. But during the post-World War II period, and particularly since 1960, more influence has been brought to bear, by more groups, with greater force than any previous time in the history of American higher education.

The reason is clear. The institution of higher education has become more central to the interests of more groups in the society than ever before. As the volume of new knowledge has increased, knowledge has become the base of wealth and power. The acquisition of knowledge has become essential to a larger and larger proportion of the population. And the university, being in the business of discovering, accumulating, and transmitting knowledge, has been moved from the sidelines where it educated a few to the center of the social scene where it educates

---

1 *Today's Academic Condition* (New York: McGraw-Hill Book Company, 1970), p. 72.

2 Homer D. Babbidge, Jr., "The Outsiders: External Forces Affecting American Higher Education," in R. J. Ingham (ed.), *Institutional Backgrounds of Adult Education*, Center for the Study of Liberal Education for Adults, Boston University, Boston, 1965.

3 In 1906 when the Carnegie Foundation initiated its efforts to build a pension plan for faculty members in higher education and inquired into the issue of church affiliation, it found only 51 colleges it considered nondenominational. In 1966 of 817 institutions classified as "church related," one-fourth had no financial support from any church and only one out of twenty derived as much as half of its income from church support, and these several institutions contained only 14 percent of the total of all students enrolled in four-year colleges and universities. M. M. Pattillo, Jr., and D. MacKenzie, *Church Sponsored Higher Education in the United States*, American Council on Education, 1966.

many, and where many other institutions within the society—the farm, the elementary and secondary schools, government, business, and the professions—come for workers trained in the professions and para-professions, and for aid in applying knowledge to the problems of society (e.g., from how to better the reading skills of elementary school children to the discovery of the cause of a disease).

Society has many ways of communicating its needs and wishes to the university, even while it superficially, at least, does not invade the autonomy of the intellectual enterprise. It communicates its needs directly through the enrollment of students and their choices of educational programs. It communicates its needs through requests for research and services and by the expressions of the professional groups for which it serves as gate tenders. It communicates its needs, in some instances, through the media—press, radio, and television—when those agencies second the wishes and opinions of various segments of the society.[4] It communicates its needs mostly through the provision of financial support by government and by the controls that accompany that support.[5]

Other segments of the society communicate their needs and wishes to the institution of higher education through various means and with markedly varying degrees of influence. This chapter illustrates the interaction with the more obvious "outsiders," particularly the influence exercised through these relationships on the decisions made by trustees, presidents, and faculties.

VOICES OF PERSISTING "OUTSIDERS"

Four groups have long exercised from without varying degrees of influence over the governance of the college or university, the alumni, accrediting associations, contractors-grantors, and donors. In the past that influence has not been large or comprehensive. How has that influence been increased, diminished, or changed in character as the college or university has become more involved in affairs outside the campus?

---

[4] The best-known illustration of the influence of the media of communication on institutional governance—and the most flagrant abuse of that influence—is seen in the relationship between the Manchester (New Hampshire) *Union Leader* and the University of New Hampshire. That newspaper, pursuing extreme rightist values, subjected the university to persistent criticism and its presidents to abuse for approximately two decades.

[5] That relationship, between government and the academy, has become of such importance in the governance of colleges and universities (especially, but not alone, the public institutions) that it will be dealt with separately in Chapter 3, "Governance within a System."

IMPACT OF ALUMNI

Consider, first, the outsiders that historically have been most sympa-
thetically linked with the college or university—the alumni. In past
decades, alumni were generically those men and women who had gone
to college and thus formed an elite in American society. As such they
tended to support unquestioningly the patterns of education with which
they were familiar and to give unwavering loyalty and some financial
support. If they challenged or criticized, it was usually on noneduca-
tional matters—often athletics, campus architecture, or campus life-
style.

The attitudes of more recent alumni—and likely future alumni—are
conditioned by their experiences as students unlike those of older alumni.
Most students of recent years attended large institutions; there they
were members of a large, nonhomogeneous student body. A large
proportion attended as commuters. There were fewer fraternities and
sororities and fewer students belonged. A substantial proportion simultaneously were earning a living and their allegiance was divided between the college, an employer, and perhaps the family they were
supporting. More students attended two or more institutions before
earning a degree and their loyalties were divided. In many newly established institutions (e.g., since 1950) students, subject to each of the
experiences cited, never became members of an ardent, loyal, and
generous body of alumni.

Consequently, a 1968 survey of recent alumni (class of 1961) revealed that only 27 percent felt a "strong attachment" to their alma
mater.[6] In choosing a college for their sons and daughters, they testified
that the quality of education to be obtained was of more concern than
whether their children attended their alma mater.

The older alumni, roughly those thirty-five or more years of age,
while manifesting a greater loyalty to their alma mater, concern for its
continued existence along traditional lines, and a willingness to provide
financial support,[7] exhibit a growing tendency to question what now

---

[6] Joe L. Spaeth and Andrew M. Greeley, *Recent Alumni and Higher Education*,
a report prepared for the Carnegie Commission on Higher Education (New
York: McGraw-Hill Book Company, 1970), p. 38.

[7] Over the past decade, alumni continued to account for nearly half of all voluntary support from individuals, i.e., for almost 25 percent of total gifts, and the
annual fund solicitations realized about the same response—20 percent—
throughout the decade, except for 1968–69, when they fell to 18.3 percent. In
the Spaeth and Greeley report on recent alumni, the authors reported that the
effect of campus unrest on contributions of the class of 1961 to alumni funds
was "essentially nil" (p. 116–119).

goes on on the campus. The alumni of many institutions reacted critically to the disturbances on their campuses between 1964 and 1972.[8] A few alumni seem content with making annual contributions, raising funds, rooting for the football team, reading class notes in the alumni magazine, taking part in student counseling and placement programs, and seeking out potential enrollees. Only an articulate minority of the alumni are asking for hard information on current issues and manifesting a continuing and substantial interest. And this minority may be of large importance to the institution when it runs into difficulty.

The critical attitude of at least an articulate minority of the older alumni and the seeming lesser affection of younger alumni have combined to make it more difficult than in the past for presidents and their staffs to mobilize alumni when their support is needed. In the private institutions their financial support is needed more than at perhaps any time in the past; in the public institutions their financial support is of less consequence, but their vocal support is needed with Congress, state legislatures, federal and state agencies, the community, and the media of communications. Where alumni have joined forces, as they have in several states,[9] they have exercised significant influence in support of their alma maters.

A traditional view has been that the alumni's "infantilism was a constant embarrassment to the college administrator, who was not long in finding out that the twin of support was control, a desire for a voice in

---

[8] Reports issued by alumni of Columbia (1968) and Yale (1970) universities after controversy had arisen on both campuses are illustrative. Both reports mildly criticized their alma maters with respect to new relationships that had developed between the universities and their students. Both reports recognized the need for alumni to continue as fund raisers; claimed a larger role in providing advice to the administration, faculty, and students; and recommended that alumni representatives be given a formal part in the institution's decision making. The Commission on Alumni Affairs at Yale University responded in December 1970 that "alumni have a right to expect a full and regular flow of information and explanation relating to policy and events.... alumni want to be heard and involved on the issues that concern them." In a similar vein, the alumni of Columbia University recommended that formal boards of visitors (composed of educators, alumni, students and others) be constituted "to maintain continuous inspection of the University's activities and to issue public reports to the trustees and to the alumni, as well as to the faculty and students" (*Alumni Recommendations for the Future Government and Operation of Columbia University*, Aug. 15, 1968).

[9] For example, the New York State Confederation of Alumni Associations has 250,000 members, and the Council of California State College Alumni Associations has 400,000 members. When such organizations speak to state legislatures about budget proposals, to the community about the approval of bond issues, or to the university on campus issues, they constitute a segment of the electorate that cannot be ignored. Other states having alumni federations include New Jersey, Oklahoma, Louisiana, Ohio, and Pennsylvania (*College and University Journal*, May 1972, pp. 5–8).

the determination of alma mater's policies."[10] Whether their association is viewed as embarrassing or as "indispensable,"[11] the greater involvement of the university in the society and its pressing financial needs have tended to compel some trustees and presidents to strive to stimulate alumni interests and to channel the alumni's influence in directions beneficial to the institution. Those directions for public institutions, and for all institutions at a time when the activities of colleges and universities are of greater public concern, differ substantially from the directions in which alumni have employed their energies in the past.

In turn, the alumni have sought a more formal means of participating in institutional decision making; and the alumni, particularly the younger alumni, have been increasingly recognized as a constituency to be represented in the councils of the institution. A number of institutions have accommodated those demands by electing alumni to the boards of trustees. Other institutions have provided for alumni representation on the newly established "community councils" or "broadly based senates" that serve as advisory agencies to the president and trustees. The inclusion of alumni representatives on these bodies promises to ameliorate an organizational problem that has arisen in many institutions, i.e., the relationship between the executive of the organized alumni and the president and his staff, and particularly the vice president for or director of development.

In summary it appears that "the role of alumni in university governance may change in the years ahead, even quite radically, and the persons who speak for the alumni may speak quite differently than in the past, but the alumni will remain an absolutely vital and integral constituency of the universities."[12]

ACCREDITATION AND DECISION MAKING

As the importance of higher education to students, parents, employers, and the society has grown, so has the impact of a second body of "outsiders"—the accreditation associations. These "voluntary membership associations" are responsible for the enforcement of standards of educational performance by secondary schools, colleges, and universities. In performing this function they have long exercised substantial influ-

---

10 Kingman Brewster has called the alumni "the indispensable ambassadors of the university to the society as a whole" (*Report of the Commission on Alumni Affairs,* Yale University, December 1970).
11 John S. Brubacher and Willis Rudy, *Higher Education in Transition* (New York: Harper & Row, Publishers, Incorporated, 1968), pp. 363–364.
12 Robert O'Neil, "Is the Role of Alumni in University Life Declining?" *Alma Mater,* October 1970.

ence, or even control, particularly over the newer and marginal colleges and universities. That influence has been enlarged as federal support of higher education has grown and federal aid has generally been made available only to accredited institutions.

This body of accreditation associations consists, first, of six regional associations[13] of somewhat varying influence that accredit both secondary schools and postsecondary institutions. Each has a "commission for higher education" and a separate "commission for secondary schools." These commissions assess the entire institution rather than a particular part (e.g., a department) or program (e.g., the program leading to a bachelor's degree in physical education). They determine when a new institution shall be deemed to have developed its faculty and facilities sufficiently to warrant "accreditation." And these commissions for higher education review the educational performance of each accredited institution once in five or ten years.

The "members" of these associations are the institutions that have been accredited. They support the associations' activities by membership fees and charges for the examinations made. Despite the continued and general use of the term "voluntary" to describe these associations, every college and university effectively must be accredited and, hence, must become a member.

The network includes, secondly, more than forty professional associations such as the American Bar Association, the American Chemical Society, the American Psychological Association, the American Medical Association (and at least thirteen agencies engaged in accrediting institutions that train individuals in the allied health professions),[14] and the National League for Nursing. These associations have as members practitioners in the respective fields (e.g., chemists, physicians) and the professors in the universities who train practitioners for these fields. They perform with respect to parts or programs of an institution similar functions, i.e., setting and enforcing standards of educational performance.

The accrediting network includes, in addition, the State University of New York (the one state agency that performs an accrediting function), Phi Beta Kappa, and the American Association of University

---

[13] These associations are: New England Association of Colleges and Schools, Inc., Southern Association of Colleges and Schools, the North Central Association of Colleges and Secondary Schools, Middle States Association of Colleges and Secondary Schools, the Western Association of Schools and Colleges, and the Northwest Association of Secondary and Higher Schools.

[14] For a critical description of the network of agencies engaged in the "Accreditation of Health Educational Programs," see *Part One: Working Papers, Study of Accreditation of Selected Health Educational Programs*, October 1971.

Women.[15] Each of these agencies performs specialized evaluations of colleges and universities. Attempts were made during 1972–73 to create a National Council on Institutional and Specialized Accrediting to interrelate the whole network of accrediting agencies. These efforts are continuing and in the meantime some coordination of standards and of practices is provided by two separate agencies, the Federation of Regional Accrediting Commissions of Higher Education and the National Commission on Accrediting.

The accreditation function generally involves appraisal of (1) the stated objectives of the institution, (2) the substance of courses and programs and the requirements for degrees, (3) the caliber of instruction, (4) standards and practices governing the admission of students, (5) the makeup of the faculty, the faculty-student ratio, compensation, tenure, leaves of absence, pensions and other conditions of faculty employment, and the protection accorded the faculty to express its own views in teaching and writing, (6) the conditions of student life, (7) evidence as to the outcomes of educational programs, (8) the facilities, particularly library and learning resource equipment, available to support the faculties, (9) the adequacy of financing, and (10) organizational arrangements for governance.

Criteria, which vary among the regional associations, guide the appraisal of each aspect of an institution's functioning.[16] The actual appraisal is made by teams consisting in principal part of individuals recruited from the staffs and faculties of other institutions. These teams visit the institution seeking accreditation (or reaccreditation) and, after studying materials supplied them and making such observations as they deem necessary over a two- to four-day period, render reports. On the basis of these reports the commissions on higher education reach judgments as to whether an institution shall be accredited or reaccredited.

For the new institution seeking accreditation, the judgments of the visiting teams and the commissions on colleges are of life-or-death consequence. Nonaccreditation greatly limits the institution's opportunity. For the established institution the reaccreditation process is a

---

15 The AAUW was one of the earliest agencies to attempt to use accreditation as a means of exerting external control over the educational standards of an institution. In a few instances alumni have been especially concerned when the illustrious Phi Beta Kappa or the AAUW challenged the quality of the educational offering of their alma maters.

16 Alexander W. Astin, in an address entitled, "Some New Directions for Accrediting," before a seminar held by the National Commission on Accrediting, Oct. 27, 1972, contended that ". . . accrediting associations have developed an elaborate set of criteria based on what I like to call educational folklore." He makes a plea for the development of new criteria for accreditation that will give greater emphasis to the measurement of the educational outputs of the institutions seeking reaccreditation.

bother. An increasing number of university presidents question whether the process accurately evaluates educational performance, and some manifest an antipathy toward the process.[17]

The bother (and cost) derive from the extensive "self-study" each institution is expected to perform, in accordance with a general format specified by the regional accrediting association, and to the relatively exacting standards maintained by the professional associations. These approaches, in the opinion of some observers, force conformity with conventional standards, materially limit the freedom of presidents and deans (especially of the marginal institutions) to allocate resources thus constraining their leadership and ability to control costs, and sometimes thwart efforts to introduce new educational approaches (e.g., the granting of a master's degree in business administration by means of instruction via television).

The linkage of the professional associations (a university may have to deal with 30 or more) with departmental (e.g., the department of psychology and the American Psychological Association) and school (e.g., the medical school and the American Medical Association) faculties constitutes a particularly irritating impact on institutional governance. At times faculty members in particular departments and schools use the standards established by professional associations (e.g., the ratio of teachers to students that should obtain and the facilities, equipment, library, volumes, and other resources that should be provided) to enforce demands within the institution for larger staffs and larger budgets. Such use of the accreditation process can seriously skew the allocation of resources among departments and schools to the disadvantage of the institution as a whole. At other times when a departmental or school faculty fails to achieve its ends by presenting its arguments within the institution (usually by requesting larger budgets), it may stimulate fellow members of the profession to bring pressure from without on the institution's administrators. Or faculty members may be aided by visiting accreditation teams made up of fellow professionals in resisting innovations proposed by deans or presidents, e.g., interdisciplinary courses or programs.[18]

---

[17] "The Puffer Study," *A Study Prepared for the Federation of Regional Accrediting Commissions of Higher Education*, an analysis of what the colleges and universities think of regional institutional accreditation, July 1970, App. III. Frederick W. Ness, "The Proper Role of the Institution in Accrediting," a paper presented at a seminar on Accreditation and the Public Interest, Nov. 6, 1970.

[18] The influence of the professions is not exercised solely through the accreditation process. The state bar association, state medical society and other professional bodies often maintain a possessive and persistent surveillance of the professional school.

Members of departmental and school faculties are legitimately concerned with the evaluation of their performance by their peers. The judgment of their peers is reflected by the standards of the professional association and by the reports of visiting committees. Faculty members do not regard the accrediting associations as interlopers, as presidents often do and as trustees customarily do if informed of their actions, but as fellow professionals. Generally faculty members see in the accrediting association, particularly the professional association, an ally and a friend. The accrediting association supports the individual faculty member—his academic freedom, his compensation, and his tenure. Simultaneously, it supports the department and school faculties—their autonomy—and claims for them the resources and facilities they believe to be needed.

The reactions of presidents, on the one hand, and of faculties, on the other, do not constitute a comprehensive and wholly objective appraisal of the accreditation process. But their view that the accrediting associations—institutional and specialized—must be expected to improve markedly their evaluation process is held also by others. The traditional measures that have focused on inputs have been proven to have limited or questionable value in appraising the educational performance of an institution.[19] This likely means that accreditation will be increasingly based on the measurement of each institution's educational outputs, e.g., evaluating the quality of graduates (as reflected by tests), analyzing admissions to graduate institutions, and analyzing "drop out" experience. And the accreditation processes must be updated to cope with such new developments as "open admissions," the granting of external degrees, and the unionization of faculties.[20]

There has emerged also the view that the federal government should put less reliance on these private accrediting associations. Congress began, in 1952, to rely on the accrediting associations to determine the eligibility of existing colleges for certain types of federal aid. Since that time, as the number of federal aid programs and the volume of federal aid has increased, the United States government has become increasingly dependent on these associations. Their repeatedly demonstrated biases in favor of the professional departments and schools and in favor of established educational forms and processes, in the eyes of key observers, disqualify them to make determinations in the public interest (as distinguished from the interest of existing discipline-oriented faculties) with regard to an institution's eligibility for receiving federal aid.

---

[19] Astin, op. cit., p. 2.

[20] Norman Burns, "New Directions in Institutional Accrediting," a paper presented to the Seminar on Validation of Accrediting Standards, Washington, Oct. 27, 1971.

Recognition of the indirect impact of accreditation, when used as a criterion of eligibility for federal aid (the recognition of the growing importance of accreditation to more students and more parents than ever before and to the public generally), led to the suggestion that the boards of accrediting associations should include individuals from other fields of study and from the general public to represent the public interest.[21] In 1971 the Newman Commission proposed that the Department of Health, Education and Welfare distinguish criteria and procedures governing eligibility for federal aid from standards and criteria for accreditation, and have separate organizations make determinations as to eligibility for federal aid.[22]

This latter proposal, if adopted, promises to stimulate a fresh and more rigorous external appraisal of the quality of the educational performance of each college and university. The strength of existing associations will likely defer or prevent as major a revision of existing accreditation processes. When functioning at their worst, these accreditation processes tend to fragment the institution and to protect obsolete concepts, methods, and forms inherited from the past. But educational evaluation is extremely difficult and no generally agreed-upon techniques are universally accepted. Using available methods the accreditation agencies have been a wholesome influence over the years, even when performing in an imperfect and sometimes oppressive fashion.

CONTRACTORS AND GRANTORS

The United States government, some business enterprises, and a miscellany of other agencies communicate the needs of the society to the colleges and universities by the purchase or subsidization of particular activities on the campus, most often research in the sciences. This form of financial support for institutions of higher education, at least on a large scale, originated during World War II, when the federal government sought the aid of especially skilled faculty members.

A decade after the war's end federal contracts and grants for research approximated $500 to 700 millions per annum and was concentrated in approximately 100 of the most prestigious universities.[23] This annual

---

21 W. K. Selden, "Dilemmas of Accreditation of Health Educational Programs," Part II: *Staff Working Paper, Accreditation of Health Educational Programs* (Washington: National Commission, 1972).

22 Frank Newman, chairman, *Report on Higher Education* (Washington: U.S. Department of Health, Education and Welfare, 1971), ED 002219.

23 In fiscal year 1969 the 100 institutions receiving the largest amounts of federal funds received 81 percent of all funds made available. *Federal Funds for Academic Science*, National Science Foundation, NSF 71-7, p. 6.

sum grew to more than $2.2 billions in the early 1970s and then declined. In the 1950s about 40 percent of all monies spent by the colleges and universities on research came from the federal government. By 1960 the United States' share had increased to 50 percent, and by 1971 it was estimated at approximately 60 percent.[24]

Colleges and universities, or more exactly their faculties, were quick to avail themselves of these research monies and of like monies from corporate and other sources. The granting of these funds not only made possible the financing of research for certain institutions, it also facilitated their attraction of scholars of repute, permitted the reduction of faculty teaching loads, tended to raise faculty salaries, and played a major part in increasing graduate student enrollment. Conversely, colleges and universities lacking facilities and opportunities for sponsored research found it difficult to attract scholars of repute and thus to bid persuasively for research monies.

During the early 1960s, some observers warned that these research funds distorted the internal governance of recipient institutions.[25] With the growth of these funds it was predicted would come federal controls and intervention. Dictation by the contractors and grantors of the types of research wanted (or at least of the types of research proposed by faculty members that the contractors would fund) tended to create an imbalance in the support available for research in the various disciplines within the institution. Money was readily available for research in the sciences, less available for the social sciences, and hard-to-come-by for the humanities. This made it difficult for deans and presidents to ensure balanced curricula. And this research money, it became clear in the 1960s, made those faculty members who obtained grants to support their research efforts substantially independent of the institutions where they are employed.

John W. Gardner commented in 1967 that universities attracted by these available monies "not only do not look a gift horse in the mouth, they do not even pause to note whether it's a gift horse or a boa constrictor."[26] Gradually university administrators came to realize that acceptance of these monies, usually granted as direct support for particular activities of a specified professor, tended (1) to undermine

---

24 Dael Wolfle, *The Home of Science* (New York: McGraw-Hill Book Company, 1972), p. 114.

25 Harold Orlans, *The Effects of Federal Programs on Higher Education,* a study conducted for the U.S. Office of Education (Washington: Brookings Institution, 1962), p. 287.

26 *Alma Mater,* 1967.

their influence as the responsible administrators of the institution[27] and (2) to eat into the finances of the university, since these contracts or grants did not meet all incidental and overhead costs incurred in carrying out the research. Those major universities that administered large federal contract research centers[28] found, in most instances, that those centers were substantially separated from the instructional effort and constituted an administrative task claiming much time of the president or of several of his vice presidents.

To counter these impacts the universities gradually developed organizational units close to the president or the senior academic officer to aid faculty members in procuring contracts or grants (i.e., they wrote proposals and supplied the "art of grantsmanship") and in controlling related costs, and to coordinate the universities' relationships with the sources of such funds.[29]

As a consequence of the substantial growth in funds available for research and for public services, an activity which had long been regarded as an integral element of the academic life assumed a substantially enlarged role particularly in the most prestigious institutions which attracted this support. But after two decades of expansion of the research activity, developments outside the university made much of the research carried on suspect, and raised crucial questions as to integral governance of the institution. Such questions as these were posed:[30]

- Can a university maintain an environment of free inquiry and permit its faculty members to contract to carry on "classified inquiries" the results of which cannot be published and shared with colleagues throughout the intellectual world?

---

27 John Morse of the American Council on Education has observed that "sponsored research has a way of putting the administration over a barrel. The system lends itself to direct negotiation between the man with the idea and his counterpart in the research supporting agency, leaving the college administration in the middle. . . . If the university official rejects the proposal that the professor wishes to submit . . . he's in danger of having that man pick up his marbles and go elsewhere" ("Can We Afford Sponsored Research?" *College Management*, April 1969, p. 33).

28 For example, the Arlington National Laboratory at the University of Chicago; the Jet Propulsion Laboratory at the California Institute of Technology; and the Human Resources Research Office, George Washington University.

29 J. Douglas Brown, "The Control of Sponsored Research," *The Liberal University* (New York: McGraw-Hill Book Company, 1969), part III, chap. 4, pp. 182–188.

30 These issues are effectively discussed in John A. Dillon, Jr., James W. McGrath, and Dale C. Ray, "Research and the Universities," *Journal of Higher Education*, April 1972, pp. 257–266; and Rodney W. Nichols, "Mission-Oriented R&D," *Science*, Apr. 2, 1971, pp. 29–33.

- Should faculty members accept support for research designed to create weapons of war, e.g., research in chemistry and biology to create noxious gases or devices for "germ warfare"?

- Should university faculties concentrate on basic research and limit or avoid opportunities to carry on applied research and to provide public services?

- Are some subjects (e.g., race and intelligence) so fraught with hazards to the peace of the society as to be avoided by university researchers?

- When large-scale research projects are undertaken for federal agencies, does the university sacrifice its ability or inclination to criticize these same federal patrons?

- Can a university manage a Job Corps Center and still be objective about the pros and cons of the government's policies for the employment and training of disadvantaged youth?

On a number of campuses the students, stimulated by opposition to the Vietnam war, forced administrators and trustees to face up to these and other questions. On other campuses, a minority of the faculty, usually from among the social scientists and humanists, forced such decisions. Presidents and trustees, faced by the loss of funds upon which the institutions had become dependent, seldom took the initiative in raising these issues. Yet in most institutions substantially involved in research, widespread antipathy to war forced trustees and presidents to prohibit the acceptance of support for research or public service projects, the sponsors of which could not be made known or the results of which could not be published. In several institutions, in addition (e.g., the Massachusetts Institute of Technology; New York University; the University of Pennsylvania; and the University of California, Berkeley), decisions were made to cut back on or to prohibit research undertaken for the Department of Defense.

DONORS: INDIVIDUALS AND FOUNDATIONS

The contributions that the variety of donors give toward the support of colleges and universities have reflected, over the years, the personal preferences of wealthy individuals, the purposes regarded as "safe" by corporations, the desire of foundation officials to effect social change, and the loyalty of the alumni. Probably no more than a third of the total financial aid donated has been made available for the unrestricted use of the receiving institution.

The total of voluntary support for higher education in fiscal year 1972–73 approximated $2.24 billions, a sum 11 percent greater than in any previous year.[31] The sources of this support and its distribution among types of institutions are shown in the following table:

Sources of Support	Proportion Donated	Proportion Donated to:			
		Private Universities	Private Colleges	Public Institutions	Other
Business corporations	14.2	33.4	25.1	33.9	7.6
Religious denominations	4.5	17.2	80.8	0.5	1.5
Alumni	23.9	47.5	33.1	15.2	4.2
Nonalumni individuals	26.8	39.7	34.8	16.4	8.1
General welfare foundations	23.4	46.7	22.0	23.8	7.5
Other	7.2	30.6	16.3	47.7	5.4
TOTAL	100.0	40.5	30.1	21.9	7.5

SOURCE: Council for Financial Aid to Higher Education.

Despite the increased amount made available, the influence exercised by these several sources is liable to decline. The aggregate contributed constitutes a small proportion of the total of the annual budgets of institutions of higher education, e.g., 6 to 8 percent. As federal and state support grows, these sources might not exceed 5 percent in the years ahead.

Of the total of all given by donors, that by individuals is perhaps the least reflective, and that by foundations the most reflective, of either the concerns of the society or the needs of the particular institution. Many contributions from individual donors and business firms are given to honor a particular individual and often in a form dictated by the donor's or the honoree's preference, e.g., a new building for the law school from which the donor or honoree graduated when a library is more needed. Business firms are generally unqualified to distribute support in relation to social needs; for instance, one chemical manufacturing company refused to make a gift to a women's college seeking support for the construction of a science building on the grounds that "we do not employ women scientists."

Much that is given by foundations is to foster those developments which, at a point in time, a foundation deems to be important for the

---

[31] A preliminary estimate by the Council for Financial Aid to Higher Education based on reports from 1,020 institutions, as reported in The Chronicle of Higher Education, Apr. 8, 1974.

society. Thus, in 1970 and 1971, the Carnegie Corporation made grants to several universities to enable them to develop programs leading to the Doctor of Arts degree. In 1972, the Ford Foundation dedicated the bulk of all funds made available for education to a small number of black colleges on the reasoning that their support constituted an especially significant social need. In some instances foundations' investments in particular programs have led to important advances—Carnegie's support of Flexner's study of medical schools—and in other instances foundations have invested substantial sums in programs generally believed to be of questionable value—the Ford Foundation support of teacher education during the 1950s and the Danforth Foundation awards to outstanding teachers during the 1960s.

The financial exigencies faced by a substantial number of private colleges and universities during the years 1963–1973 forced an intensive effort to seek additional funds from these several external sources. These efforts were often in the form of capital fund-raising campaigns for which considered statements of the institution's needs were formulated. The results achieved by most institutions during these years has been moderately successful. Over the longer run the funds available from these sources, and particularly from business enterprises, may be expected to grow,[32] but the funds available from foundations may grow less as a consequence of increasingly restrictive federal tax legislation.[33]

THE IMPACT OF NEW FORCES

In addition to these "outsiders" that in the past have influenced in varying ways the internal governance of colleges and universities, "new forces" have emerged as the role of these institutions has expanded and as the society about them has changed. The newness and vigor with which these new forces have stated their views has given them a significant influence in advocating actions, often in their own interest, but reflecting trends dominant in the society in the early 1970s.

WOMEN SPEAK UP

By the late 1960s an active and essentially new force for change was brought to bear on those responsible for the governance of institutions

---

32 Corporations give approximately one-third of the total of all corporate giving or approximately 0.45 percent of their pretax net income to education as compared with an allowable 5 percent under prevailing tax legislation (*College Management*, February 1972, p. 25).

33 F. Emerson Andrews, "Foundation Influence on Education," *Educational Record*, Winter 1972, pp. 26–29.

of higher education—organized women. That force manifested itself on a number of campuses in the spring of 1969. In the early 1970s, armed with Executive Order No. 11246, which prohibits sex discrimination by federal contractors,[34] women's groups pressed their demands through legal channels and with few demonstrations. "Women," one observer noted, "are aware that it is not through addressing emotional appeals to the president or scaling the administration's walls, but through the cultivation and exercise of power that they will make lasting gains."[35]

That approach is based on the belief that discrimination by colleges and universities is rooted in a deeper problem—the attitudes and norms prevailing in the American society as to the role of women.[36] Feminists contend that these attitudes and norms—i.e., that it is wrong for women to excel over men, that the woman's role is that of wife, mother, and homemaker, and hence that educating women is a waste of educational resources—are wrong. The college and the university serves as one battlefield over which this basic problem, as with other issues, is being fought. In the opinion of some advocates of women's rights, however, "the producer and the refuge of the male intellectual, the university, [has] turned out to be one of the most sexist institutions in this country."[37]

Executive Order No. 11246 is of no help to women in bringing about greater equality in undergraduate admissions. Even before this order was issued, some formerly elite preserves of male students had opened their undergraduate programs to women, among them Yale, Princeton, Dartmouth, Notre Dame, and Johns Hopkins. The decisions of these institutions were influenced by several forces: the desire of male students for the more natural environment of a balanced student body, the pressure of admissions officers and the need to attract more students to help meet annual budgets, and, of course, in some instances, the pressure of women's groups. The Executive order does provide aid for those seeking greater access to graduate education where employment

---

34 This Executive order also forbids discrimination based on race, religion, age or national origin. The women's rights movement gained further strength when the jurisdiction of the U.S. Civil Rights Commission was extended by Congress in late 1972 to include women, and at least psychological support as a consequence of the submission of the Equal Rights amendment to the states for ratification.

35 Constance Holden, "Women in Michigan: Parlaying Rights into Power," *Science*, Dec. 1, 1972, p. 964.

36 A. Y. Lewin and L. Duchan, "Women in Academia," *Science*, Sept. 3, 1971, p. 892.

37 A statement by Patricia Roberts Harris, quoted by Constance Holden, op. cit., p. 964.

as teaching assistants is involved, and its use will be referred to later.

Demands for special women's studies have also been successful. Courses on the historical and social roles of women were introduced and are now offered at several large institutions; and at least one college was, in 1973, considering offering a major in women's studies. These gains, and those in undergraduate admissions, must be attributed to the effectiveness of women's organizations and to the prevalent trend throughout the society of granting greater rights to disadvantaged groups.

The drive for equality in employment encompasses four major complaints: Far fewer women than men are hired to serve on faculties, from the level of teaching assistant to full professor; among the non-faculty members, women are often placed in jobs far beneath their capabilities; women receive lower salaries across all ranks; and promotions come more slowly to women than to men. These charges are not difficult to document.

Evidence on which these complaints are founded include such data as these: In 1971, in all colleges and universities only 32 percent of the instructors, 19 percent of the assistant professors, 15 percent of the associate professors, and 8 percent of the full professors were women. These facts are supported by the following specific illustrations: Harvard had no women among its 411 tenured graduate school professors; in 1970 at the University of California at Berkeley only 3.6 percent of the faculty positions were held by women; at the University of Michigan in 1969 more women (52 percent) than men served as temporary faculty members, but only 10.5 percent of more than 2,000 faculty members were women; at Wayne State University, in 1970 only 8 percent of all full professors were women and these women were paid, on the average, $2,000 less than their male colleagues, and it had taken them, on the average, twice as long to obtain tenure.[38] In that same year, the American Council on Education reported that 63 percent of faculty women were paid less than $10,000 a year as compared with 28 percent of all male faculty members.

The defense of such disparities offered by most administrators was effectively expressed by Allan W. Ostar in these words: "It is true that there are significant faculty salary differences between men and women. This is due in part to educational attainment, academic responsibility, and career interest."[39]

To reverse these trends, women's rights groups lodged during 1970

---

[38] Holden, op. cit., p. 964.

[39] *U.S. News and World Report,* op. cit., p. 80.

and 1971 more than 350 complaints with the Contract Compliance Office of the U.S. Department of Health, Education and Welfare.[40] In the first three months of 1971, the Women's Equity Action League alone demanded investigations at more than 200 colleges, including the entire state systems of New York, California, Florida, and New Jersey. According to the Association of American Colleges, about 40 schools had federal contracts delayed while discrimination charges were being investigated. Harvard and Columbia universities and the universities of Maryland, Michigan, Illinois, Pennsylvania, and Wisconsin, among others, were involved in costly and time-consuming investigations and negotiations with United States authorities.

In addition, on particular campuses women's groups waged vigorous campaigns. At the University of Michigan, Focus on Equal Opportunity for Women and PROBE, a coalition of faculty, staff, and students, first succeeded in getting the university to create a women's commission and an affirmative action post. In addition these groups hired a worker for the women's commission to search the university's personnel files and notify departmental chairmen of the women in their departments who were being paid at least 10 percent below the norm, and over 100 adjustments were made in women's salaries.[41] As a result of a further effort of these groups, the University of Michigan pledged itself to achieve salary equity between men and women in the same jobs, to pay back wages—retroactive to the day of hiring—to any women who should have been earning more, and to undertake vigorous recruitment of females for academic posts.[42]

At Michigan State University, the focus of the women's activities shifted to a drive to get the clerical-technical workers unionized; there were some 2,200 of them—mostly women. When a policy of "no merit increases" was announced in the spring of 1972 at MSU, the women's groups went to work; discussions were held with the American Federation of State, County, and Municipal Employees local of the AFL-CIO. As a result of these activities, MSU is now the first university to have a separate contract with an international union.

In late 1971, the University of Wisconsin granted $500,000 in

[40] U.S. News and World Report stated in its Dec. 13, 1971, issue that Professional Women's Caucus groups existed on 100 campuses, that organized women's committees existed on the campuses of a substantial number of member institutions of the American Association of Colleges, and that the American Political Science Association and about twenty other professional organizations have formed action groups to press for equality for women.

[41] "Women in Michigan: Academic Sexism under Siege," Science, Nov. 24, 1972, pp. 841–842.

[42] The New Republic, Mar. 20, 1971, p. 12.

salary increases to 600 women and was considering making the raises retroactive. In Florida, the Women's Caucus has mobilized for action on the campus of the University of Florida, Gainesville. Women on campus and the professional women in Gainesville have attacked the university's nepotism law, which won't allow a husband and wife to work in the same department. (The universities of Michigan, Minnesota, Maine, and Stanford, and Oberlin College yielded to demands for a change in such nepotism rules and now allow husbands and wives to work in the same department so long as neither is involved in employment decisions about the other. At Florida Atlantic University in Boca Raton, the Women's Caucus succeeded in winning the administration's agreement to drop all sex designations from job placement forms. On several other campuses in the country, women have forced academic administrators to post all job openings; they have also publicized cases of discrimination by campus officials, have forced the institution's administrators to write affirmative action programs, and have won the establishment of women's commissions and the hiring of affirmative action officers.

Many female activists view the incidents that have been cited as evidence of the prevalence of discrimination in many other institutions and of the need for aggressive action on many other campuses. They complain that the federal enforcement agencies, particularly the Department of Health, Education and Welfare, are groping their way slowly and are not able to investigate complaints promptly and thoroughly.

Experience in coping with the impact on governance of this relatively new force has been limited. But that experience suggests that trustees and presidents will be pressed continually for the assurance of equal opportunities for women in all aspects of campus life, and that those pressures will increasingly be reinforced by federal government efforts to eliminate discrimination. This prospect will necessitate difficult adjustments in long-standing educational and employment practices and may be expected to add materially to the cost of operations.

STUDENTS AS CITIZENS

The role of students in relation to the college or university has become an ambivalent one. In the past they related to the institution substantially as wards: during the 1960s they insisted upon being recognized simultaneously as citizens and upon bringing pressure to bear on those responsible for institution decision making—federal and state officials as well as university officers and trustees. That pressure was focused on the role of the institution in society as well as on the status of students within the academic community. Here we picture the influence they have exerted as citizens and the methods used in exercising that influence. In Chapter 6 we treat the changing role of students as wards of the institution.

THE UNIVERSITY AND SOCIAL ISSUES   Students had been involved in racial affairs, in voter registration, in presenting views to political leaders in Washington at least as early as 1960, but the event that initiated a period of unprecedented student activism was the Free Speech Movement outbreak on the Berkeley campus of the University of California for three months in the fall of 1964. This incident was touched off by restrictions on the use of the campus "to support or advocate off-campus political or social action."[43] National attention was attracted by the students' flaunting of university discipline and the violent tactics employed in effectively closing down the university. More significant, in retrospect, was the issue posed for the president and regents of this university as to the position the university should take, or allow its facilities to be used in support of, on social issues of the moment.

The Berkeley incident released a mounting concern of students on other campuses as to American involvement in Vietnam. Simultaneously it provided a rallying theme for what became the most effective of the student activist organizations—the Students for a Democratic Society (SDS).[44] The Berkeley incident and widespread concern with Vietnam precipitated SDS's call for a national student march on Washington in April 1965 in protest of the war.

The role of the university in support of what the SDS branded as an immoral national policy became a major issue for students. They made cooperation with the ROTC, the Selective Service Commission, military defense contracting agencies, and the recruiters for industrial companies engaged in supplying the military the targets for action. In the spring of 1966, a student sit-in at the University of Chicago, led by the SDS, forced closing of the university's administration building and touched off similar protests on other campuses. At issue were student demands that administration officials refuse to transmit male class rankings to the local draft boards. The Chicago students, and others as well, were successful in winning the administration's agreement that a student's rank in class would not be disclosed without his consent. On scores of

---

43 Letter from Dean Katherine Towle to student organizations, Sept. 14, 1964.

44 In 1962, SDS had 10 functioning chapters and about 200 dues-paying members. By 1969, there were at least 300 chapters and 7,000 paid members, and conservative estimates placed the number of other students who regularly participated in SDS activities at 35,000 (Jerome K. Skolnick, *The Politics of Protest*, Washington: U.S. Government Printing Office, 1969, p. 94).

campuses demonstrations forced the cancellation of or rendered unsuccessful visits on campus by employers' recruiters—Dow Chemical at Brown University, the Institute for Defense Analyses at Harvard and Princeton, the Navy at Berkeley, the Marines at Columbia.

The outbreak at Columbia University in the spring of 1968 was touched off in part by SDS demands that the university sever its affiliation with the Institute for Defense Analyses (IDA)—a nonprofit corporation organized to conduct research for the Department of Defense. Columbia, and each of the eleven other universities formally affiliated with IDA, severed their relationship as a result of these student protests. At other universities these same protests resulted in the adoption of policies prohibiting the acceptance of government contracts or grants for classified research.

At the heart of these and related student protests was a question well warranting the consideration of the university community: Do such ties with governmental agencies compromise the intellectual independence of the university and its teachers? By their actions—unpleasant and in instances unjustifiable—the students forced those responsible for the governance[45] of these institutions to grapple with such questions as: Should their institutions—openly or covertly—take sides on controversial social issues? Should they accept contracts or grants for research the results of which cannot be disseminated?

THE FUTURE OF STUDENT ACTIVISM The proportion of all students who were involved in campus disorders and who were members of the student activist organizations that led these disorders has never been determined. The consensus is that it was small, but simultaneously it is clear that on particular issues the small minority of activists could mobilize substantial student support.[46] The relative quiet experienced on the campuses during the early 1970s provoked questions as to the extent of student activism and organization in the future.[47] Some students likely were, in the vernacular of this era, "turned off"

---

45 The pros and cons of student participation in decisions on various aspects of governance will be presented in Chapters 5 and 6, and a prescription as to the role students should play in governance will be presented in Chapter 12.

46 Kenneth Keniston (*Youth and Dissent*, New York: Harcourt Brace Jovanovich, Inc., 1971) points out: "Whatever we say about student dissenters is said about a very small minority of America's 7 million college students . . . even at the colleges that gather together the greatest number of dissenters the vast majority of students—generally well over 95 percent—remain interested onlookers or opponents rather than active dissenters" (p. 145).

47 See, for example, Robert A. Blume, "Quiet on the Campus?" *Today's Education*, May 1972, pp. 38–40; Alan E. Bayer and Alexander W. Astin, "Campus Unrest, 1970–71: Was It Really That Quiet?" *Educational Record*, Fall 1971, pp. 301–313; and "Has SDS Ceased to Be Relevant?" *College and University Business*, February 1971, p. 14.

by the excesses of the 1960s. But the greater maturity, sophistication, and relative independence of the student bodies of the 1970s seem to make it likely that students will continue to expect a larger role in the making of decisions that affect them.

A demonstration of that prospect is afforded by the National Student Lobby formed in the early 1970s, partly as a consequence of the stimulus provided by granting all who were eighteen years of age and over the right to vote. "If the college students of this country can effectively organize," a pamphlet issued by this organization states, "this bloc of 8.6 million newly-enfranchised voters can have a dramatic impact on the politics and society of the United States."[48]

Statewide student lobbies have been organized in at least eight states and have demonstrated some effectiveness in influencing legislation. The Associated Students of the University of California, for example, maintain offices in the state capitol, where they have lobbied actively for university appropriations and other measures. The National Students Association, which was prohibited from undertaking lobbying activities by its tax-exempt status, appealed to the IRS for a change in status to permit it to lobby. Their power has been used in instances in opposition to university officials and the representatives of higher educational associations.[49] Their effectiveness has been limited.

THE DEMANDS OF MINORITIES

Still a third body of "outsiders" emerged, during the 1960s, as a force to be recognized by those responsible for university governance. This group was made up of the nation's minorities, particularly the blacks. Their spokesmen generally concentrated on the admission of more black students, increased financial support for these and other students from minority groups, more black teachers, more aggressive involve-

---

[48] The National Student Lobby, with headquarters on Capitol Hill, brings students to Washington to present the student view on pending legislation to members of Congress. A "consensus" student opinion is determined by an annual referendum on legislative issues. The Lobby is supported by the dues paid by member student governments, and in addition to its national activities it keeps students informed on the issues through a "Legislative Report," which goes to every campus in the country, and helps students organize their state-level lobbying activities.

[49] In the Congressional debates that preceded passages of the 1972 higher education bill, Senator Claiborne Pell, Chairman of the Senate Education Subcommittee, and the National Student Lobby pressed for tying institutional aid to federal assistance to needy students. Rep. Edith Green, Chairman of the House Education Subcommittee, and some of the higher education associations sought to link institutional aid to enrollments. Senator Pell and the students won and succeeded in inserting an additional provision that made it impossible to direct student aid money to general assistance for institutions (*Change*, October 1972, p. 62).

ment by the university in righting the social wrongs that disadvantaged minorities, and the incorporation of black or ethnic studies in the curricula.

The admission and preparation of an increased number of individuals for better paying jobs and entry into the professions, it became clear, is not a sufficient response by the college or university in the eyes of minority groups. The institutions, they held, should lead the effort to establish a more equitable society.[50] Consequently blacks and other minorities participated vigorously, though often independent of other student groups, against the war in Vietnam and segregation and for university concern with other social issues. Trustees and presidents were presented with lists of demands by black student groups, sometimes supported by external organizations. If they refused to discuss or to accede to the demands as presented or in the presenters' view "to negotiate in good faith," they were confronted with protests, demonstrations, and strikes.[51]

By their insistence upon the introduction of black or ethnic studies in the curriculum,[52] these groups posed additional, new, and critical issues of governance. On a number of campuses they would not accept the adaptation of existing courses or the inclusion of a few courses on black history by established departments. Rather, spokesmen for blacks insisted upon the establishment of separate programs. They refused, in a number of instances, to have their needs determined by white officials or the courses developed by white professors, and demanded that they be given control over decisions as to course offerings. In a few institutions black students adopted the Black Power credo[53] of the Student

---

[50] James W. Turner, for example, wrote: "Presently, black students are being trained to live and work in a white middle-class environment. They are compelled to study and learn about the politics, art, economics and culture of white people as if black people, their community, and their problems did not exist." "Black Studies: Challenge to Higher Education," in G. Kerry Smith, ed., *The Troubled Campus* (San Francisco: Jossey-Bass, Inc., Publishers, 1970), for the American Association of Higher Education, p. 203.

[51] Such a confrontation at Berkeley in 1969 brought about the declaration of a gubernatorial state of emergency.

[52] During the first four months of 1969 students demanded black studies programs at 140 colleges and universities, according to a report of the American Council on Education (*New York Times*, May 15, 1969). The 1971 Newman Report observed that "most minority-student programs through recruiting, tutoring, counseling, etc., attempt to adapt the minority student to conventional colleges. More ingenuity and effort must go into experimenting with varying forms of education that adapt college to the minority student" (p. 103 of advance draft).

[53] The concept of Black Power rests on a fundamental premise: *Before a group can enter into the open society, it must first close ranks"* (italics in original). Stokeley Carmichael and Charles V. Hamilton, "Black Power: Its Needs and Substance," in James McCray and Abraham Miller, eds., *Black Power and Student Rebellion* (Belmont, Calif.: Wadsworth Publishing Company, Inc., 1969), p. 244.

Nonviolent Coordinating Committee and demanded that the college or
university establish separate, nonwhite enclaves with complete autonomy from the parent institution on their campuses.

The critical issues posed by these demands had to be resolved by
trustees and presidents in a number of instances under crisis conditions.
In their haste to meet these demands college and university administrators often did not take, or were not allowed, time to explore basic
issues and to formulate considered approaches to such questions as
these:[54]

- What are the chances of survival of a minority student who cannot pass an admissions test but is nonetheless admitted? Does he
  have any chance of surviving without special remedial classes?

- What is the impact on other students concerning special considerations for some, e.g., open admissions, dual systems of grading,
  differing course requirements, and minority-student control of
  their own programs?

- Should the university agree to hire faculty members who do not
  possess traditional academic credentials?

- Should the university take the lead in changing society?

As a result, many black studies programs have been criticized as "too
politically oriented," "not academically respectable," and "uncon-
trollable." Uncritical propagandizing for a particular culture, many
have recognized, can prevent mutually beneficial interaction of different ethnic, racial, and cultural groups. Some black studies programs,
hence, were abandoned after a short period of experimentation, either
because of questions as to their academic integrity or the lack of financial support. Other programs persist, although they have not yet been
in existence long enough to be thoroughly tested.

The demands for black separatism on the campus posed particularly
difficult—and dangerous—problems of governance. Black leaders Roy
Wilkins and Kenneth Clark vigorously opposed acceding to such

---

[54] "It must candidly be said that black studies programs arrived on campuses in a
context of fear and disorganization on the part of essentially white administrators. . . . Before the mimeograph paper was dry on many of these demands,
colleges and universities were saying, 'Yes, that's right. We'll be very glad to
move ahead with that' " (Vincent Harding, "The Future of Black Studies," in
Smith, ed., *The Troubled Campus*, p. 213). Harding raises an interesting question. Instead of asking, "What black students are qualified to be on our campuses?" he asks, "What campuses are qualified to deal with black students?"

demands.[55] The National Association for the Advancement of Colored People, which Wilkins headed, threatened court action against any institution that used public funds to set up racially exclusive programs. The U.S. Office of Education threatened to withhold funds from Antioch College under Title VI of the Civil Rights Act when it established a "blacks only" Afro-American Studies Institute.

In the aggregate the demands of blacks—and in some areas Puerto Ricans, Chicanos, and American Indians—posed in even more extreme, form the issues raised by student activism as well as additional questions of large significance. While some actions taken seem in retrospect to have been unwise, the longer term impact of these demands, as with the demands of student activists, forced upon trustees and presidents an awareness of the views of a relatively new part of their constituencies and broadened the scope of institutional governance.

THE IMPACT OF URBANIZATION

As the new youth culture, the movement for women's liberation, and the drive for racial equality gave rise to critical problems of governance, so too has the urbanization of the American population. This social force has imposed great pressures on trustees, presidents, deans, and faculties to modify the curricula offered, to undertake research in new areas, to provide unprecedented services, to accept new obligations when citizens of an urban center, and to adapt to altered relationships with students.[56]

EDUCATOR FOR THE URBAN CENTER Urbanization has forced two distinguishable kinds of curricular adaptation on the institution of higher learning: (1) the inclusion of programs and courses to meet the needs of disadvantaged students seeking admission and (2) the development of courses dealing with the particular problems of the metropolis and programs to train the kinds of workers needed in the city. Urban groups have looked to the urban university to provide special programs for the educationally disadvantaged, tutorial services, consumer education, programs for adults, and a wide variety of courses

---

55 In "The Case against Separatism: 'Black Jim Crow,'" in *Black Power and Student Rebellion*, op. cit., p. 236, Wilkins suggests that in view of the costs involved and the shortage of qualified personnel, an alternative to scores of inadequate black studies centers would be the establishment of "two centers of genuine stature," one on the West Coast and one on the East Coast. Kenneth Clark resigned as a trustee of Antioch College because of its establishment of such an enclave.

56 A fuller and well-reasoned assessment of the impact of urbanization is provided in *The Campus and the City*, a report of the Carnegie Commission on Higher Education (New York: McGraw-Hill Book Company, 1972).

adapted to the needs of the work force of the community (for example, the University of Toledo has for many years offered courses in the technology of the glass industry, a principal opportunity for employment in that city).

RESEARCH IN URBAN PROBLEMS Just as the development of agriculture, once this country's dominant industry, attracted the interest of university scholars for more than a half century, so the emergence of large urban centers has attracted the curiosity of scholars. Simultaneously, even as the business and military segments of the society had turned to the universities for assistance in finding solutions to their problems the spokesmen for American cities followed suit. Together the interests of their scholars and the demands from city officials and civic leaders posed for those responsible for the governance of this country's colleges and universities tough problems of adaptation and of finance.

The "Urban Observatory Program" was an effort by the federal government to assist institutions in coping with these demands. Supported jointly by the U.S. Department of Housing and Urban Development and the U.S. Office of Education, this program, in 1968, provided that in six cities in which local government officials and local college or university administrators worked out a collaborative program the federal government would provide financial support. This program was designed to enable the local institution to help the local government cope with problems it identified, and thus to enable the educational institution to develop its own understanding of urban problems.

SERVICES FOR THE CITY The cities wracked by problems during the 1960s have increasingly looked to the local colleges and universities for assistance. This has resulted in the development of a variety of services provided by students, faculty members, and institutions. These include tutoring, child care, legal assistance, and many other services provided by students. Faculty members have contributed their expertise as consultants to local business and civic enterprises, and as board and committee members for planning, welfare, educational, and other agencies. The institutions have provided, depending upon their individual capabilities, assistance for the local schools, legal and health services for the poor, and technical assistance in support of such governmental activities as the "model cities" program.[57]

---

[57] Several observers contend that the demand for services is excessive. Robert C. Wood and Harriet A. Zuckerman, "The Urban Crisis," in R. H. Connery, ed. *The Corporation and the Campus* (New York: Praeger Publishers, Inc., 1970), p. 5, contend that the universities should not accept responsibility for meeting the deficiencies of other social agencies.

An illustration of the demand for services is provided by the effort of the U.S. Chamber of Commerce through local chambers to explore how the colleges and universities can provide those services which business leaders of the communities deem needed. A second illustration was provided in late 1972 when Senators Frank Church (Idaho) and Harrison Williams (New Jersey) introduced a bill providing support for "community education centers" to be established or expanded by the colleges or universities located in major metropolitan areas in order to provide a variety of educational, cultural, and vocational services tailored to the needs of the particular area.

OBLIGATIONS AS A CITIZEN Historically American colleges and universities were not located in the larger cities or, if located there, maintained a "walled-off" mien toward the community. As the cities have grown and as the institutions have expanded, this separateness, physically or functionally, could not be maintained. Hence, trustees, presidents, and financial officers have been confronted with a succession of problems as to how the institution shall treat its neighbors and as to what obligations it has as a citizen of the community. An enumeration of such problems is impracticable here but the identification of two that have had to be dealt with in many cities is illustrative.

The first is the problem of the institution's financial liability for services provided by the city: its properties being tax-exempt, the institution constitutes a burden for the local government, which is met in a number of cities by the voluntary payment of a sum calculated to cover the costs of services provided by the local government, e.g., streets, fire protection, etc. The second is the impact of the institution's development upon surrounding property, and often upon slum areas and the homes of lower-income peoples.

RELATIONS WITH STUDENTS In addition to the adaptation of educational programs (including admissions) to meet the particular needs of many who enroll in the urban institutions, college and university administrators have had to rid their minds as well as their institutions of conventions and practices rooted in the functioning of a smaller institution, serving residential students in a relatively rural location. In preponderant part, the students served in the institutions located in large cities are commuters and workers. This fact has posed for deans of students, presidents, and trustees the need for providing parking, eating, and other facilities and, in some instances, the need for finding alternative uses for dormitories no longer needed. It has necessitated the adaptation of class schedules to permit working students to attend in the early morning, late afternoon, and weekend hours. And it has necessitated the modification of course loads, and the development of relationships with major employers in the community, including arrangements for offering courses in students' work places.

For each institution in each urban center, the impact of urbanization on governance is distinctive. The facets of that impact have been identified, but the compulsiveness with which that impact confronts those responsible for governance depends upon circumstances prevailing in the community, the capabilities of the institution, and its financial status. That urbanization is a force that has and will shape this country's institutions of higher education is very clear. The task for trustees, presidents, and faculties is to recognize that impact and maintain the educational integrity of the institution while it makes inevitable adaptations.

THE OVERALL PROBLEM

The problems imposed on internal governance by each group of "outsiders" is in principal part the consequence of the spilling over of problems besetting the American society. The problems of war and peace, of racial equality, of crime and drugs, of rising unemployment and inflation, of decaying cities of the developing countries and this country's efforts to aid them and still others affect decisions as to admissions, curriculum, faculty membership, the functions to be performed, the funds required and how they can be allocated within the institution.

In the aggregate the questions posed by the interactions with these several outsiders can be stated succinctly. How can those responsible for the governance of the college or university:

- Be responsive to those who can contribute to its well-being?

- Be alert to the changes taking place in the world outside the campus, which are reflected by the actions and desires of "outsiders"?

- Maintain the independence, detachment, and impartiality essential for an institution's persistent obligation to seek new knowledge, transmit objectively what is known, and voice critical judgments as to prevailing problems and trends?

To respond effectively to such questions, trustees, presidents, academic officers, and faculties must hear, interpret, and correlate the messages conveyed by each body of outsiders—and must have a considered philosophy to guide their response.

Governance within a System

*A characteristic of modern societies is their inter-
dependence. Important institutions cannot be expected
to remain indifferent to the impact of even ostensibly
independent institutions on political and social processes.
In the contemporary context, the only question worth
discussing is not whether the university is part of society
at large, but the respective limits of academic freedom
and political interference.* R. K. A. Gardiner[1]

3 It was practicable during the 1950s, when studying the nature of
institutional governance, to view the college or university as a free-
standing, independent institution. By the 1970s such was no longer
the case. Public colleges and universities had become, in practically
every state, parts of a statewide system[2] of higher education. Simultaneously, most had become entangled in a federal system in which,
in return for financial support, they became subjected to controls. Many
private institutions were participants in the federal system by virtue of
the federal monies they received, and were gradually being drafted
into state systems. And a proposal included in federal legislation (i.e.,
the Higher Education Amendments of 1972) suggested that what have
been separate state and federal systems will likely be merged into a
single system.[3]

This shift in the status of the college and university is a consequence
of the much needed financial support by state and federal governments.
Increasingly, the colleges and universities have been impelled to play
the tune their patrons call.

But this shift in status is also a consequence of the public utility
character these institutions have attained, of the reactions of legislatures
and citizens to the behavior of some students and some faculty members, and, in some instances, of the failure of the institutions to recognize society's interest in their affairs.

---

1 "The University in Africa," the keynote address before a meeting of the Association of African Universities, Kinshasa, Nov. 19–21, 1969.

2 The term "system" is used to describe "a set or arrangement of things so related or connected as to form a unity" (*Webster's Unabridged Dictionary*, 2d.
ed., 1968).

3 The association of what were essentially separate state and federal systems
seems likely to result from the establishment of so-called "1202 Commissions"
created by Section 1202 of the Federal Education Amendment of 1972.

Colleges and universities provide services that are essential for a rapidly growing proportion of the total population—the young, the not-so-young, employers, and the society as a whole. Thus the disturbances experienced on some campuses between 1964 and 1971 provoked substantial public reaction. So did the occasional failure of individual institutions to weigh the society's various interests in formulating their own decisions to establish—or not to establish—new medical schools, social work schools, or other adjuncts.

The result of this shift is that many or most institutions have lost much of the autonomy once deemed essential for the functioning of a center of learning. Their boards of trustees and their presidents have lost much of the power to make those decisions that determine the caliber and quality of the institution's educational program. Institutions, their governing officers and their faculties have lost autonomy in the sense that they are being held accountable by external agencies, most often agencies of the state and federal governments.

THE SIGNIFICANCE OF AUTONOMY

A basic tenet of higher education has been that the individual institution must be autonomous.[4] Many institutions, notably those which are church-related, never enjoyed autonomy in a literal sense, and few observers of the American scene would contend that in the 1970s a college or university can insist upon an unlimited right of self-government. What then is involved in the claim for autonomy in the 1970s?

Autonomy involves more and less than the right of the responsible administrative officers—trustees and presidents—to govern the institution free of outside controls. The concept and tradition of autonomy comprehends, in addition to the latitude required for administrative action required by executives, the freedom of the academic department, of the professional school, and of the research institute within the institution to make most of the decisions of academic management. They comprehend also the freedom of the faculty as a body to set institutional goals and to have its views heard on all matters that affect the educational process, and the right of the individual faculty member to decide work patterns, to actively participate in major academic decision making, to have work evaluated by professional peers, and to be relatively free of bureaucratic regulations and restrictions.

---

[4] J. Victor Baldridge, David V. Carter, George P. Ecker, and Gary L. Riley, "The Impact of Institutional Size and Complexity on Faculty Autonomy," *Journal of Higher Education*, October 1973, p. 532.

Definitions of "autonomy" usually contend that the trustees, president, and faculty should be free to make those decisions that determine the essential character of the educational institution.[5] Those responsible for an institution's performance should be free to decide:

1. Which students shall be admitted and to what discipline they shall be subjected

2. Who shall teach, how much they shall be paid, when they shall be promoted, and whether they shall have tenure

3. The substance of the courses, the nature of the curricula, and the standards for degrees

4. The relative emphasis on instruction, research, and public service

5. How the institution's resources shall be allocated among departments, schools, and activities

The freedom of trustees, presidents, and faculties of public institutions to make unilateral decisions in any of these areas has been substantially eroded.

SPECIFICS OF THE EROSION

ACADEMIC DECISIONS[6]

Decisions as to which students to admit were once made almost solely by the faculty. Those decisions, by the 1970s, were substantially delegated to professionally trained admissions officers advised by faculty committees. Admissions decisions were also influenced by federal provisions about eligibility for student financial assistance and, in some states, by (explicit or implicit) requirements that all graduates of state high schools be admitted to public institutions. Private institutions are relatively free to make admissions decisions as they deem best, but that freedom is constrained by financial pressures that dictate liberal stand-

---

5 The best reasoned explanations of this article of faith are those of Sir Eric Ashby in *Universities: British, Indian, African* (Cambridge, Mass.: Harvard University Press, 1966) and Logan Wilson's address, "Institutional Autonomy," in *Shaping American Higher Education* (Washington: American Council on Education, 1972), pp. 232–242.

6 Consideration of the locus of responsibility for making admissions decisions must take into account the relative number seeking admission. Prior to 1950 most public institutions accepted all high school graduates. Most private institutions had no more than one applicant per available space in the institution, and even the prestige institutions were operating at about 2½ applicants to each space available. Hence, decisions as to admissions became much more selective as the number seeking to enroll increased rapidly during the 1950s and 1960s.

ards to bring in needed income. Admissions to both public and private institutions are substantially influenced by social pressures to admit more blacks, more poor, and more women.

Decisions about who shall teach, how much they shall be paid for which services, and whether they shall have tenure once were shared by faculties and administrators. In the public institutions of some states such decisions are governed by civil service rules (often conceived for nonacademic application); and, of late, some state legislatures have intervened to fix hours, limit compensation, and circumscribe the granting of tenure. Robert M. O'Neil has forecast:

> Legislative intervention of various forms will probably continue into the foreseeable future. For several reasons, . . . the scarcity of funds and the change in the academic market place, . . . lawmakers . . . have become far more sophisticated about the internal workings of colleges and universities. . . . The development of state wide coordination and control is likely to intensify legislative activity. . . . Having taken the first step with impunity may embolden lawmakers. . . . Regardless of the level or recurrence of student protest, legislative regulation of academic life is likely to persist up to the point it is checked by the courts.[7]

PROGRAM DECISIONS

The professional—lawyer, doctor, or professor—increasingly claims an expanding right to determine how his skills shall be applied and what actions shall be taken. But decisions about courses, curricula, and degrees are increasingly constrained by the requirement of state coordinating agencies that they review and approve all new programs in public institutions. In private institutions, decisions are made with greater freedom. However, the freedom of both private and public institutions to make program decisions is limited by the accrediting associations. The influence of these associations (see Chapter 2, p. 26) is heightened because the majority make decisions on which eligibility for federal aid is based.

RESEARCH DECISIONS

In both public and private institutions, research, where it is carried on, is supported in principal part (i.e., 60 percent or more) by the federal government. This means, in practice, the individual faculty member's

---

[7] *The Courts, Government, and Higher Education,* a paper prepared for the Committee for Economic Development, New York, 1972.

decision as to what research he will undertake must conform with federal decisions that determine what funds are available, and means that the federal government plays the major role in the financing of doctoral degree programs, and influences not only decisions as to what and how much research will be done, but decisions as to the development of graduate study as well.

During the 1950s and most of the 1960s, research was the main vehicle of federal support for higher education. During those years (and the earlier war years), federal support for research produced noteworthy scientific achievements and advances in the teaching of sciences and engineering. However, by tying this support to individual research projects, federal agencies caused some faculty members to focus their attention on research (to the detriment of teaching) and weakened their loyalties to the institution that employed them. This reduction of institutional loyalty was furthered by a heightened demand for instructors which made the individual faculty member all the more independent.

The president and trustees often learned, after having approved requests from faculty members for federal support of research projects, that they had mortgaged some institutional funds and their own influence within their own institution. The availability of federal support created an imbalance in institutional programs, gave rise to a dependence on federal research funds, and, as federal funds "dried up" in the early 1970s, made institutional budgets less stable.[8]

FINANCIAL DECISIONS

The ability of deans, presidents, and trustees to allocate funds, with the advice of faculties and students, as they deem desirable, is affected by the particular mix of revenue sources on which their institutions depend. The manner in which their freedom to allocate is limited by the rigid formulas used by several states to determine appropriations for particular purposes, e.g., instruction and libraries is described in Chapter 8, "Change and the Financial Process." Here it will suffice to make clear that within the prevailing systems much revenue available to an institution is tied to particular activities, i.e., funds come from different sources for specified purposes: instruction research, student aid, construction. In general, private institutions have greater freedom

---

8 For analysis of the impact of federal support, see Harold Orlans, *The Effects of Federal Programs on Higher Education* (Washington: The Brookings Institution, 1962), chap. 18, "The Project System," pp. 250–280; and William G. Bowen, *The Federal Government and Princeton University* (Princeton, N.J.: Princeton University, 1962), pp. 305–319.

in using their funds, but the principal sources ensuring that freedom (student fees, private gifts and grants, and endowment e nings) are likely to provide a smaller proportion of all revenues in the future. This, in turn, will mean less elbow room for presidents and trustees in governing those institutions.

In short, as the social utility of higher education has become increasingly recognized and the cost has grown apace, institutions have become embroiled in a complex system of bureaucratization and centralization. Both the legislative and executive branches of federal and state governments have focused increasing attention on the policies, programs, and performances of colleges and universities, as well as on their costs. New legislative and investigative committees have been established, state coordinating agencies have been strengthened, some governors have intervened in operations, and political campaigns have been waged on issues of higher education. And the federal government stressed, during the early 1970s, the legal obligation of these institutions to provide greater opportunity for blacks and women as members of the faculties.

JUDICIAL INTERVENTION

A spate of legal decisions has further circumscribed the freedom of those who head, private as well as public, institutions to manage institutional affairs. These decisions have substituted the judgments of courts for those of presidents, trustees, and faculties in such matters as the handling of campus disorders (e.g., when officials of an institution are justified in closing or keeping it open); student discipline; the hiring, firing, and conditions of employment of faculty or the president; the recognition and privileges on the campus of student groups; and the equality of opportunity in employment, admissions, financial aid, and academic evaluation.[9]

The extension of judicial rule has pushed the colleges and universities (and particularly the public institutions) from their informal and paternalistic ways of the past to a heavy dependence on formal regulations and procedures. This tendency is rooted in the realization that the courts are more accessible than ever before to aggrieved members

---

[9] For elaboration of the nature and impact of court decisions, see Robert M. O'Neil, "Law and Higher Education in Imperfect Harmony," a paper prepared for the CED Sub-committee on the Management and Financing of Colleges, Feb. 2, 1972, pp. 15–22; T. R. McConnell, "Accountability and Autonomy," *Journal of Higher Education*, June 1971, pp. 451–452; and Wilbur J. Cohen and Philip S. Gartenberg, "New Challenges in Higher Education: The Rule of Law in the Academy—Help or Hindrance?" an unpublished paper prepared in January 1971.

of the academic community and that the courts (as well as some administrative agencies, e.g., the U.S. Department of Health, Education and Welfare) have manifested a readiness to challenge long-standing processes of student discipline, faculty membership, admissions, and even academic grading and degree granting.

ACCOUNTABILITY AND GOVERNANCE

In the aggregate the system that has evolved constitutes an explainable response to the changed context in which higher education has come to operate. As both the public and private colleges and universities have required more public funds, interacted in many more ways with the society about them, and played an increasingly central role in the lives of *not* an elite few, but the majority of all young people, governors, legislators, and the courts have been impelled to require of these institutions an increasing accountability.

On the one hand, legislators and public executives are concerned with such questions as these:

- When society promises equal educational opportunity, can it rely on the institution to seek ways to admit all who can benefit? Given the freedom to decide, will the institution cling to admissions standards that ape those of prestige institutions, or will it fix standards and tuition rates to maximize income with little concern for avowed social policy?

- Does the college or university any longer desire to retain authority to discipline its students? Or has much of that function been ceded to civil authorities?

- Can institutions, after delegating to faculties substantially unqualified authority to make decisions about teaching, promotion, and tenure, be free to make such decisions when faculties are unionized? Or shall such decisions become the prerogative of the state board or the governor's office?

- Can faculties granted substantial freedom to design courses and curricula be relied upon to seek out the particular needs of the institution's geographical region? Can they be expected philosophically to accept the limitations on the educational program implicit in a state's master plan?

- So long as the country's prestige institutions emphasize the importance of research and public service, can the new and expanding public college or university, competing for faculty members and students, be expected to content itself with the instruction of a predominantly undergraduate student body?

- Do the processes of internal governance generally enable trustees and presidents to allocate resources to serve society's ends when they conflict with the conventions of discipline-oriented faculties? Can trustees be relied upon, as theory dictates, to represent society's views in such allocational decisions, or do they become the proponents of the institutional objectives as framed by faculties and presidents?

On the other hand, the autonomy that society has granted to institutions of higher learning in the past is rooted in two fundamental beliefs. The first is that higher education is a creative, intellectual activity and if scholar-teachers are to carry on such an activity they must be assured the freedom to pursue their inquiries wherever they may lead and to express their reasons and beliefs no matter how they may vary from conventionally held opinions. Furthermore if their wills, interests, and imaginations are to be continually stimulated to "package" their expanding knowledge in courses and programs relevant to society's current needs, they must be allowed a substantial and effective part in decisions as to educational programming. Hence, the concept of autonomy comprehends the freedom of the department, of the professional school, and of the research institute within the institution to formulate most academic decisions, as well as the freedom of the scholar-teacher, i.e., academic freedom.

The second is a belief that the higher education institution should be relatively free to make its own decisions as to the allocation of resources within; the selection, work assignments, and promotion of personnel; and the details of operations (e.g., where and when supplies and equipment shall be purchased). This belief rests on two facts: few other enterprises—except perhaps the theater and the arts—are so largely continually dependent upon creative, intellectual effort; and no other enterprise is more exposed to general criticism as colleges and universities have become more and more involved in instruction, research, and services that challenge conventional standards, traditionally held beliefs, and some long-established policies. Hence, academic administrators claim that "a portion of [the university's] institutional life and development . . . is not within the bailiwick of anyone else to prescribe or control or even touch."[10]

---

[10] Samuel B. Gould, "The University and State Government: Fears and Realities," in W. John Minter, ed., *Campus and Capitol* (Denver, Colo.: Interstate Commission for Higher Education, 1966), p. 9.

FEASIBILITY OF AUTONOMY

Autonomy in the literal meaning of the word is no longer an acceptable concept. In the 1970s it is clear that the general public, various interest groups (e.g., teachers, blacks, farmers, businessmen), and state and federal officials outside the academic community, as well as trustees, administrators, faculty members, and students within, have legitimate interests in college and university decision making. What is needed, given that intermixture of interests, is a framework that will satisfy the legitimate interests and responsibilities of each.

State governments must be concerned with the roles and objectives and the operational and capital expenditures of each institution primarily because they are concerned with finance.[11] They are also obligated to see that the total offering of all institutions meets the needs of the state's residents.[12] Because the federal government is increasingly concerned with changes concerning access to higher education and the level of particular programs (e.g., teacher training), it may enforce those changes through the mechanisms of the state governments[13]— mechanisms which limit the authority of those within the institution to make decisions that determine institutional character.

The mechanisms include the master plan and the review of proposals for new programs which constitute the implementation of this plan; the state budget and the detailed formulas to calculate appropriations; the capital expenditure programs and the specification of space and design characteristics; and the requirements to use centralized personnel, purchasing, and many other services created for state agencies which are not educational institutions. When these mechanisms are supplemented by legislation that stipulates the number of class hours, provides for an annual assessment of courses or curricula, monitors student discipline, and prohibits class suspension without prior approval by the state board, not only is the freedom of the individual institution to shape its own program and to respond to the initiatives of faculty members and students diminished but admission standards and educational programs may be drastically and unwittingly altered by the minor alteration (perhaps by an uninitiated legislator) of budgetary formulas

---

11 For elaboration of this point see Robert O. Berdahl, *Statewide Coordination of Higher Education* (Washington: American Council on Education, 1971), chaps. 5, 6, and 7, pp. 73–172.

12 The capacity and desirability of having agencies of government determining what educational programs should be offered is questioned by many observers.

13 Lanier Cox and Lester E. Harrell, "The Impact of Federal Programs on State Planning and Coordination of Higher Education," Southern Regional Education Board, 1969.

by which appropriations are calculated. In one state, for example, the basing of appropriations on the average number of students enrolled *at the beginning and at the end of the year* influenced public institutions to retain students who richly deserved to be "busted out" to the year's end. The setting of this budgetary formula illustrates a generally applicable axiom of administration: administrative absurdity increases directly with the square of the distance between principle and context.

More important, the aggregate system that has evolved violates a principle applicable to the management of any human endeavor—bureau, church, firm, regiment, or ship: if an enterprise is to enlist the creativity, enthusiasm, and collaboration of its members, these individuals must have a sense of participation. They must be assured that their voices will be heard by those who make the decisions that affect their work and their lives. They must have confidence in and be respected by the decision makers.[14] As responsibility for the decisions that determine the essential character of an institution has been moved effectively out of the institution, administrators, faculty members, and students have lost some part of the basis upon which loyalty to and identification with the university was founded.

Substantially, the college teacher's freedom to express himself, as his mind and conscience dictate, and to define goals and activities and evaluative standards for his students has not been invaded from without. The autonomy of the department to choose members and to specify courses has been curtailed where state civil service regulations impinge and where state coordinating boards extend their controls over courses and programs. More substantially and more generally abridged has been the authority of trustees and presidents to participate in decision making and to exercise the controls required to hold the institution together and to keep it on course.

The business enterprise, the government bureau, and the military forces are held together as organizations by structure—by an authoritarian system of rules and processes which dictates who shall make decisions about what. The college has been held together less by structure and authority and more by shared beliefs, attitudes, and values: beliefs about the importance of learning; attitudes on the responsibility of the scholar to his discipline, his peers, and his students; and values concerning the worthiness of the academic life, devoted to the conservation and discovery of knowledge and to the development of

---

[14] Chester Barnard, *The Functions of the Executive* (Cambridge, Mass.: Harvard University Press, 1948), pp. 161–184; Rensis Likert, *The Human Organization: Its Management and Value* (New York: McGraw-Hill Book Company, 1967).

youth.[15] When decision making is centralized in the hands of individuals remote from those who share these beliefs, attitudes, and values, the collegial organization becomes particularly susceptible to disintegration.

Moreover, the larger the enterprise—and in the mid-1970s the typical college or university is relatively large—the more difficult it is to define beliefs that claim the zeal of faculty members, students, clients and alumni of several colleges and many departments. Such a normative system of governance is substantially negated when the institution is part of a centralized system.

A GUIDING PHILOSOPHY

The fault is not in the mechanisms used by the state or federal governments. Statewide plans, budgets, and capital expenditure programs are required. The controls accompanying most federal legislation are inevitable. It is not possible to specify the decisions to be made by government controllers and by institutional administrators; in increasing measure, most decisions are simultaneously social and educational decisions. Consider, for example, admissions standards. A philosophy is needed to guide state officials, institutional administrators, and faculty members in utilizing those mechanisms constructively. Such a philosophy can be expressed in five relatively simple guidelines.

1. The integrity—the wholeness—of the individual institution must be a prime concern both of government coordinators-controllers and of those within the institutions.
The grant-making processes of the federal government; the devotion of faculty members to their disciplines; and the demands of organized nurses, chemists, lawyers, farmers, blacks, and women have demonstrated how readily the institution can be fragmented.

Some coordinating boards, unwittingly, are now demonstrating this same propensity. For example, one state board called upon educational institutions to revise and resubmit the basic statements of their missions, in terms and on a schedule that made manifest it did not intend the presidents to seek the concurrence of their trustees. In that same state, the faculties made obvious that since the state board approves or dis-

---

15 Burton R. Clark, "Belief and Loyalty in College Organization," *Journal of Higher Education*, June 1971, pp. 499–515, and Allen Wallis, "Institutional Coherence and Priorities," in *Whose Goals for American Higher Education?* (Washington: American Council on Education, 1967), pp. 93–11.

approves their proposals for new educational programs, they see little purpose in the trustees' review.

Simultaneously, many colleges and universities have demonstrated that, while traditional processes of academic governance are incapable of coping with the complexity of large institutions and with the interventions of external forces, they are unwilling to modify these processes to permit those theoretically responsible for leadership—trustees and presidents—to lead.[16]

2. The colleges and universities have attained the status of a public utility; their affairs must be conducted in recognition of that status.
Trustees must face their obligations to represent society to the institution as well as the institution to the society. They are the allies of the president, but they do not exist simply to support the president and his administration. Presidents, department chairmen, and faculties must recognize, more fully than in the past, the social dimension of the decisions they make, decisions they have tended to view as exclusively educational.

State and federal coordinators-controllers must be aware that a dynamic, innovative faculty can be reduced to the pulp of a time-serving bureaucracy by remote "coordination." The effect of the heavy hand of external regulation has been demonstrated in this country in the electric, communication, transportation, and other utilities. That heavy hand may be simply persisting demands for detailed information which gradually draws the regulatory agency into internal decision making. A current example is the demand on offices of institutional research to provide enrollment projections and statistical analyses and to complete questionnaires requested by state and federal agencies.

3. College and university administrators must be welcomed to and aggressively take part in those state and federal councils where socio-politico-educational decisions are now made.
As the cost and importance of higher education grow, the locus of decision making about admissions, educational programs, faculties,

---

16 Dwight R. Ladd, *Change in Educational Policy*, Carnegie Commission on Higher Education (New York: McGraw-Hill Book Company, 1970): "As universities have grown larger and more heterogeneous and as faculties have become more a part of the department and of a national scholarly guild, as opposed to the central institution, the power of decision making has tended to move outward and to become more diffuse. It has become primarily a veto power which cannot be offset by the rhetoric of collegiality" (p. 214).

and facilities drifts "away from the educational institutions toward political structures."[17]

To many administrators habituated to the academic life, participation in the hurly burly of state political life is distasteful. In several states, state university trustees and presidents have looked down their noses at those state officials responsible for coordination, and generally have lost stature for their institutions as a consequence.

If the decisions made increasingly by "political structures" are to reflect a full understanding of the educational implications, they cannot be made by state or federal functionaries removed from first-hand concern with the educational process and from contact with faculties whose spirits must be kindled if the decisions are to foster educational advance.

4. *Diversity—a much treasured characteristic of American higher education—cannot survive in a system in which institutions conform to a common mold, either through subtle force or abjection.* Despite all that is said about diversity, the generally vacuous statements of mission filed with coordinating agencies reveal little distinctive purpose. The statements of trustees, administrators, and faculty members often reflect an addiction to how it was at Old Siwash more often than they demonstrate fresh and individual programs and processes. Few institutions with as valid and innovative a program as that of the University of Wisconsin at Green Bay have reared their heads in recent decades.

The institutional forces that induce conformity can be reinforced or combatted by federal regulations and the processes of state coordinators and budget officers. The review of new programs by state coordinating boards and accrediting agencies and budgets fixed by formulas are perhaps the principal processes that now impel conformity. Adaptation of educational offerings to current social needs requires faculty and student involvement to a degree not yet attempted by state bureaucracies or accrediting associations.

The hope for a diversity that will include new, imaginative, pragmatic approaches lies in focusing accrediting, budgeting, and coordinating processes on measures of institutional outputs rather than on measures of inputs. When governors and budget officers, for example,

---

17 James A. Perkins, "The Drive for Coordination," an essay included in *Higher Education: From Autonomy to Systems* (New York: International Council for Educational Development, 1972), develops this thought and cites a particular decision as to the internal operation of Cornell University that was finally made in the executive office of the President of the United States.

limit institutional dollars, manpower, space, and equipment by niggling controls over salary levels, faculty-student ratios, space standards, and operating procedures, educational programming is constrained.

> 5. *The structure and processes of internal governance must be so strengthened as to ensure the responsible exercise of such freedom as is granted the individual institutions.*

Those concerned with higher education require the same freedom to exercise their professional judgment as other professionals even though they function within an organization that constitutes a part of government; so too does the judge.[18] These guidelines (pp. 60–64) are designed to provide that freedom. But these institutions need insulation from interference by state bureaucracies, even as the courts have traditionally been insulated. It is not isolation that they need, nor can afford.

If they are to function responsibly, granted that insulation, and if they are to function responsibly within today's context, the structure and processes inherited from the past must be modernized. The nature of that modernization will be spelled out in subsequent chapters. Here, however, it can be noted that this modernization will mean that:

1. Authority shall be redistributed among the several constituencies that make up the institution—that is, among students, the faculty and units of the faculty (e.g., schools and departments), the administration and trustees—in relation to their concerns and competencies, to mobilize the continuing loyalty and zeal of each.[19]

2. The faculty shall be so organized, and so committed to responsible discharge of the authority delegated, as to enable it to fulfill its obligation for the formulation of admissions policy, for the continuing redesign of curricula, and for the choice of its own members in a manner consistent with the public interest as well as with the personal conveniences and preferences of individual members. The form of organization that meets this test will provide for concurrence with officers of administration and participation by students in decision making by the faculty.[20]

---

[18] For analysis of the evolving relationship between the professional and his employer see Wilbert E. Moore, *The Professions*, "The Professional and His Employer" (New York: Russell Sage Foundation, 1970), chap. 11, pp. 187–206.

[19] For elaboration of the reasons for such decentralization, see Morris Keeton, ed., *Shared Authority on Campus* (Washington, D.C.: American Association for Higher Education, 1971), pp. 148–152.

[20] Arnold Weber, et al., *Faculty Participation in Academic Governance* (American Association for Higher Education, 1967), voices the view that academic senates dedicated to and effective in bringing about faculty and administrative collaboration will be the most productive vehicle for achieving the ends itemized in this paragraph (pp. 65–66).

3. The president shall be entrusted—by faculty[21] and students, as well as trustees—with such fullness of authority as to enable him to make promptly and firmly those decisions that are essential to the on-going effectiveness and economy of a large enterprise.

4. The board of trustees shall be reconstituted (or recreated in those state colleges and universities where it has been abandoned) to provide a membership that:

   a. Possesses an understanding of the nature and functions of a college or university

   b. Can and will give the time required to develop an intimate awareness of the need and views of each constituency it serves—the public, the faculty, the students, and the alumni

   c. Particularly will examine and reexamine the quality of the educational program and its relevance to the university's clientele

   d. Will assume responsibility for the autonomy that is delegated, as well as the funds that are provided

These guidelines present no new or radical concepts. But the behavior of state coordinator-controllers, on the one hand, and institutional trustees, administrators, and faculties, on the other, has reflected little acceptance of these principles.

ORIENTED LEADERSHIP

However, more is needed than a restatement of principles if the trend toward centralization and bureaucratization of higher education is to be rationalized. The locus for this rationalization is in each state government. There the debate must produce answers to questions such as how to control increasing expenditures, how to coordinate competitive and ambitious institutions, including the private colleges and universities, and how to make the aggregate of public and private institutions responsible to social needs.

If that debate is to stem the tide of bureaucratization, three needs must be met. First, broad-gauged political leadership that understands the distinctive nature of a college or university, and can distinguish it clearly

---

21 "The *autonomy and freedom of action* of presidents and trustees have been surrendered ... to the faculty itself," in the opinion of Vernon R. Alden, former president of Ohio University. They (presidents and trustees) must assume control, he contends, over the curriculum, the quality of teaching, and the selection and promotion of teaching personnel if they are to be held accountable.

from the state highways department or a chain of retail stores, must emerge in each state. Experience suggests that governors have not often provided such leadership. It could come from a senior legislator, from a state university president who has earned political status in his state and who can rise above identification with a particular institution. In Indiana, it could be a Theodore Hesburgh; in Michigan, a John Hannah; in North Carolina, a William Friday; in Ohio, a John Millett.

Second, such leadership should produce a reaffirmation in legislation, or even in the state constitution (as now obtains in a few states), of a guarantee of independent action for each college or university. Eulau and Quinley have suggested that state legislators could be persuaded to provide such statutory guarantees. Reporting on a survey of the opinions and experiences of policy makers in nine states, they found that state legislators generally consider their responsibilities fulfilled by a review of the educational budget and that "it would be improper for them to get entangled in educational decision making."[22] Legislative reaffirmation would not automatically ensure independent action and institutional integrity, but it would be a persistent reminder that political interference is not in the interest of the public or the institution. More important, the debates that would produce such a reaffirmation would provide the citizenry a sorely needed education. Reaffirmation will depend upon the ability of the individuals who accept the politico-educational leadership to hammer out fresh agreements on autonomy. How much autonomy is, in fact, needed by the individual institution? How can an institution's responsiveness to state needs be ensured?

Third, the function of the state coordinating agency must be redefined before a determination is possible on whether a "statewide governing board" or a "coordinating council" will best do the job.[23] Although the current trend is toward establishment of statewide governing boards (such as those established in North Carolina, Wisconsin, and Louisiana in 1972), analyses of the two types of agencies argue strongly that boards may not provide the needed control and coordination *and* the needed assurance of institutional integrity and vitality.[24]

---

[22] Heinz Eulau and Harold Quinley, *State Officials and Higher Education: A Survey of the Opinions and Expectations of Policy Makers in Nine States,* Carnegie Commision on Higher Education (New York: McGraw-Hill Book Company, 1970), p. 65.

[23] The experience in Michigan (and perhaps Indiana)—where laissez-faire tolerance prevails in substantial measure when compared with the experience in California and other states where more rigid controls over institutional operations have been exercised—raises a question as to whether state government coordination results in educational quality at lesser cost.

[24] Berdahl, *Statewide Coordination;* Carnegie Commission on Higher Education, *The Capitol and the Campus: State Responsibility for Postsecondary Education* (New York: McGraw-Hill Book Company, 1971).

AGENCY RESPONSIBILITIES

The following guidelines suggest the functions the state coordinating
agency should perform (primarily but not exclusively) in relation to
public institutions:[25]

- Consult continually with the trustees and president of each institution and with legislative leaders and their staffs.[26]

- Reframe the state master plan regularly, with a maximum participation by key administrators and faculty members from the state
  institutions; review institutional proposals for establishing new
  degree programs and courses, with full recognition that judgments
  about educational worth will be made within the institution and
  that heavy-handed decisions will discourage initiative, limit diversity, and induce costly conformity.

- Provide a forum in which representatives of public and private
  institutions can participate with state officials and leaders of constituencies (e.g., physicians, secondary school administrators,
  blacks, women) to study evolving needs for higher education, to
  devise means for special educational services, and to extend inter-
  institutional collaboration. The Southern Regional Educational
  Board provides, at the regional level, an example of such a forum
  in action.

- Assess the financial needs of each institution and serve as the
  advisor for allocating state and, perhaps, federal appropriations
  for construction, student aid, and general institutional support.
  According to the Carnegie Commission:

  External budget control should be limited to the total amount of the
  budget and to post-audit for purposes of determining fiscal responsibility and should not involve line-item approval, involvement in budget management, or specific allocation of resources within the institution.
    Salary scales for individual classifications should not be set by

---

25 See also *Institutional Rights and Responsibilities* (Washington: American Association of State Colleges and Universities, 1972). The relations of the state
   coordinating agency is more limited and increasingly complex, particularly for
   the private college or university that operates in more than one state.

26 A brochure entitled "Institutional Rights and Responsibilities" (Washington:
   American Association of State Colleges and Universities, 1972) provides a logical and useful analysis of the distribution of responsibilities as between institutions and statewide governing or coordinating agencies.

external authority, nor should mix of faculty or staff at various levels be determined by external authority.

General levels of admission may be determined externally, but external authorities should not be involved in the development of a policy to meet those levels or in the application of admission policies to individual cases.

The hiring, firing, and assignment of faculty and staff should be within the internal control of the institution.

While space utilization standards and maximum costs per square foot are legitimately a matter of external policy, building and equipment design should not be.[27]

- Protect the autonomy and diversity of state institutions, by striving to expand the freedom of each from ill-suited fiscal constraints, procedural controls, and civil service rules and practices.

- Finance management advisory service for both public and private institutions, i.e., enable institutions to bring to their campuses individuals or firms qualified to assist in improving management and administration.

FUNCTIONING WITHIN THE SYSTEM

As the costs of higher education continue to rise, the public will increasingly demand accountability from colleges and universities, and these institutions will be inextricably entrapped in a centralized bureaucracy. Conventional cries for autonomy will not lead to the needed rationalization of the governance of individual institutions within the state and federal systems. That rationalization will require recognition first that the individual institution cannot expect absolute autonomy in governance, that decisions in each critical area of institutional governance will be shared between government controllers and institutional trustees, presidents, and faculties; and second that unless a philosophical framework is accepted not only by government controllers and trustees but also by presidents, and faculties for making shared decisions, the vitality and dynamism of higher education will be snuffed out.

---

[27] Carnegie Commission on Higher Education, *Capitol and Campus*, p. 106.

PART TWO

SUBSTANTIVE PROCESSES

Unique Organizational
Characteristics of
the Academic Enterprise

*The American college or university is a prototypic
organized anarchy. It does not know what it is doing. Its
goals are either vague or in dispute. Its technology is
familiar but not understood. Its major participants wander
in and out of the organization. These factors do not make a
university a bad organization or a disorganized one; but
they do make it a problem to describe, understand, and
lead.* Michael O. Cohen and James G. March[1]

4 If one would believe the charts, manuals, and catalog descriptions
by which universities tell others what their organizations are like,
one would conclude that the university is organized much as the
corporation or the governmental agency, or even the hospital. Graph-
ically, each has a similar hierarchy: a governing board on top, a chief
executive, several levels of subordinate officers, and in the background
unpictured customers, investors, bankers, and suppliers for each. But
anyone who has been exposed to such organizations as the U.S. Department of Transportation, the International Paper Company, the United
States Army, the Protestant Episcopal Church, the Danforth Foundation, and the University of South Carolina know that this depiction is
misleading. The individuals in these and like organizations are banded
together to achieve common objectives in quite different ways, despite
the seeming similarity in structure.

The purpose of this chapter is to look beneath the superficial similarity portrayed by the organization charts, to look at the environment
depicted in the two preceding chapters, and to look within and identify
the unique characteristics of the organization of the academic enterprise. Simultaneously, it will indicate how the pressures for formaliza-
tion and routinization imposed upon the academic enterprise by the
changes in function, the reduction of autonomy, and the insistence
upon fuller accountability are altering that organization.

---

[1] Michael O. Cohen and James G. March, *Leadership and Ambiguity: The American College President* (New York: McGraw-Hill Book Company, 1974), p. 3.

To accomplish these ends, this chapter will consider in turn:[2]

1. *The charter of the organization*: Not the formal words of a musty document, but what in fact does the university exist to do?

2. *The activities the organization performs*: How and to what extent do the university's activities interrelate, or fail to interrelate, the individuals who make up the organization?

3. *The character of the organization*: What kind of a world does the university provide for those who are part of its structure?

4. *The membership of the organization*: What is distinctive about the individuals and groups that make up the university?

5. *The bonds of the organization*: What ties hold the members of the university together and with what degree of consanguinity?

CHARTER AND GOVERNANCE

It is an axiom of management that to be effective an organization must have a clearly stated purpose and generally understood objectives that can be translated into more precise goals against which performance can be measured. But few colleges or universities have clear, tangible objectives that are generally understood.

Statements of objectives are found in most catalogs but they are so general and so vacuous as to provide little or no guide for the individuals who make up the institution. Here are some examples: "to develop the individual"; "to provide each student with the opportunity to develop intellectually, morally, culturally and vocationally"; "to produce ornaments of the church and the state"; and "the advancement of knowledge and the education of young men."[3]

The accrediting associations force institutions "to formulate . . . statements of purposes for the institution as a whole that will provide a guide for educational planning" that the faculty "may understand, accept and support."[4] Some institutions are able to translate noble objectives into particular educational tasks; other pronouncements remain so vague as to be devoid of operational utility. For example, a

---

[2] This framework for analysis is patterned after an approach described by E. Wight Bakke in "Concept of the Social Organization," in Mason Haire, ed., *Modern Organization Theory* (New York: John Wiley & Sons, Inc., 1959).

[3] These examples are taken from an article by William C. Fels, *Columbia University Forum*, Spring 1959.

[4] "Guide for the Evaluation of Institutions of Higher Education," North Central Association of Colleges and Secondary Schools, Commission on Colleges and Universities, 1967.

large urban college recently reported to its accreditation agency that through its Student Services Division it would strive to help students "find more flexible ways of living," "become excited about being alive," and "increase one's capacity to love." These may be worthy objectives, but they provide a lame "guide for educational planning"; they do nothing to convert broadly stated objectives into goals, strategies, programs, and plans of action.[5]

In a large number or majority of all colleges, available evidence (and most of that empirical) suggests that broad and nobly stated objectives are *not* supplemented by more manageable educational goals and plans, and there obtains but little and superficial agreement among faculty members as to the educational strategies and programs they are jointly pursuing. As a consequence, the college's educational program tends to be a congeries of little-planned and little-related departmental or divisional efforts. Planning is usually limited to forecasts of enrollments and of admissions efforts, and to administrative (e.g., space needs) and financial (e.g., the instructional budget, per student food costs) matters. A number of institutions are striving to install program budgeting and cost-benefit measurement techniques, but as yet the difficulties of identifying the objectives to be programmed for and of quantifying the goals set have limited the extent to which educational planning has accompanied and guided resource allocation.

THE ADMINISTRATIVE FUNCTION OF OBJECTIVES

Yet the college needs, if it is to utilize limited resources effectively in producing worthy educational outputs, objectives that provide a frame of reference within which trustees, administrative officers, deans, and departmental chairmen, in consultation with faculty and students, may:[6]

- Set goals and policies as to admission and retention of students

- Fix standards for the selection and promotion of faculty members

- Fashion the curriculum and other educational experiences to be made available to students

- Plan innovations in the instructional function

---

[5] Marvin Bower in *The Will to Manage* (New York: McGraw-Hill Book Company, 1966), pp. 146–147, states that "the total planning process . . . consists of determining objectives, establishing goals, developing programs or broad plans for carrying out strategy, and developing more detailed operational plans for carrying out the programs."

[6] Cohen and March, op. cit., p. 3.

- Establish policies as to the allocation of time and resources for research and the provision of other than instructional services

The community college, for example, may in the light of the needs of the community it serves set objectives in terms of numbers of individuals to be trained for specific occupations (e.g., medical technologists), the numbers to be started on their way toward baccalaureate degrees, and the numbers (principally, adults) to be provided with further training in locally needed skills (e.g., accounting or teaching) or to be provided opportunities for enrichment in music or drama. The four-year college may similarly define objectives in terms of the constituencies served [e.g., the student body of Trenton (New Jersey) State College will likely have different needs than the female students enrolled in aristocratic Sweet Briar (Virginia) College]. A Princeton or a University of Chicago may well define the objectives of its college of arts and sciences, as in effect each does, as the education of students for entry into graduate work, with emphasis on particular fields (e.g., mathematics, physics, history). And each institution—community college, four-year college, or university—can pursue such objectives while striving to develop such outlooks, attitudes, personalities, and values in the students as it may deem important.

But why do explicit and understood objectives seldom exist to guide the management of colleges? A very obvious answer to this question is that the framing of objectives, that is, clear-cut goals for which strategies and plans can be formulated, is a more difficult task for the university than for a shoe factory, a supermarket, or an insurance company. This difficulty will be discussed below.

REASONS FOR LACK OF OBJECTIVES

A central reason for the lack of objectives that can be translated into precise educational goals and neat plans is that "a true university like most marriages is a unity of diversities."[7] If education were simply a matter of transmitting an accumulated and limited body of knowledge inherited from the past (even though that knowledge is comprehensive), the definition of objectives and the conversion of objectives into action would be relatively simple. But the diversities it comprehends include "the clash between new visions of promoting technological efficiency and old traditions of nurturing human individuality," the

---

[7] A statement made to the author by Harold W. Dodds. See also his book entitled *The Academic President—Educator or Caretaker* (New York: McGraw-Hill Book Company, 1962), pp. 6–8.

contention of many faculty members who hold that only an education that involves heavy concentration in a discipline is worth while and the contention of others who would encourage students to equip themselves with interdisciplinary programs in American studies or European studies, and opposing views as to the desirability of education in the liberal arts and sciences and in career-oriented training. And academic administrators, particularly in large institutions, shrink from the divisive effects of trying to gain approval of objectives that choose between opposing views.

A second reason is that the process of helping a broadening variety of more sophisticated students[8] understand a broadening variety of problems of an increasingly complex world in which a growing variety of specialists offers an increasing variety of interpretations makes the definition of objectives readily translatable into tangible goals difficult indeed. And that process is made still more difficult in this country by a seeming inability to agree on where higher education commences: the improvement of the high school has illuminated the extent to which college curricula contain much that duplicates what the student encountered in secondary school, and many community colleges have tended to vacillate as to whether they offer in fact two additional years of secondary schooling or higher education in a meaningful sense.

A third reason for the lack of objectives that are translatable into educational goals and plans is found in the succession of pressures that society imposes on the colleges and the universities.[9] When the typical higher education institution is a large enterprise with 10,000 or more diverse, commuting students, meeting demands for contract research and public service, as well as providing a "way station" for many uninterested and some unteachable young people for whom the society has no alternative, it is carrying on activities that have been thrust upon it; it is not carrying out objectives it has chosen for itself and which its administrators and faculty generally understand and approve.

A fourth reason lies in the even more varied concerns of the several constituencies that make up the college and especially the university— the faculty, the students, the trustees and administrators, the alumni,

---

[8] Calvin B. T. Lee wrote in "Whose Goals for American Higher Education?" in Dobbins and Lee, eds., *Whose Goals for American Higher Education?* (Washington: American Council on Education, 1968), p. 5: "Students are demanding more freedom both inside and outside the classroom. Refusing to be treated like products on an assembly line, they conceive of learning as a process that entails action and participation."

[9] Alan Pifer has explicated this theme in an essay entitled "The Responsibility for Reform of Higher Education," in the annual report of the Carnegie Corporation, 1971.

and, last but not least, the institution's clients, particularly the government agencies that look to it to perform research or provide services, and the professions (e.g., medicine, law, engineering) that look to it to guard their gates of entry. Only the most broadly stated purpose—one encompassing the objectives of each faction—would be generally acceptable.

In the well-managed business enterprise, objectives are translated into operating plans that specify for the immediate future, in quantifiable terms, what is to be accomplished and when. The government bureau's activities are made specific from year to year by a legislatively approved budget; when the appropriation process works well, that budget spells out, in conformity with the originally legislated purpose, what will be accomplished within a specified fiscal period. And the philanthropic foundation with a known annual revenue can and often does formulate strategies as to the social objectives it will perceive and allocates proportions of its funds to be used in pursuing each objective —e.g., research in the natural sciences, archeological exploration, experimentation in public health, or research in early learning.

Planning for the college or university—and particularly for its core activity of teaching and research—is less feasible and, despite the noble efforts of some proponents of academic "management," less often practiced than in the business enterprise, the government bureau, or the foundation. Plans can be and are developed for the college's or university's physical facilities (the development of the campus), for its financing (the raising of funds, expenditures, and the investment of endowments), and for its business affairs (housing and feeding of students, purchasing, maintenance of grounds and buildings, keeping of accounts, and construction). But teaching and research are so little quantifiable and so subject to the varying approaches of different teachers and scholars that institutionwide plans are seldom formulated.

Few departments have plans that clearly set forth teaching (undergraduate and graduate), research, service to business and government, and student advising missions, and provide a grand design to guide the formulation of courses and teaching.[10] This lack of departmental planning is due in many instances to a lack of data even as to number of student hours produced, number of majors, and number of funds available and expended and to the lack of standards or limits on size of class and to the lack of firm teaching-load standards. But often departments do not have plans because faculty members have their own

10 Paul E. Dressel, F. Craig Johnson, Philip M. Marcus, *The Confidence Crisis* (San Francisco: Jossey-Bass, Inc., Publishers, 1970), pp. 71–77, 190–192. An excellent schema for departmental planning is outlined on pp. 196–206.

objectives which may or may not coincide with those of their colleagues. In general such planning as departments do is only the planning of incremental additions to the work of the department, e.g., the addition of an assistant professor in a field not covered by the teaching of the several members of the department.

In summary then, for reasons that stem from the basic nature of an institution of higher learning, the college or university functions with only the most general understanding as to goals to guide the individuals who carry out its activities.[11] In this respect the university differs significantly as an organization from its counterparts—the business enterprise or the military unit and some (e.g., the Social Security Administration), but not all, governmental agencies.

ACTIVITIES, STRUCTURE, AND PROCESS

The architecture of organization is fashioned to accommodate the activities to be carried on, even as the architecture of buildings reflects the activities for which they are constructed. The activities to be performed dictate the kinds of personnel required, the roles and influence accorded different categories of personnel (e.g., the production executive in the manufacturing company, the buyer in the department store, and the actuary in the insurance company). Together the nature of the activities to be performed and the personnel mobilized to carry them out shape organization and modes of functioning.

Colleges and universities have traditionally carried on two primary activities. The core activity was and is, of course, teaching. Integrally related to this activity has been research, an activity more generally claimed than carried on in fact, but nonetheless integral to the core teaching activity.[12]

Society, as well as the individual institutions, have recognized the large importance of these activities and have accorded to those who perform them certain protections that influence the structure and processes of the college and university. Those protections are customarily summed up in the term "academic freedom"—the guarantee to the teacher of the freedom of expression (i.e., the right to interpret in his

---

[11] There are notable exceptions. A few colleges, usually of modest size, have established a distinctive purpose that is generally accepted by faculty, students, administration, board, and alumni. Perhaps the best-known examples are Antioch, Reed, and Swarthmore.

[12] Ralph W. Tyler has declared that "The notion that every professor is a competent research scholar is a fiction and an effort to bring this ideal to reality seems destined to fail" ("Can a University Determine Its Future?" *Proceedings of the Higher Education Colloquium*, Chicago, March 1973. Mimeographed).

teaching the knowledge accumulated as he sees it) and to the researcher the freedom of inquiry (i.e., the right to pursue his research wherever it may lead him). To assure these protections for those who perform these roles, the college and university have traditionally claimed, and society has generally granted, autonomy, i.e., the right of the institution to govern its internal affairs without undue interference by the state or by any powerful group within the society. As knowledge has been accumulated, the individual teacher or researcher has gained an additional dimension of freedom, which flows from possession of so specialized an understanding of a particular area of knowledge as to make impracticable or impossible the direction or control of his activities by others.[13] This high degree of specialization means, in addition, that much of what the individual does in teaching and research is only generally related to what fellow members in the organization do. Together these two factors—(1) the possession of a unique knowledge, skill, or experience and (2) the lack of relatedness among the work of many faculty members—limit the authority[14] of superiors in the academic enterprise and substantially limit the applicability of the concept of hierarchy.

The reflection of the nature of these academic activities, their social importance, and the protections consequently accorded the institution, its teachers, and researchers can be seen in three aspects of the college and university structure. The lay board (with broad powers of governance in theory and limited powers in fact) exists to represent the concerns of society in the autonomous institution and to ensure that the teachers and researchers are accorded the freedoms essential for the performance of their functions. The simultaneous existence of two internal structures within the college or university—the academic structure, made up of departments, schools, and colleges, and the administrative structure, responsible for supporting services and business affairs—reflects the self-governance granted the teaching and research staffs. And the flat organization of the academic structure (i.e., the limited

---

13 Talcott Parsons writes that "in a sense probably not true of most bureaucratic organizations, it is not possible for academic men, competent as they may be in their own fields, to understand each other's specialties at a very high level" ("The Strange Case of Academic Organization," *Journal of Higher Education*, June 1971, pp. 486–495).

14 The organizational theorist recognizes this problem in his distinction between formal and functional authority: formal authority is derived from the organizational position an individual occupies and the sanctions associated with that position; functional authority is derived from professional competence, unique understanding or experience, personal charisma, and human relations skills possessed by the individual. See, for example, Robert L. Peabody, "Perceptions of Organizational Authority: A Comparative Analysis," *Administrative Science Quarterly*, vol. 6, pp. 463–482, March 1962.

organizational distance vertically between professor and senior academic officer) reflects the relative independence accorded the individual teacher and researcher.

The nature of these academic activities simultaneously conditions the internal processes of governance. Decisions as to who shall teach are highly diffused, i.e., are made, in the large university, by each department (e.g., the departments of history, physics, or sociology) and in the smaller college by the department with the concurrence of the dean and sometimes the president; decisions as to what shall be taught, largely by the individual teacher in concert with his departmental colleagues; as to how it shall be taught, predominantly by the teacher; and as to what research shall be undertaken, almost exclusively by the individual researcher and his sponsor. The processes of control—i.e., of seeing to it that classes meet and are taught effectively, and that research undertaken is carried out competently and as scheduled—are substantially self-administered; the conscience of the individual teacher or researcher and the desire to gain the esteem of peers constitute the primary, and a self-imposed, control.

Will these differences in organizational structure and processes persist or disappear? Will the uniqueness of university structure and processes persist as the university grows larger? As the business enterprise performs an increasing array of functions important to the society (e.g., employing the hard-core unemployed, producing drugs on which many individuals depend for the maintenance of life itself) and as the business enterprise and the governmental bureau utilize increasing numbers of highly specialized workers (who claim for themselves substantial self-determination of what they shall do and how), will their structure and processes become more like those of the university? Will the spread of external degree programs and other forces making for prepackaged educational modules undermine the extensive diffusion of authority that has existed?

CHARACTER OF AN ORGANIZATION

The character of an individual organization—be it a business firm, governmental agency, church, or institution of higher learning—is molded primarily by the basic purpose and the activities it is established to perform.

The purposes for which colleges and universities exist—the transmission of knowledge to the young (and, incidentally, the shaping of the values of a major segment of the upcoming generation), the discovery of new knowledge and its application to the ills and problems of the society—are purposes that receive general social approbation. This approbation has been reflected in the financial support accorded these institutions and in the willingness of individuals of better-than-average talent to devote themselves to academic life despite alternative opportunities. The academic world provides faculty members with ego satisfactions greater than those enjoyed by the manager of the rent-a-car station or the engineer in the public highway department. That social approbation is based on the presumption that the education of people and the findings disclosed by research are, in the long run, of great benefit to the society. The intangibility of that presumption makes the college and university vulnerable at times when happenings on the campus run counter to the conventions of society. But traditionally it has been held that the college or university should enjoy freedom from external interference to assure the academic freedom of individuals, and that it may well be located physically separate from the rest of society. The location of many colleges or universities in days gone by in rural communities, removed from the work-a-day world, and the physical separation of the campus from that community emphasize this separation.

Detachment—intellectual as well as physical—has been markedly reduced by the changes of recent decades. The increased importance of the college's and university's function of certifying their graduates for entry into employment is one of such changes. As new individuals become dependent upon the holding of a degree to obtain the jobs they seek, the college and the university perform a function of increasing essentiality to both their graduates and to employers. Hence, the institution has assumed some of the obligations of the public utility and has lost some of the detachment it has deemed essential. This detachment has also been eroded as the institution of higher learning has become increasingly involved in the study of, and the application of knowledge to, problems of business, government, and the community. The teacher and researcher have more and more recognized their need for interaction with the community, not for detachment from it. Autonomy, both the personal autonomy of the scholar and the autonomy of the institution, has been reduced.

One characteristic associated with this earlier detachment persists in the colleges and universities that still serve residential student bodies. The institution of higher learning has been (and to a degree still is) a "total institution."[15] That is, it tends to encompass for many of its

---

15 For a stimulating discussion of the organizational implications of the "total institution," see Erving Goffman, "On the Characteristics of Total Institutions," *Asylums* (Chicago: Aldine Publishing Co., 1961), chap. 1, pp. 3–124.

members (principally students, but also faculty members) not only the work-associated aspects of their lives, but the social and recreational aspects of their lives as well. In this respect, the residential college or university located in the rural areas did provide for many of its members an environment more akin to the monastery, the convent, the prison, or the asylum than to the business enterprise.[16] In the "total institution" all aspects of life are conducted in the same place, in association with the same individuals, and under the same authority; the work, social, and recreational phases of the individual's life are, in varying degrees, scheduled in relation to one another in an overall plan purported to accomplish the purpose of the organization. (Such conditions prevailed in the smaller residential institutions of the past more than they do in the 1970s in the large urban institutions.) An organization that is a total institution in this sense maintains a distinctive relationship with and interdependency among its members.

Generally the college or university has "a notably loose kind of social organization." These organizations vary markedly between institutions (e.g., faculty members at the City University of New York operate under greater constraints than do faculty members at the University of Michigan or at the University of Chicago) but in most institutions the college or university organization is highly decentralized, and the individual faculty member—and, increasingly, the student—is relatively free to determine his own activities, free of supervision and direction, and free of evaluative controls in comparison with analogous members of counterpart organizations.[17] That freedom, when coupled with the kinds of individuals that make up institutions of higher learning, is central to the debates of the early 1970s as to the proper focus for the making of various kinds of decisions (e.g., the establishment or abandonment of particular courses), who should be involved in the making of decisions (e.g., the faculty, junior faculty members, students), and what controls should be maintained (e.g., criteria specifying faculty productivity and workloads, formulas to determine the allocation of funds.) [18]

---

16 "The Man from Mars" (*Dun's,* February 1971, p. 41) pictures the kind of world provided by one industrial enterprise for its employees.

17 Such freedom was not always the case: many universities, during the early 1900s, were quite authoritarian in their administrative style, e.g., Columbia University under Pres. Nicholas Murray Butler or the College of William and Mary under Pres. J. A. C. Chandler. The change to "a notably loose kind of social organization" is likely attributable, in principal part, to the increased professionalization of faculty members.

18 For elaboration of this reasoning and a citation of useful references see Kenneth P. Mortimer, "Accountability Dilemmas," a paper prepared for the Committee on Economic Development, May 1972.

MEMBERSHIP AFFILIATION

The university is, in economic jargon, a "labor intensive" enterprise. It is dependent, as are many businesses (a high technology firm—IBM, Polaroid), professional enterprises (a hospital or a law firm), and governmental agencies (such as the National Institutes of Health or the Atomic Energy Commission), upon the caliber, the effectiveness, and the zeal of the several categories of individuals that make up the membership of the staff of the university. These categories include: trustees, administrators (the president and his staff), academic administrators (deans and department chairmen), faculty members (tenured and untenured), the emerging semiprofessional staff (librarians, computer operators, laboratory directors, and others), the nonacademic staff (the accounting, purchasing, building-operation, and maintenance and other staffs), students, and alumni.

It was Chester Barnard who pointed out a quarter of a century ago that to be effective an organization must persuade the individual member that his personal interests are in accord with, and will be furthered by, accomplishment of the objectives of the employing organization.[19] Measurement of the identity and depth of the interest of each category of "members" by this yardstick reflects a fundamental characteristic of the university as an organization.

INTENSITY OF AFFILIATION

Consider first the affiliation of the trustees with the institution of higher education. The men and women who serve in this role, in major part, are attracted to these boards by the social distinction the role of trustee grants, a desire to contribute to the public good, or the emotional attachment of the alumnus. Their interests and zeal are not unrelated to the objectives of the college or university, but in most instances, the institutions are necessarily a secondary or peripheral interest. Most trustees can give neither the time, the understanding, nor the depth of concern to the college or university that the corporate directors devote to the enterprises in which they (or their principals) have a substantial economic stake, or that elected legislators are impelled by public exposure to give to the affairs of the government they serve.

Passing for the moment the president and his affiliation with the college or university he serves, consider the nature of the academic

---

19 *The Functions of the Executive* (Cambridge, Mass.: Harvard University Press, 1948), pp. 163–165.

administrators. The interests and depth of concern with the success of the institution manifested by those who serve in these posts (from departmental chairman to provost) are limited by two factors. The first is the notion prevailing in many institutions that scholars should not give an undue proportion of their time to administrative tasks, i.e., that after a limited period of years they should return to their roles as teachers and scholars. That notion is underlain by the individuals' identification with the academic discipline in which they were trained. The values of the academic man dictate that he is first a chemist, second a professor in the XYZ University, and third a department chairperson.

The scale of values that limits the academic administrators' depth of concern with the interests of the institution they serve affects even more clearly the attachment of faculty members. Many or most see their future in terms of advancement as a physicist or an historian rather than as a member of the faculty of the XYZ institution.[20] The depth of their attachment will vary as between those academics who serve on the faculties of prestige institutions and those who serve in less prestigious institutions, and as between those older teachers who have served an institution for an extended period and those younger men and women "on their way up" who have served in a particular institution for a relatively few years. In general, the intensity of the individual's concern with the institution as an enterprise is limited by his primary concern with his academic discipline.

The students of a residential college tend to have a substantial concern for the institution in which they are enrolled; the students who commute to the large urban universities tend to develop a lesser allegiance. This differentiation, recent studies indicate, will be reflected in the nature of the attachment of alumni to their alma mater; the older alumni (e.g., those who graduated before 1950) tend to exhibit a greater allegiance to their alma mater than those alumni who completed their student lives during the period 1964–1974.

The professional and nonacademic staffs can be and usually are attracted to the college or university and their zeal is heightened and maintained by the conditions of employment that are provided. For

[20] D. B. Truman has written ("The Academic Community in Transition," *NASPA Journal*, July 1970, p. 7) that "there has been a kind of atrophy of intra-institutional contacts and identifications as we now have a situation, perfectly familiar in most universities, where a man will have more intimate and close contact with colleagues three thousand miles away and will share more loyalty and affection with them than he will with a colleague who occupies an office three doors down the corridor. There has been, in consequence of this, a weakening of concern for the collective educational enterprise that spans any such professional boundaries or should span them."

them, the level of compensation and the permanence of employment are major factors influencing their attachment to the institution.

The president and his immediate staff, in contrast to each of the other categories of individuals that make up the staff of the college or university, have a clear identity of interest with the institution as an enterprise and a presumed permanence of attachment. His success or failure is commensurate with that of the institution; he is primarily responsible for shaping the objectives of the institution, and presumably shapes them toward ends in which he fervidly believes, or finds acceptable.

IMPACT ON GOVERNANCE

The secondary nature of the concern with the affairs of the college or university as an enterprise of both trustees and faculty members, and the impermanence or transitory nature of the concern of students and alumni, concentrate the responsibility for the success of the institution on the president and his staff. Yet the president is constrained in the discharge of that responsibility by the insistence of each of these categories of members of the university's staff (and oftentimes of factions among each category) that they have a part (and in crucial areas of governance a controlling part) in decision making.[21]

Despite their secondary concern with success of the university as a whole enterprise, faculty members claim, in increasing measure, a voice in decisions as to educational program, in the selection and promotion of their colleagues, and in decisions as to their compensation and working conditions. Students claim an increasing right to determine their individual course of study, their own living patterns, and claim a voice in a widening range of decisions as to educational program, admissions, and, in a few instances, faculty membership. And both claim the right to participate in shaping the policies of the whole institution. Do they possess the requisite talent for the roles they claim?

"The American professoriate today is a diverse assortment of professionals, very much divided collectively—and in many cases, uncertain, individually—about what they and their institutions should be doing."[22] This diversity must be recognized in attempting to answer the question

---

21 Michael D. Cohen and James G. March, op. cit., p. 2: "...the president has modest control over the events of college life. The contributions he makes can easily be swamped by outside events or the diffuse qualities of university decision making." For further development of this idea see these authors, chap. 9, "Leadership in an Organized Anarchy," pp. 195–230.

22 Seymour Martin Lipset and Everett Carll Ladd, Jr., "The Divided Professoriate," *Change*, May–June 1971.

stated above. Yet some relevant generalizations can be drawn. The faculty member was trained over an extended period for service as a scholar. That training involved for most an extended period of financial stringency and the necessity for rigorous and persistent application of mind and time to a narrowing range of problems. The individuals who eventually emerge tend to be characterized by a singlemindedness, a sense of intellectual superiority, and "a latent hostility to that which is nonintellectual," e.g., raising funds for the college endowment.[23] In addition, in comparison with the salesman or the accountant in business or the bureau chief in government, professors are likely to hold as important for organizational decisions such choices as absolutism versus relativism, objectivity versus commitment, freedom versus authority, and orthodoxy versus secularism. Concern with such fundamental values may limit the individual's capacity to contribute to the making of decisions on practical matters central to the institution's needs at the moment.[24]

Students come and go, bringing little experience or accumulated wisdom and having, perhaps, little time to involve themselves in matters of governance. Yet their right to participate in governance has been recognized by many institutions.[25] Why? Because most decisions of the institution affect them; because students believe that if education is of fateful significance to them, they should have a voice in its character and quality; because students have strong social and educational motivations and have demonstrated that they can provoke desirable educational change; because participation in governance is preparation for responsible citizenship in the larger society; and because students can play a refreshing role in the improvement of institutions.[26] In considerable part, students have won their right to participate by demonstrating the raw power to close the institution. The stimulus to the exercise of that power is the general revulsion to paternalism in the American

---

[23] See Allan M. Cartter, "All Sail and No Anchor," *The Key Reporter,* Winter 1970–71, p. 2, for a supplementary point of view. See also, George Williams, *Some of My Best Friends Are Professors* (New York: Abelard-Schuman, Limited, 1958), for a similar point of view, more dramatically put.

[24] Mrs. Ewart K. Lewis presented a supplementary point of view in a Phi Beta Kappa Address at Oberlin College in 1956: "For it is also characteristic of those who are steeped in philosophia that they are always disagreeing on its significance; if they agree on a principle, they disagree on methods. In an academic community, the love of wisdom seems scarcely distinguishable from the love of argument. An academic community is in a perpetual condition of war...."

[25] See, for example, James J. Hearn and Hugh L. Thompson, "Who Governs in Academia?" *Journal of Higher Education,* July 1970, pp. 132–135.

[26] Earl J. McGrath, *Should Students Share the Power?* (Philadelphia: Temple University Press, 1970), pp. 51–62.

society. But only organized labor with the strike has rejected paternalism or authoritarianism as vehemently as students have by their actions on a number of campuses between 1964 and 1974.

The president of the college or university is continually confronted with the necessity of maximizing the interests of these several categories of "members" in the objectives of the *whole institution*, in maintaining their interests over time, and in reconciling conflict as among various groups within the faculty and between students and alumni, among faculty and students and trustees, and as between public governing authorities and the faculty or students. The task is fundamentally one of political leadership. It involves the diagnosis of the obligations of the institution he heads; the assessment of the power structure within and surrounding the institution; and the continual reconciliation of conflict among the several categories of the institution's membership, striving always to achieve ends his judgment dictates are in the best interests of the institution he heads.[27]

THE BONDS OF ORGANIZATION

The business enterprise, the government bureau, and the military organization are held together as organizations by structure. Each has as its organizational skeleton a hierarchy that relates one unit to another and establishes "clear lines of authority." Each has a supplementary system of superordination and subordination, which is reflected in the vital processes by which decisions are made as to the allocation of resources; the appointment, promotion, and evaluation of personnel; and the control of performance. And in each, as size grows and as the power of the apex of the hierarchy to direct and control the whole declines (whether because of unionization or geographical dispersion), rules and procedures are developed to constitute a system of due process that ensures the articulation of each unit with the whole.

Traditionally, the college was held together as an organization by

---

27 J. Victor Baldridge in presenting a similar view of the nature of the university as an organization (*Power and Conflict in the University*, New York: John Wiley & Sons, Inc., 1971, pp. 15–18) describes the relevance of three bodies of theoretical reasoning not customarily applied to the problems of university governance. These bodies of theoretical reasoning are the writings of (1) sociologists in the field of "conflict theory" (e.g., Dorwin Cartwright, "Influence, Leadership, Control," in James G. March, ed., *Handbook of Organizations*, Chicago: Rand McNally & Company, 1956, pp. 1–47), (2) political scientists relative to "community power structure" (e.g., Robert A. Dahl, *Who Governs?* New Haven, Conn.: Yale University Press, 1961), and (3) organizational theorists as to the functioning of "informal organizations" within an organization (e.g., Chester I. Barnard, *The Functions of the Executive*, Cambridge, Mass.: Harvard University Press, 1948, pp. 114–123).

normative values: the individuals who made it up, and particularly the faculty and, less cognitively and more emotionally, the students, "shared beliefs, attitudes and values."[28] Those beliefs had to do with the large importance of learning for learning's sake. Those attitudes had to do with the responsibility of the scholar to his academic discipline, to his peers, and to his students. And those values included the worthiness of the academic way of life, of a life devoted to the conservation and discovery of knowledge and to the development of youth. Analogous beliefs, attitudes, and values contribute to the integration of some governmental bureaus for periods of time (e.g., the Social Security Board, 1936–1939; the Economic Cooperation Administration, 1945–1959; and the Peace Corps, 1960–1963), some foundations when launched on a new mission, and a few business enterprises.

In the college that has hammered out a distinctive and respected purpose and has stuck to it over a period of years such "shared beliefs, attitudes and values" constitute a "social cement" that links departments and schools, emphasizes the whole, and commits individual faculty members, students, alumni, and trustees to the institution. In those colleges in which no distinctive purpose was achieved, or in which common beliefs, attitudes, and values were not cultivated by a more authoritative president, such "social cement" is replaced by greater emphasis on hierarchical structure and by a system of superordination and subordination.

As we have moved over the past five decades in this country from the small college (less than 1,000 students), to the medium-size university (3,000 to 5,000 students), to the multiversity (10,000 to 100,000 students), the normative basis for governance has slowly but implacably been replaced by increasing emphasis on hierarchical structure, on refined processes of superordination-subordination, and on rules and procedures that will ensure due process for the individual or for the subunit.

The larger the academic enterprise, the more difficult it is to maintain a set of beliefs that will claim the interest and zeal of the faculties and students of several schools and many departments. The large urban institution with many professors and students who commute from the suburbs and spend a limited time on campus find the building and maintenance of common beliefs especially difficult. On most campuses common beliefs are found only in the departments, and only in those

---

[28] "Sociologists commonly conceive of two broad dimensions of social bonding: the structural, consisting of patterns of relation and interaction of persons and groups; and the normative, consisting of shared beliefs, attitudes and values" (Burton Clark, "Belief and Loyalty in College Organization," *Journal of Higher Education*, June 1971, p. 499).

departments that can claim some standing in their particular disciplines. The maintenance of common beliefs is even more difficult when both faculties and student bodies are subdivided into political factions. And a normative system of governance is substantially negated whenever the institution is a part of a state system in which governance decisions are made by an authority removed from the educational process on the campus (i.e., the state coordinating board).

The key problem of governance in the mid-1970s is to determine what changes in the structure and processes of governance need be made (*a*) to better adapt prevailing forms of governance to the unique characteristics of the academic enterprise and (*b*) to adjust to a changed environment in which these institutions function and to some fundamental changes in the academic enterprise itself.

The search for such a mode of governance is taking place when the institutions of higher education face a "no growth" or a declining future.[29] If a mode of governance, particularly appropriate to the functions of academic institutions in the 1970s and early 1980s, is to be developed, answers to at least these five questions must be found.

1. Do the unique characteristics of the college or university as an organization require new structural arrangements to provide efficient means for the expression of opinion and/or participation in decision making of groups which have had little voice in decision making?

2. Should the processes of decision making be made more explicit and decision-making bodies more visible to all within the institution affected by decisions?

3. Are the structures for faculty decision making and student government that have obtained to be abandoned as new structures are conceived, or will there continue to be a need for these structures?

4. What power will remain with trustees and president as the faculty and students are granted a larger share in decision making?[30]

---

29 Lyman Glenny has forecast, in contrast to forecasts of the U.S. Bureau of the Census, the Carnegie Commission on Higher Education, and the U.S. Office of Education, that the growth in enrollments during the late 1970s will increase less rapidly, that enrollments during the 1980s will tend to decline more, and that the decline in enrollments will continue during the 1990s ("The 60s in Reverse," *The Research Reporter*, The Center for Research and Development in Higher Education, University of California, Berkeley, 1973, no. 3, p. 2).

30 Michael D. Cohen and James G. March, op. cit., p. 4, contend that ". . . organized anarchies require a new theory of management. Much of our present theory of management . . . assumes the existence of well-defined goals and technology, as well as substantial participant involvement in the affairs of the organization. When goals and technology are hazy and participation is fluid, many of the axioms and standard procedures of management collapse."

5. What processes of accountability by each constituency that participates in decision making need be established as structural changes endow each with larger responsibilities?

Answers to these questions must be based on consideration of two conditioning forces. The first is the evolution of organizations, not colleges and universities alone, but all complex organizations. The second is the nature and evolution of the several processes that are involved in the functioning of a college or university.

Successive chapters will describe the governance of each of these basic processes, as it is carried on in colleges and universities, most of which now function as parts of larger systems. Before going on to the consideration of those processes some speculation as to the future of organizations generally will be relevant.

Some scholars question a theme that has run through this chapter, i.e., that the college or university is an organizational entity that can be compared with other types of organization—a bank, an industrial firm, a government.[31] Other scholars have classified organizations and have contended that colleges and universities are comparable with other types only in a very broad sense.[32] My observation of organizations over three decades suggest that the college or university as an enterprise has certain unique characteristics and operates in an environment which dictate significant modifications in the manner in which authority is distributed and individuals and subunits relate one to another, but that one need not abandon what is known of organizational theory to interpret the functioning of the institution of higher education.

Indeed, others forecast (and persuasively, I think) that organizations generally will evolve in ways similar to the changes that have been apparent in the colleges and universities. James D. Thompson, for example, predicts that complex organizations by the year 2000 will be "much more fluid, ad hoc and flexible" and will rely less on authority "as the glue that holds them together."[33] The "notably loose organization" found in most colleges and universities is more fluid, ad hoc, and flexible than the organizations typical of business enterprises and governments. The need is for the rational modification of organizational forms and processes which the colleges and universities have inherited from other fields of endeavor.

---

31 John D. Millett, *The Academic Community: An Essay on Organization* (New York: McGraw-Hill Book Company, 1962).

32 See, for example, Peter M. Blau and W. Richard Scott, *Formal Organizations* (San Francisco: Chandler Publishing Co., 1962); and Amitai Etzioni, *Modern Organizations* (Englewood Cliffs, N.J.: Prentice-Hall, Inc., 1964).

33 "Society's Frontiers for Organizing Activities," *Public Administration Review*, July–August 1973, pp. 327–335.

Change and the Instructional Process

*Throughout history, educational institutions have
continually become inadequate for the intellectual demands
of their time and as a result have suffered from the shocks
of drastic adjustment.*   J. B. Lon Hefferlin[1]

5 "We are at a moment in history," that wise observer Eric Ashby
wrote in 1973, "when the balance of forces in systems of higher
education all over the world is upset by social changes. . . ."[2] In the
United States his diagnosis is obviously true; seven elements of change
can be identified that have forced alterations in what is taught, how,
and by whom.[3]

The first of these elements is the great increase in the number and
variety of students to be educated. This has forced the introduction of
new kinds of courses, new methods of instruction, and the use of young
and relatively inexperienced instructors to offer much of the instruction
in the lower divisions of the universities.

Second, the ever more rapid discovery of new knowledge in every
discipline—from anthropology to zoology—has necessitated a substantial and repeated revision of course content and curricula. This accumulation of new knowledge tested the adaptability of many teachers and
required the enlistment of more teachers with understanding in new
areas of knowledge. It has as well prompted the substantial growth in
graduate, professional, and vocational education.

Third, the increase in the range of the abilities of students has
induced modification of the subject matter offered, and has challenged
the conventional view that higher education necessarily involves the
development of the intellectual curiosity, the capacity for precise reasoning, and the assimilation of a body of historically evolved ideas. Higher
education, it has become clear, to be useful for some now enrolled, con-
centrates on the development of those affective skills that enable the

---

1 *Dynamics of Academic Reform* (San Francisco: Jossey-Bass, Inc., Publishers,
1969), p. 2.

2 *The Structure of Higher Education: A World View*, International Council for
Educational Development, occasional paper no. 6, January 1973, p. 9.

3 Carnegie Commission on Higher Education, *Reform on Campus: Changing Students, Changing Academic Programs* (New York: McGraw-Hill Book Company,
June 1972), chap. 4, pp. 23–26.

individual to "get along" in the organizational world in which he or she will spend time.[4]

Fourth, recognition of the greater maturity, better preparation; and greater sophistication of many students (when compared with those enrolled a decade earlier) forced the updating and enrichment of courses and curricula. Simultaneously these students demanded "relevance"; they sought in the courses and curricula they were offered material that would aid them in understanding the problems of their time and themselves. This demand for relevance reflects an unwillingness to accept the academics' concern for learning for learning's sake, for wisdom as a valuable good in and of itself. And, as Jacques Barzun has written, it is likely attributable to the fact that "the spirit has gone out of whatever is being taught,"[5] or as Riesman and Jencks have argued: "Today's students . . . have been bored in class since they were six, and very few even entertain the idea that this is necessary. Their anger and resentment focus on other problems [such as] . . . poverty, racism, the War in Viet Nam, etc."[6] Whatever the cause, it is associated with an insistence that students be given a part in the making of decisions as to what shall be taught, and a less often pressed claim that students be privileged to participate in decisions as to who shall teach.

A fifth element of change is found in the nature and volume of jobs prospectively available to graduates and dropouts. The undergraduate educational programs offered in four-year colleges and universities were originally designed to provide the fundamental understandings for individuals who would eventually enter professional or managerial jobs.[7] As the proportion of all young people going to college has grown, and as the job market has changed, the nature of the educational training they require has been altered.

The sixth element of change is the financial stringency that attacked the colleges and universities in the early 1970s and that promises to constrain these institutions for the foreseeable future. The paucity of resources necessitated the paring of the most sacrosanct of all categories of expenditures—"instructional costs"—or, in simpler terms, necessitated the reduction of the number of teachers. This has involved

---

[4] For a supporting view see George Shea, "The University: A Longer View," *Liberal Education*, December 1970.

[5] *The American University* (New York: Harper & Row, Publishers, Incorporated, 1968), p. 210.

[6] *Atlantic Monthly*, vol. 22, February 1968, p. 54.

[7] Carnegie Commission on Higher Education, *College Graduates and Jobs: Adjusting to a New Labor Market Situation* (New York: McGraw-Hill Book Company, April 1973), chaps. 3 and 4, pp. 25–68.

a "hard look" at the number and variety of courses being offered, the number and capabilities of teachers, and even at the very educational objectives[8] being sought and the essentiality of subcategories of instructional costs to those ends. This hard look has involved the faculty, but has been impelled, in many instances, by deans, presidents, and even trustees who, obligated to maintain the financial viability of the institutions over which they preside, have been forced to delve into areas of governance long regarded as the exclusive province of the faculty.

A seventh element of higher education's environment that has induced change in the content and method of instruction is the change in values and attitudes that has taken place throughout the society, and particularly among the young. Manifestations of this change are seen in the greater readiness to accept the eighteen-year-old as an adult, in the egalitarianism accorded women, in prevailing sexual mores, in the general acceptance of a cultural pluralism in lieu of the earlier melting-pot theory of a good American society, in the evaluation of experience outside this country's borders, and in attitudes on war. Together these shifts in the ethical outlook of the American society have constituted a force that teachers consciously or unconsciously have taken into account.

The prospect for the future is continual change. It will require a persistent effort to create new and varied environments, more stimulating and more relevant programs, and more effective instruction for a diverse student body.

The student is being trained for a world that can only dimly be foreseen, but that will surely differ from today's world. A curriculum, hence, must be a living, growing instrument, and teachers must be alert, enthusiastic, and self-renewing individuals. Thus, this chapter focuses on the capacity of these institutions, as presently governed, to make the decisions involved in adapting the intellectual menus they offer to the changing demands of the society about them and the students they enroll. It will identify the major alterations made in curricula and instructional methods. With respect to each it will consider who, within

---

8 Alvin C. Eurich has suggested that the "new frontier" found in the appraisal of objectives (*Reforming American Education*, New York: Harper & Row, Publishers, Incorporated, 1969) "lies in the humanistic area of the curriculum." The present spectacular revival in the U.S. of concern with humanistic and cultural matters will, he believes, have an impact "almost comparable to the impact of Sputnik." Noting that schools and colleges "have dealt systematically with students' development in skills and subject matter," he suggests that the time has come to do the same "with students' grasp of major ideas" with emphasis on the thinking process rather than indoctrination or a preordained way of coping with ideas" (chap. 8, "The Humanities: New Frontier of Curricular Reform," p. 117ff.)

or without the academic community, promoted and who resisted such alterations as the supplementation of the traditional four-year curriculum by the offering of a three-year curriculum, the granting to students of greater freedom in determining their course of study, the introduction of new interdisciplinary programs, and the granting of degrees based on independent study and college equivalency examinations. And with respect to decisions as to who shall teach what, it will consider the efficacy in terms of the effectiveness of instruction of existing decision-making processes.

ADJUSTING PROGRAMS

The need to adjust educational programs and instructional practices suggested by the elements that have been enumerated was affirmed during the 1960s by a rash of studies initiated by colleges large and small. These institutional self-examinations revealed numerous weaknesses in educational programs and proposed new approaches. The results of studies in eleven institutions are helpfully summarized and evaluated by Dwight R. Ladd in his book entitled *Change in Educational Policy*.[9] Ladd's findings are supplemented and substantially affirmed by an earlier study of changes in curriculum in 426 departments in 110 colleges and universities by J. B. Lon Hefferlin.[10] Together these studies depict four principal directions of reform.

1. REFORM OF THE CURRICULUM

"The primary measure of institutional vitality of a college or university," Hefferlin declares, is the considered updating and enrichment of its curriculum, and he reports that the amount of change disclosed by his study is not large. Yet four kinds of reform are apparent in a goodly number of institutions.

Perhaps the most important reform is the revision of individual courses. This is necessitated to incorporate the persistent accretion of new knowledge and the interpretation of current issues, and was forced by the better preparation and greater sophistication of students. A companion reform has been the introduction of interdisciplinary courses and programs designed to help the student relate what he

---

[9] A general report prepared for the Carnegie Commission on Higher Education (New York: McGraw-Hill Book Company, 1970).

[10] Op. cit., pp. 54–63. See also Michael Buck and Earl J. McGrath, *Innovation in Liberal Arts Colleges* (New York: Teachers College Press, Columbia University, 1969), chap. 2, "New Approaches to the Curriculum," pp. 7–47.

learns to his life and current problems. A third type of curricular reform has consisted in the introduction of new fields of study as new social issues reared their heads, e.g., urban studies, black studies, environmental studies. A fourth kind of reform is reflected by an increase in that content which emphasizes the conceptual and theoretical as distinguished from the specific, e.g., the appraisal of a historical era rather than the events and personalities of the era. Perhaps even more important in their impact on the learner than these four kinds of change in curricula are the changes, whether planned or by chance, that have taken place in fewer institutions in the learning environment. These latter changes include the broadening of the mix of students; the introduction of new types of individuals to the faculty; the establishment of new patterns of interaction between students and faculty, and students and work and travel experiences. These changes have likely brought about greater changes in learning than more specific changes in what is taught. Still a fifth kind of reform suggested by a number of educators is the reduction of the overall period of schooling—twelve years in elementary and secondary schools and four years in college—by the introduction of a three-year curriculum and by the better articulation of the secondary school and college curricula.

2. REFORM IN MODES OF TEACHING AND LEARNING

Equipping more students of diverse levels of academic ability and academic preparation and from a wider assortment of cultural backgrounds than in previous years for a greater variety of careers has prompted a number of changes in instructional approach. These range from changes in the long-standing nine-month–two-semester program (e.g., perhaps the most common modification has been the introduction of a short "intersession" between the Christmas holidays and the commencement of the second semester) to the offering of an "external degree" based upon independent study and the taking of college equivalency examinations.[11] Some institutions have experimented with the offering of courses in sequence (e.g., instead of the student's taking five courses simultaneously, he devotes himself intensively to a particular course for a period of weeks and then turns to the next course). Other institutions have experimented with work-study programs and with the relation of study to experiences in the community, e.g., assignments with local social agencies or with the Federal Neighborhood Youth Corps or Vista.

---

[11] For a description of the revamping of academic calendars at illustrative institutions see Buck and McGrath, op. cit., pp. 118–126.

A substantial number of institutions, induced by recognition that the bulk of all students can accept responsibility for their own intellectual and personal growth and for framing the design of their own education, have granted substantially greater freedom in the selection of courses and have modified requirements for "majors" and for degrees. This recognition of student maturity and the granting to students of greater freedom of choice promise greater learning and predict still further change in the future in the structure of the college and university.

3. REFORM IN THE MECHANICS OF INSTRUCTION

Simultaneous with the acceptance of modifications in modes of teaching and learning have come changes in grading practices, course-credit policies, testing, and the use of new instructional aids. The impetus for the replacement of letter or numerical grades by "pass-fail" grading has been a desire to emphasize learning for its own sake and to reduce the competitive pressures created by grading. The objective of policies that focus on the completion of courses rather than the accumulation of credits is similar in that it also emphasizes learning. The principal modification of testing practices has been the greater use of comprehensive examinations to force the student to better integrate and relate the knowledge he accumulates in course "packages." The introduction of television, the computer, cassettes, and various other instructional aids has had two ends in view: to curtail expenditures for instruction (an end not always achieved) and to facilitate learning by providing means with which the student can supplement or reinforce learning. Indeed in 1972 it was forecast that by the year 2000 a significant proportion of all instruction will be carried on with the aid of or through instructional technology.[12] The introduction of the new technology gives promise of materially enriching the instruction of large classes and of making independent study more feasible, and will offer little threat to faculty members because it can be used to reinforce rather than replace instructors.

4. REFORM OF THE CAMPUS

The impersonality of the large institution and the different life-styles of many members of the diverse student bodies that inhabited the colleges

---

[12] Carnegie Commission on Higher Education, *The Fourth Revolution: Instructional Technology in Higher Education* (New York: McGraw-Hill Book Company, 1972). For a description of illustrative introductions of instructional television, see Buck and McGrath, op. cit., pp. 50–58.

and universities during the 1960s induced still other change. To overcome the bigness that, in the minds of many, had depersonalized the relation of the student to the institution and had created a major obstacle to learning by extending the distance between teacher and student, several institutions (e.g., the University of California at Santa Cruz, the University of the Pacific) established "cluster colleges," i.e., smaller living and/or learning units on a single campus or in proximity to each other.[13] These "cluster colleges" were designed to pool intellectual resources and preserve the character of the small college. The introduction of coeducation on other campuses (Dartmouth, Princeton, Wesleyan, Williams, and Yale) represented a similar effort, induced in some instances by financial pressures, to provide a pattern of student living in keeping with mores in the society as a whole. Finally, the establishment of a few experimental colleges reflects a further effort to adapt traditional forms of higher education to current life-styles. These experiments (New College at the University of Alabama, Monteith College at Wayne State University in Detroit, and Hampshire College in Massachusetts) each offered students and faculty members new approaches to learning and living which emphasized small size, substantial faculty and student involvement in curricular planning, more flexible requirements for majors and degrees, and courses of study focused on the needs of the student rather than the interests of discipline-oriented professions.

ORGANIZATIONAL DYNAMICS

Two decades' experience as a consultant engaged in analysis of the functioning of organizations in business, government, academia, and other nonprofit enterprises (hospitals, social agencies) has convinced me that change in the product, service, program, structure, and process is always found in the truly effective, responsive, and dynamic organization. The essentiality of change is not only dictated by forces in the society being served, but by the needs of the human beings that make up the staffs of such organizations as well. An individual's enthusiasm, zeal, and productivity are sapped by the persistence of the status quo. They are stimulated when one is confronted with orderly, considered change; they are maximized when that change originates in one's ideas and is effected with his participation.

---

[13] For an analysis of several such attempts to overcome "bigness," see Ann Heiss, *An Inventory of Academic Innovation and Reform*, Carnegie Commission on Higher Education, Berkeley, 1973, chap. 2, "Institutions within Institutions," pp. 19–34.

FACULTY RESISTANCE

Yet, as John W. Gardner has written: "Much innovation goes on at any first-rate university—but it is almost never conscious innovation in the structure or practices of the university itself. University people love to innovate away from home."[14] That observation has numerous seconders. Irving Kristol, for example, has declared that "the university has been —with the possible exception of the post office—the least inventive (or even adaptive) of our social institutions since the end of World War II."[15] Others have contended that the behavior of faculties has been characterized by "drift, reluctant accommodation, belated recognition that while no one was looking change had in fact taken place."[16] "College teaching," still another observer has stated, "stands out as one of the few fields in which innovation and improvement are neglected. . . . Clearly, a very large majority of our institutions of higher learning and faculty members have no commitment to change or to improve college and university teaching."[17]

Howard R. Bowen, in contrast, contends in a note to this author that "enormous changes, especially improvement in quality of staff and in the vitality of institutions have occurred." The majority of observers, however, hold that the college and university resist change. Why? In the face of demographic, social, and economic changes that dictate the need for revision of educational programs, a need that has been reaffirmed by studies in scores of institutions, and in light of the relationship of change to institutional strategy, why does this alleged unwillingness to modify curricula, requirements, instructional practices and arrangements persist?

Why are faculties so slow to change what is taught, or to permit change? For in the governance of colleges and universities, decisions as

---

14 *Self-Renewal: The Individual and the Innovative Society* (New York: Harper & Row, Publishers, Incorporated, 1965), p. 76.

15 "A Different Way to Restructure the University," *The New York Times Magazine*, Dec. 8, 1968, p. 50.

16 Frederich Rudolph, *The American College and University* (New York: Alfred A. Knopf, 1962), pp. 491–492.

17 Alvin C. Eurich, "The Commitment to Experiment and Innovate in College Teaching," *Educational Record*, vol. 45, no. 1, Winter 1964, pp. 49–50. See also Lewis B. Mayhew, "Higher Education—Toward 1984," *Educational Record*, vol. 53, no. 3, Summer 1972, pp. 218–220; *Report of the Commission on Governance*, Vanderbilt University, October 1970, ". . . the curriculum both in structure and scope, particularly on the undergraduate levels, still functions within the confines of parameters laid down several decades ago. And one can hardly fail to note that despite the technological advances and discoveries regarding the learning process, the format of instruction, particularly in the classroom, is essentially that of a previous century" (p. 76).

to what is taught are clearly the prime province of the faculty.[18] The content of the individual course is substantially the province of the individual teacher, circumscribed (in varying degrees in relation to the rank of the teacher) by the departmental faculty. Decisions as to the variety of courses offered and the requirements for majoring in a program are customarily made by departmental faculties. Decisions as to the requirements that students must meet to earn a degree and as to regulations such as attendance, tardiness, and conduct are usually made by the faculty of the institution as a whole.

Eric Ashby attributes this resistance to two "hereditary forces": (1) "the inertia of the system to any change" and (2) "the belief in the purpose of the system which is held by those who are engaged in it." "These forces constitute," he has written, "the inner logic of the system." He justifies this resistance to change by these words: "When one comes to analyze the governance of universities one reaches the conclusion that on certain essential and basic issues (what shall be taught? what research shall be done?) there should really be no governance at all. These are decisions each individual ought to be left to make for himself, observing only one principle: that he is considerate to the whole academic community and does not make decisions about his own teaching or research which run counter to its aims."[19] But consideration, not only of "the whole academic community" but of the students whose careers and values are being shaped and of the society whose prime resource is being developed, requires some abridgment of the freedom from any "governance at all." The justification for such abridgment becomes clear when one illuminates the reasons for faculty resistance to change.

REASONS FOR FACULTY RESISTANCE[20]

A primary reason for the failure of faculties to modify curricula, requirements, instructional practices, and arrangements is that the bulk of all professors are more concerned with substantive issues of the discipline in which they have been trained, with the concerns of the

---

18 J. Victor Baldridge, *Power and Conflict in the University* (New York: John Wiley & Sons, Inc., 1971), pp. 183–188.

19 Carnegie Commission on Higher Education, *Any Person, Any Study* (New York: McGraw-Hill Book Company, 1971), p. 69.

20 Jarold A. Kieffer provides a sympathetic and understanding view of the reasons for faculty resistance in App. C, "Obstacles to Curriculum and Teaching—Learning Innovation in Higher Education," in Howard R. Bowen and Lloyd T. Douglas, eds., *Efficiency in Liberal Education* (New York: McGraw-Hill Book Company, 1971), pp. 121–132.

"guilds" of which they are members, than with the whole curriculum imposed on the undergraduate.

David Riesman has written that the "academic guilds or disciplines have become the main intellectual and emotional homes of that minority of faculty members who set the modern style and, correspondingly, that the institutions where they happen to be teaching . . . have somewhat less call upon their interest and dedication. . . . The guilds are oriented to their substantive subject matters and hardly at all to the question of how these are taught. . . ."[21] In short, he suggests that faculty members cannot be relied upon to make decisions considerate of the aims of the "whole academic community."

A second reason is the nature of the individual professor. Study of the opinions of professors at more than 300 institutions revealed that these men and women are "deeply divided . . . on virtually all important matters . . . confused and uncertain . . . as to their roles and responsibilities in the vastly altered setting in which they find themselves."[22] This very division, it should be noted, may be a source of energy and change.

The professoriate of the pre-World War II era was made up of men and women committed to a lifetime of teaching, closeted to a greater degree than now within the campus, trained by a very similar process in a limited number of institutions, emanating from similar social backgrounds. In 1972 they represent a greater range of fields and substantive interests, have various outside associations, reach their posts through various career lines, and come from many different social backgrounds. The division and confusion they now reflect is the consequence of these conditioning forces—and prevents their developing a consensus as to what shall be taught and as to educational policy generally.

A third reason for the failure of faculties to modify curricula, requirements, and instructional practices and arrangements is the dominant influence of the department.[23] Hefferlin in his analysis of curricular

---

[21] In an essay entitled "Alterations in Institutional Attitudes and Behavior," Logan Wilson, ed., *Emerging Patterns in American Higher Education* (Washington, D.C.: American Council on Education, 1965), pp. 66 and 72.

[22] Seymour Martin Lipset and Everett Carll Ladd, Jr., "The Divided Professoriate," *Change*, May–June 1971, p. 54. See also Dwight Ladd, op. cit., p. 205. There Ladd writes: "Faculty members have strong feelings of independence—ideological ones derived from the traditions of academia and supported by the tenure system and, increasingly, practical ones, based on the relative independence from a particular institution which the contemporary mobile professor has."

[23] "Our failure to develop a more coherent and educationally effective curriculum reflects the inertia of departmental structure and faculty avoidance of wider perspective in undergraduate teaching" (Philip C. Ritterbush, "Adaptive Response within the Institutional System of Higher Education and Research," *Daedalus*, Summer 1970, p. 656).

change found that only 73 of 426 departments (17 percent) studied were substantially receptive to change.[24]

The department usually offers, in decisions on curricular reform, the mobilized view of a discipline or of a closely knit small group. The individual professor, when separated from the familiar ground of his discipline or from his "work family," becomes insecure. He joins his colleagues in fighting for the preservation of his intellectual "homeland." Hence, the department often constitutes the bastion of resistance to proposed reforms that would introduce an interdisciplinary approach.

These blocks to change—the lack of concern for the total educational program, the intellectual differences among professors, and the mobilized resistance of the departments—prevent adaptation. They combine to discourage that small minority of the faculty who would propose innovations. Thus, the very democratic processes of faculty decision making that were established to provide for the expression of faculty members' opinions limit advance.

The record of faculty decision making as to educational programs has provoked an effort to protect the more innovative professors and has raised doubts as to the willingness of faculties generally to serve the public interest. Dean Carl Sellinger of Bard College has proposed the formulation of a "Bill of Rights for Innovative Faculty Members." Hefferlin has concluded that "no priesthood, it has been said, ever institutes its own reforms; no military service can be expected to do so; no professional association is so altruistic that it will not at some point confuse public welfare and its own; and colleges and universities tend, as do all other public trusts, toward serving the interest of their personnel—their teachers and administrators—before those of their clientele."[25] These observations have led to the further suggestion that colleges and universities may "have reached the limits of collegiality as the basis for policy formulation—at least in the larger and more diverse institutions."[26] This tradition-shaking conclusion is supported by the record of faculty decision making; the adaptations and advances that have been made have largely been those that required little change in the traditional thinking and behavior patterns of individual faculty members.

---

[24] *Dynamics of Academic Reform*, pp. 112–113.

[25] Op. cit., p. 150.

[26] Dwight Ladd, op. cit., p. 212.

WHO SHALL TEACH WHAT?

"If we want to improve American education, we ought to aim first at improving the quality of the faculty."[27] No decisions involved in the governance of a college or university affect the quality of the educational program more than those that determine the makeup of the faculty. In choosing those young men and women who shall teach, in assigning courses among members of the faculty, in evaluating the performance of individuals,[28] those responsible for governance shape the intellectual and moral character of the institution. What is the nature of these decisions and what impact do they have on the instruction provided?

SELECTING NEW FACULTY MEMBERS

The individuals who make up a college faculty are customarily called "members." Use of this term has meaning. It distinguishes the process of selecting a new teacher from that of recruiting an employee, even for a professional assignment. The process is substantially identical in the concern of the decision maker as to the basic qualities of the individual —innate intelligence, physical vigor and appearance, and social adaptability; it is similar in terms of the evaluation of the individual's training for the work to be undertaken; but it differs in terms of the appraisal of the individual's goals and commitment. Will the applicant be content with the academic life? Will he derive real satisfaction from the rewards of academic life—the success of students, the publication of the product of his scholarship?

The selection decisions that are made over a period of time determine not only the range of the institution's educational offering, e.g., its capacity to offer individual training in vocational fields as well as in general education, but the "balance" of the intellectual menu it provides students (e.g., is the social science faculty predominantly "liberal" or "conservative"), the relative emphasis that will be given to teaching versus research, and the concern that will be devoted to the development of the whole student. These decisions determine also the proportion of women and of blacks, Jews, and other minorities that will be included on the faculty.

---

[27] Robert F. Byrnes, "Effective Teaching Is Our First Need," *The Challenge of Curricular Change* (Princeton, N.J.: College Entrance Examination Board, 1966), p. 73.

[28] How these and other "personnel decisions" are made is discussed in Chapter 8 as elements of the institution's personnel administration. Here we are concerned with the impact of such decisions on the instructional process.

The nature and the importance of such decisions argue for the devotion of the time and attention of those in the institution who accept responsibility for the shaping of its character and quality. Victor Butterfield devoted substantial time and energy to traveling to the campuses of the major universities in search of the ablest individuals about to receive graduate degrees and thus over the years from 1942 to 1967 markedly influenced the fitting together of a distinguished faculty at Wesleyan University. But as institutions have grown large, the selection of new appointees has been delegated, first, to deans, subsequently to departments, and within the largest departments to senior faculty members in subject matter areas.

The caliber of the selections made within the departments is influenced in the better academic institutions by the pride of its members. In addition, the departments are customarily subjected to reviews of varying degrees of thoroughness by deans, by provosts (or vice presidents for academic affairs), occasionally by presidents, and often to a final (and substantially meaningless) approval by trustees. The maintenance of consistently high standards of selection, when the primary authority to select is delegated as broadly to the departments, is difficult or impossible. The result is, on most large campuses, marked variation of departmental faculties.

TEACHING ASSIGNMENTS

Most departments, and particularly those which usually include the larger number of professors (e.g., English, mathematics, chemistry, and economics), enroll relatively large numbers of first- and second-year students in introductory courses. These courses are often offered in multiple sections and require a significant proportion of the department members' time. Responsibility for teaching these introductory courses in those institutions which give emphasis to the quality of undergraduate education is rotated among the department's senior professors. More frequently, particularly in the larger universities and in those which train large numbers of graduate students, responsibility for the conduct of these large introductory courses is assigned to young, inexperienced teaching assistants, under the guidance of one of the younger men of professional rank. The senior professors opt to teach only the more advanced courses that fall in their particular areas of interest.

The decisions as to who shall teach the lower-division courses are of major consequence in shaping the character and caliber of undergraduate education. These decisions are in considerable part made by the individual faculty member; teachers are specialists, and increasingly narrow specialists; they are particularly qualified to teach the more advanced courses that coincide with their special interests. Department chairmen and deans are faced with the alternatives of enlisting a portion of the teaching time of the more senior professors for the conduct of lower-division courses or of assigning these courses to young, less experienced teaching assistants. In the universities offering graduate work, such decisions are materially influenced by the necessity of providing financial support for graduate students. As teaching assistants they have been employed at approximately one-third the cost of a better prepared full-time faculty member and the more senior professors are relieved of a chore many regard as onerous. The individual teaching assistant, in some instances, benefits from the tutelage of senior professors, but the system generally reduces the quality of undergraduate education and imposes a heavy burden on the aspiring graduate student whose immediate and primary concern is the earning of the Ph.D. degree.

Determinations as to who shall teach the more advanced courses are, in substantial measure, made by the individual professor. Those faculty members who attain the rank of associate and full professor have either succeeded in conducting courses in a particular subject-matter area (e.g., labor economics within the field of economics) or were recruited from without to offer courses in the particular area. To the extent that such self-determinations focus the individual's teaching on that subject matter in which he is conducting research they offer some assurance of zealous and sophisticated handling of these courses.

Decision making as to teaching assignments is analogous to the fitting together of a crossword puzzle. Departmental chairmen and their colleagues have an obligation, with such resources as are made available to them, to provide an array of courses that offer a comprehensive view of the whole discipline. They fulfill this obligation by selecting individuals, each of whom has particular interests and competences, and by agreeing with, assigning, or cajoling each to offer those courses that provide a full and balanced menu. The task is a continuing one, requiring the skill of a person broadly abreast of developments throughout the discipline and artful in the persuasion or leadership of his of her colleagues.

EVALUATING PERFORMANCE

"The academic tradition," John Millett has written, "has belittled any form of work supervision and of evaluation . . . [and] has tended to ignore job training and development for staff members."[29] This conse-

---

[29] *Personnel Management in Higher Education*, Management Division, Academy for Educational Development, October 1972, p. 11.

quence is rooted in the belief that the scholar who attains the doctor of philosophy degree will engage in continual scholarship and teaching and thus will grow in understanding and in the capacity to interpret and transmit what he knows.

These beliefs are closely associated with a prime attraction to the academic profession—the right of self-determination or, in other words, freedom to fulfill responsibilities in ways that the individual determines to be appropriate. These beliefs effectively limit or deny the department chairperson's or the senior professor's right to supervise or to develop, even though these individuals must make decisions as to the effectiveness of the individual.

Decisions as to the teaching effectiveness of an individual and his capabilities as a scholar are made when the term appointments of teaching assistants, instructors, and assistant professors expire and their renewal is considered, when inquiries from other institutions relative to the younger individuals are answered, when promotions are considered, and, of especial importance, when individuals are granted tenure. These decisions are of great consequence in determining the quality of each academic department and of an institution's faculty. Such decisions are made on a paucity of chance information derived from the occasional comments of students, in some institutions, of late from more ordered evaluations by students, sometimes by the analysis of grade distributions, and from the "impressions" of fellow faculty members.[30]

The distressing consequence is that decisions of vital significance to the individual and which markedly affect the quality of instruction offered by a faculty are made on inadequate bases. The personal traits of the individual or his visible publications or administrative service are overemphasized, and inadequate emphasis is given to his undetermined capabilities as a teacher.

In summary, trustees, presidents, academic vice presidents, and, to a lesser degree, deans, in most institutions, have little impact on decisions that directly effect the quality of teaching—the core activity of an institution of higher education. Responsibility for such decisions rests with the departments—the departmental chairmen, the departmental faculties, and the individual members. In considerable part the decision-making pattern is founded in the belief that the department (and the

---

30 See John A. Centra, *The Utility of Student Ratings for Instructional Improvement*, Educational Testing Service, August 1972; J. W. Gustad, "Evaluation of Teaching Performance," in C. B. T. Lee, ed., *Improving College Teaching* (Washington: American Council on Education, 1967), pp. 268–279; and Kenneth E. Eble, *The Recognition and Evaluation of Teaching*, the report of a Conference on Evaluation sponsored by The Project to Improve College Teaching, Washington, Apr. 10, 1970.

college) is a "community of scholars" whose members are studying, inquiring, teaching, and exchanging ideas, experiences, and opinions among each other. In practice each faculty member has a job to do and a life to live, and he goes about it. He relies on his colleagues to mind their classes, their articles, and their consulting and to allow him to mind his. The specialization of an individual's interests deter interchange, and few institutions provide mechanisms that bring teachers together for intellectual (as distinguished from administrative) interchange.

OTHER VOICES TO BE HEARD

In view of mounting questions as to the ability of faculties—as individuals, as departments, and as corporate institutions—to provide the direction and dynamism needed to ensure the continual improvement of the instructional process, there are pressures to permit others within the college or university to have larger voices in deciding what shall be taught and who shall teach. Two pressures are apparent.

STUDENT PARTICIPATION

The first is that students be given a greater voice in determining what is taught and who shall teach. The arguments in behalf of student participation are essentially these:[31]

1. Students recognize the large importance of education to the individual's future, and they seek a larger voice in determining its character and quality.

2. Students in the 1970s are the product of better secondary schools than earlier generations; they are more sophisticated as the consequence of exposure (a) to television and supplementary forces of communication and (b) to an urbanized shoulder-to-shoulder civilization. They bring to the institutions of higher education a more serious and informed interest in economic, social, political, and racial issues than any predecessor generation.

3. Participation in decision making as to what shall be taught and who shall teach constitutes an educational experience that could contribute materially to the development of the individual student.

---

[31] For a thoughtful analysis of proposals for student participation, see Earl J. McGrath, *Should Students Share the Power?* (Philadelphia: Temple University Press, 1970), pp. 51–70; see also Louis T. Benezet, "Should Students Have a Voice in What They're Taught?" *The Chronicle of Higher Education*, Nov. 20, 1972.

4. Students, because they are continuingly exposed to the present educational processes, because they are not handicapped by the narrow disciplinary focus of many professors, and because many are concerned with today's problems, can contribute fresh and useful ideas to the curricular considerations.

In opposition to student participation in decision making as to curricula, it is contended that:

1. Students are young, immature, and inexperienced.

2. Students are transitory; they are not associated with the institutions long enough to acquire understanding and perspective.[32]

3. Students would find the task of participating with faculty members in committee consideration of curricular questions dull, tedious, and fruitless.

The brief experiences in those institutions where students have been given the opportunity to participate is inconclusive.[33] There are evidences that students have contributed meaningfully to some considerations of course content and curricular makeup, and that student evaluations have contributed meaningfully to teaching effectiveness. There is also evidence on some campuses that after gaining the right to participate, students gradually lost interest and did not persistently participate.

A FULLER ROLE FOR ACADEMIC ADMINISTRATORS

The second suggestion for ensuring more progressive decision making as to the instructional process is that the academic administrators—president, provost or vice president for academic affairs, and the deans—should have a fuller and more influential voice than in the past. In many institutions they have exercised a substantial influence in the past. Previously Victor Butterfield's concern with the quality of the Wesleyan faculty was mentioned; his concern was matched by the interest and attention of scores of other deans, provosts, vice presidents for academic affairs, and presidents in curriculum improvement, as well as faculty development. But as institutions have grown larger, and faculties have

---

32 In view of the declining length of service of college and university presidents and of the mobility of university professors, this argument is less valid than it was in earlier decades.

33 Morris T. Keeton has commented to the author that the contribution of students is directly related to the effort of the institution's leadership to understand and provide the conditions for effective student participation in curricular and instructional improvement.

grown more independent and more powerful, the influence of these officials has declined.

Now it is proposed, in view of the general inability of faculties to provide the decisions that make for dynamic adaptation of program and strengthening of faculty, that the academic administrators reinvolve themselves—and substantially—in the tasks of educational programming and faculty development. This is primarily the responsibility of deans and secondarily of provosts and vice presidents for academic affairs. The responsibility of presidents and trustees is not to specify how curricula or courses shall be modified (for such tasks they lack needed capabilities), but to ensure that the faculty is continually involved in the evaluation and adaptation of courses and of curricula in light of both the expansion of knowledge and the changes taking place in the society.

One development that has tended to facilitate the reinvolvement of academic administrators is the development of institutional research. Institutional research is the study of the instructional process.[34] It usually comprehends analyses of (1) input, e.g., studies of student characteristics, faculty characteristics, finance, and the curriculum; (2) process, e.g., examinations of the effectiveness of remedial and special purpose instructional programs, student counseling services, resident hall systems, and of instruction in the classrooms; (3) context, e.g., studies of university structure, organization and climate, and of the impact of size on functioning; and (4) output, e.g., analyses of graduates by field, student credit hours provided, speeches given, and articles written by faculty members. The techniques of institutional research are relatively new; the personnel in the field is earning its spurs; a minority of all institutions have staffs working in this field, and the product is not yet impressive. But in some institutions, presidents, provosts, and deans have been enabled by fresh facts served up by their institutional research staffs to persuade faculties to make significant changes.

A second development that has impelled academic officers (and in a few instances trustees) to involve themselves in the making of decisions as to educational programs is the critical nature of the institution's finances. Such action by trustees was prescribed more than a decade ago by Beardsley Ruml in his provocative volume entitled *Memo to a College*

---

[34] John W. Hamberlin, "Institutional Research Today, Systems Analysis Tomorrow," *AEDS Journal*, March 1970, pp. 70–78; see also Stanley O. Ikenberry, "Institutional Research and the Instructional Process," a paper privately circulated, April 1971.

Trustee.[35] In 1974, substantially the same course is implicit in the discerning analysis by Bowen and Douglass of the financial plight of the smaller colleges;[36] their analyses suggest that unless trustees and presidents "move in" and provide leadership for faculty restructuring of curricula, a number of institutions cannot survive financially.

A CONCLUSION AND PROGNOSIS

Two conclusions are apparent: there is need for meaningful curricular and teaching-learning reform, and progress in meeting that need will not be made by demanding the recentralization of authority that now lies in the hands of the faculty. As in other areas of governance ways must be found of making the continuum of trustee–president–academic administrator–faculty–student decision making effective.[37]

That effort will involve the perfecting of means for fuller and more regular consultation with students, at the departmental level, in the making of decisions as to curricula and the greater use of student evaluations in the making of decisions as to faculty promotions. The prospect is as well that the finality of departmental decisions will be reduced; it is likely that both curricular and faculty selection and promotion decisions will be subjected to more substantial review and approval by stronger deans and provosts or presidents, with or without the advice of broadly based senates or councils that include faculty members, students, and perhaps others. A further prospect is that trustees will be expected to play a stronger role in determining the character and mission of their institutions and in appraising decisions as to "what shall be taught" and "who shall teach" in terms of those basic determinations.[38]

---

35 New York, McGraw-Hill Book Company, 1959.

36 Howard R. Bowen and Gordon K. Douglass, *Efficiency in Liberal Education*, a report prepared for the Macalester Foundation and issued by the Carnegie Commission on Higher Education (New York: McGraw-Hill Book Company, 1971), pp. 95–105.

37 Daniel Bell in *The Coming of Post-Industrial Society* (New York: Basic Books, 1973), forecasts that throughout the society decision making is moving from the individual (in whose hands organizational theorists have long contended it must reside) to the "political system." What is happening in the college and university can be viewed as a parallel development impelled by the same forces of technology and increasing interdependnce.

38 If collective bargaining becomes the rule the growth of administrative oversight by deans, provosts or presidents, and trustees will likely be negated, at least in the public institutions, by the efforts of organized faculty members to deal directly with the state legislatures.

Decision Making:
Student-Oriented Processes

*Any proposed curriculum change designed to improve the
intellectual atmosphere of a college that ignores the social-
personal lines, the living and dining arrangements of its
students, is likely to be futile. . . . To consider only the
academic aspects of curricular change as factors that
promote educability is to limit our understanding of what
makes an educable person more mature and a mature
person more educable.*   Douglas H. Heath[1]

6 Walter Lippmann has commented that the end purpose of the
modern college or university is to equip the individual student—
deprived of the guidance, the support, and the discipline that was
provided earlier generations by ecclesiastical and civil authority and
undergirded by tradition—to function as an emancipated, truly free
individual.[2]

How does the institution of higher education meet this obligation?
It can by instruction develop the individual's capacity to reason while
it introduces him to some of the accumulated knowledge that will
enable him to function as a citizen, employee, and parent. But for most
late adolescents adjustment from a status of childhood to self-sustaining
adulthood in the complex, urbanized world of work requires more than
lectures, textbooks, examinations, and grades can provide.[3]

In the pre-World War II era, the college assumed the parents' responsibility for the young people who enrolled. It provided for its residential student body discipline and an environment in which young men

---

[1] "But Are They Mature Enough for College?" *The Challenge of Curricular
Change* (New York: College Entrance Examination Board, 1966), pp. 39
and 41.

[2] "The University and the Human Condition," in Charles G. Dobbins and Calvin B. T. Lee (eds.) *Whose Goals for American Higher Education?* (Washington: American Council on Education, 1968), pp. 233–234.

[3] "College," Paul Dressel has written, "is not like a winery—simply an aging
and maturing process. I believe that, unlike bottles of wine, students must be
shaken as well as pressured if they are to benefit from college. And, with students as with bottles of wine, some will go sour or even blow up under such
ministrations. I do not trust faculty members generally to be either sufficiently
sensitive, concerned or knowledgeable to deal with such possibilities" ("Measuring the Benefits of Student Personnel Work," *Journal of Higher Education,*
January 1973, p. 24).

(and fewer young women) "grew up" in the company of a homogeneous group of peers. Those fellow students, equipped with an "upbringing" that had benefited in most instances by life in a family that inculcated its youth with the traditional values, provided much of the understanding the individual obtained of the relatively narrow segment of the world to which parents could in most instances assure a relatively easy transition.

What have come to be known as "student-personnel services" were of limited scope then. They comprehended the work of an admissions office; supervision of living arrangements in fraternity houses, boarding houses, or dormitories; the disciplining of those students who violated established rules and conventions; and the maintenance of an orderly, cultured, and Christian environment. Then a very few individuals in the admissions office and in the dean's office, usually former faculty members, served as disciplinarians and informal advisers. The student personnel function had its origins, after World War I, in the then *en vogue* concern with the "whole student," and reached its high point during the 1950s.

In the 1970s the need to aid students to adjust from childhood to adulthood remains, but the environment within which that adjustment is made and the nature of the aid that is needed and is acceptable are strikingly different. The array of activities that is described as student-personnel services in the 1970s encompasses a much broader scope.[4] Generally, the activities described by this term include admissions, registration of students, maintenance of student records, provision of financial aid, operation of residence halls, assistance to student organizations and the student government, counseling, placement, and efforts to orient or assist students on such matters as study habits, sex relations, marital problems, the dangers of drug abuse, and current political and social issues. On numerous campuses these activities require staffs including hundreds of individuals, many of whom are highly specialized professionals. Relatively few institutions can, in the 1970s, accept the responsibility institutions once claimed for the development of the "whole student." The scale on which, and the context within which, they operate makes that impossible. But each institution must recognize

---

4 As enrollments have grown, the number of student-personnel workers and expenditures for student-personnel services have markedly increased. In 1956 there were some 7,500 full-time student-personnel workers in institutions of higher learning (William H. Cowley, "Student Personnel Services in Retrospect and Prospect," *School and Society*, Jan. 19, 1957, p. 21). By 1972, the number had risen to between 35,000 and 40,000 (U.S. Department of Labor, Division of Manpower and Occupational Outlook, Bureau of Labor Statistics, draft manuscript, 1972).

that the bulk of its students are going through a period of life during which they will develop such ethical orientation, such sense of identity and personal integrity, and such autonomy and social intelligence as they will acquire.[5] If they are to become responsible, effective individuals, they must be provided an environment that will help them acquire such qualities.

By whom are decisions made as to the kinds and intensity of services to be provided to facilitate these aspects of student development? For example, who determines how vigorous an effort shall be made to seek out and to facilitate, financially and educationally, the enrollment of disadvantaged young people? Who decides what kinds of supportive services—health care, personal and psychodiagnostic counseling, student unions, and campus stores—shall be provided? What disciplinary, cultural, and educational programs shall be carried on? And how much time, effort, and money shall be invested in record keeping and in research into the content, processes, and benefits of student services? This chapter describes how decisions on such questions have been made and poses questions as to whether the most appropriate decisions are made and whether the appropriate constituencies are involved in the making of such decisions.

FORCES CONDITIONING SERVICES

The evolution of student-oriented services within the college or university and the complexity of the problems faced by those who provide these services are attributable to three obvious developments: the growth of the student bodies, the changed character of the society from which students come and into which they graduate, and a strikingly different culture among the young people who enroll.

GROWTH IN ENROLLMENT

The growth in enrollments that has been depicted earlier[6] converted many small and "homey" colleges into large and impersonal institutions. It made difficult or precluded close personal contact between teacher and student. It brought to the campus a wide diversity of students—the young, less scholastically capable, blacks, foreign students, older students in the graduate schools, and middle-aged businessmen

---

[5] Carnegie Commission on Higher Education, *The Purposes and Performance of Higher Education in the United States: Approaching the Year 2000* (New York: McGraw-Hill Book Company, 1973).

[6] Chap. 1, p. 5.

and housewives. Other forces—the advance of science and the advent of the fashion of "going on" to graduate and professional schools— brought to the campus an increased number of relatively mature and especially qualified individuals. The larger size of the individual institution (in 1940 only two institutions enrolled 20,000 students; by 1970, 65 institutions had attained that size and more than 40 percent of all students attended institutions with enrollments of 10,000 or more),[7] the greater diversity of the student body, and the urbanization of the population destroyed characteristics of the earlier college that had contributed much to the socialization of those who graduated in the 1920s and 1930s.

A CHANGED SOCIETY

Much of the welter of change that transformed the American society during the post-World War II period and its consequences for the institution of higher education have been described. Here the especial force with which this change bore on the student and on his relationship to the institution must be noted.

The individual who came to the college or university as an enrollee brought with him a sophistication bred by at least a decade's exposure to the institutions of the large city and particularly to the newer media of communication. He brought attitudes fashioned by the war in Vietnam and the revolution at home in racial relationships. And he was prepared to assert a claim for freedom from paternalistic supervision. That posture was consistent with the revolution against established authority apparent in the conduct of blacks, workers, members of and younger priests within the Catholic Church, and others. His tendency to insist upon recognition as an individual was founded in the rebellion in other segments of the society against the impersonalization that characterizes the "mass society."

These social trends and the frame of mind they created in the new and large student bodies that occupied the campuses beginning in the 1960s forced alterations in many or most relationships between the institution and the individual student. They forced changes in admissions policies and in housing operations. They resulted in the abandonment of the doctrine of *in loco parentis* and the marked delimitation of disciplinary efforts. They compelled the granting of a greater voice for

---

[7] Data derived from U.S. Office of Education, National Center for Educational Statistics, *Digest of Educational Statistics, 1970* (Washington: U.S. Government Printing Office, 1970), table 113, p. 85.

students in the management of all services provided for their use and convenience and in the governance of the whole institution.

A CHANGED CULTURE

The student-oriented processes of the college and university also bore the impact of the changed youth culture that has been described in Chapter 1. That changed culture is reflected in the attitudes of mind (discussed above) that many students brought with them to the campus. But youth—on and off the campuses—reflected, commencing in the early or mid-1960s, (a) a questioning of the American society—its willingness to live up to professed values; (b) a rejection of the professed values of their elders and of the knowledge that these elders had presumably accumulated; and (c) a degree of alienation from the society and its authority structure, e.g., "the establishment," that seemed to be substantial in 1965–1970 and in 1975 appears to be less sub stantial.

This changed culture undermined the authoritarian relationship between teacher and student and created a need for student personnel activities in fields and in ways not earlier performed.

DECISION MAKING AS TO STUDENT-ORIENTED PROCESSES

Together these developments dictated that those processes of the college or university which focused on the student, as an individual rather than as a student, would undergo change. That change necessitated a succession of decisions as to how policies governing the institution's relations with its students should be altered. In subsequent sections the nature of the decisions in each of the distinguishable areas of student personnel activity will be described and the changing locus of authority for decisions pictured.

EDUCATIVE ACTIVITIES

The educative activities that commonly fall within the purview of student personnel activities are those concerned with (a) determining who shall be admitted, (b) maintaining a record of the individual's personal and educational accomplishments, (c) providing those educational and cultural experiences that supplement the formal educational program, and (d) counseling the individual on questions that arise in his or her personal life, on educational plans and programs, or on career matters.

Together these several activities consume from 4 to 5 percent of the general educational expenditures in four-year colleges, somewhat less in larger institutions.[8]

ADMISSIONS

The prime issue in this area has revolved around the question, who shall be accepted as students?[9] In the dim past these decisions were made by the institution's faculty. The decision was viewed as a determination of the applicant's educability and logically as a function of those responsible for his education. The growth in enrollments and the development of a substantial body of technology with which to assess the individual's educability resulted in the shift of decision-making responsibility from faculty members to a professionally trained director of admissions and his staff. This shift was tempered by the retention of a faculty committee on admissions that set policies to guide the director of admissions and his staff, but pragmatically the decision-making responsibility was shifted (as in many other areas of the American society) to the individual who possessed the relevant technical expertise.

But developments within the society by the late 1960s had altered the nature of the decision to be made. The growing belief that every individual, regardless of race or income status, should have the opportunity to continue his education beyond the high school meant that in many institutions, and particularly in the expanding ones, the decision was less one of educability and more one as to how more students from the ethnic minorities could be recruited and could be financially aided to make attendance feasible. And as these institutions entered the 1970s, the nature of the admissions decision changed still more. There simply were not enough applicants from families with annual incomes of $16,000 or more capable of scoring well on the admissions tests to fill available places in the colleges and universities. Faced with this reality and having to make ends meet, many institutions further diminished

---

8 For an analysis, see Donald Robinson and Richard C. McKee, "Expenditures for Student Personnel Services in Higher Education," in Laurine E. Fitzgerald, Walter F. Johnson, and Willa Norris (eds.), *College Student Personnel, Readings and Bibliographies* (Boston: Houghton Mifflin Company, 1970), pp. 144–146.

9 The answer to this question no longer involves merely the selection of those most educable from among secondary school graduates. A more comprehensive answer to this question is suggested by the recommendation of the Carnegie Commission on Higher Education that "colleges should develop admissions programs to seek out new constituencies, including high school juniors as well as adults and transfers from two-year colleges" (*Continuity and Discontinuity*, New York: McGraw-Hill Book Company, August 1973, p. 40).

the emphasis on the educability of the individual student. Their primary concern was to enroll a sufficient number of students capable of meeting the costs of attendance.[10]

The need was for a balanced consideration of these several aspects of the admissions problem—the educability of and the ethnic mix of applicants for admission, the financial ability of each individual applicant, and the need of the institution for additional enrollees. In many institutions the responsibility for these interrelated decisions was diffused. Consequently the question as to who shall be accepted as students tended to be decided by the constituency faced with the most exigent problem. The students, sometimes supported by a portion of the faculty and sometimes opposed by a portion of the alumni, pressed the admissions office to make a more aggressive effort to enroll more black students and in some instances to refuse to enroll women. The president often took the lead in pressing for the admissions of blacks and females, often motivated by the financial aspects of the admission problem as well as a sense of justice. He tended to turn more and more to the director of financial aid, who, by managing a complex of governmental aid and work programs, made an increasing proportion of admissions decisions. Trustees most often were concerned with the financial aspects as viewed by the institution rather than the applicant, particularly the level of tuition charges.

It has become increasingly apparent that decisions as to who shall go to college are social decisions. They are no longer decisions to be made solely on the basis of the applicant's educability and membership in an elite. Hence, the federal government has exercised a substantial influence to ensure that women and blacks were granted equal opportunities to gain admittance. The function of the admissions office has been altered; the role of the financial aid office has been enlarged; the faculty has evidenced little concern with the ethnic and economic mix of the student body; and students, in many institutions, have manifested an increased interest in who shall be admitted. The need, as in other areas of institutional governance, is for ways and means of achieving a consensus that is educationally and socially sound.

That need will best be met if the director of admissions—throwing

---

10 K. Patricia Cross, in a statement titled "Planning for New Students to Higher Education in the 70s," prepared for the Select Education Subcommittee of the Education and Labor Committee of the House of Representatives, traces the evolution of three successive philosophies that have prevailed in the United States about who should go to college: the aristocratic philosophy, which prevailed until about 1925–1930; the meritocratic philosophy, which held sway from about 1925 to 1965; and the egalitarian philosophy, which has been gaining acceptance since about 1965.

off the shackles of his astigmatic professional skills—can formulate a broad-gauged admissions program; coordinate the interests and efforts of the financial-aid office, the faculty, students, and alumni; and measure up as the president's right arm in this area. It is the obligation of trustees and presidents to see that such a balanced program is formulated and that such coordination is achieved.

RECORDING EXPERIENCE

The role of the "registrar" has been affected by the large increase in enrollments. His has become a mass-production task requiring the utilization of the most modern office technology and imaginative efforts to recognize the individual while processing thousands of records on a demanding time schedule. Those efforts include the maintenance of meticulous accuracy; safeguarding the confidentiality of personal records, including making their contents known to public authorities or other inquirers only with the student's knowledge and agreement; and striving to avoid having the student feel that in relation to the institution he is no more than "an IBM card number."[11]

When the registrar has failed to achieve these ends, the president and trustees are confronted with complaints from the faculty that grades they have reported have not been recorded, and more urgent protests from students that records vital to them are incomplete. On more campuses for more of the time the registrar is "left alone." That treatment is often less than is needed. The responsibility of trustees and presidents to students is to ensure the integrity of this record-keeping function. Periodic evaluation of the performance of these functions by (or for) the president is desirable.

BROADENING EXPERIENCE

The responsibility of the institution to the individual student once he is enrolled includes that of fostering the development of his identity and autonomy. The commuting student in a large city who is compelled to divide his time between a job and his classes epitomizes this need. He

---

11 In May 1973 a Committee on the Privacy of Student Records at Cornell University recommended that students be allowed to know what records the university maintains, that most data in those records (academic, disciplinary, medical, financial, or counseling) be regarded as qualified privileged or privileged, and that such data be available to external agencies including parents only with the approval of the student or when subpoenaed by civil authority after informing the student. The committee further recommended that a continuing committee be established to monitor the security of record keeping and to evaluate requests for research data (*The Cornell Chronicle*, May 3, 1973, p. 2).

recognizes his dependence upon the "transcript" that will eventually serve as his passport to a better job and that will give him access to higher levels of the society. He less often recognizes his need for information and insights that will guide his social adjustment and maturation, including his understanding of sexual relations and the dangers involved in the use of alcohol and drugs and his understanding of the community and its institutions.

The efforts of student personnel workers to aid students in moving from adolescence to adulthood include on many campuses the conducting of informal discussions. These have, on most campuses, a twofold objective: to relate the individual more closely to the institution and to help the individual reason out urgent problems of adjustment of self and the society. Illustrative of such efforts are a series of noncredit "short courses" offered in the student center at the University of South Carolina. Within a single month this program involved discussions of bartending, using the library, the draft laws, lovemaking, politics, and the use of drugs.

In the smaller institutions where a substantial portion of the student body resides on or close to the campus, the need for such efforts is less and the carrying out of such efforts is relatively simple. In the larger institutions where most of the students are commuters, the need for such efforts is large and the difficulty of reaching and involving a significant portion of all students great. The imagination exhibited by leading student personnel officers during the climactic years 1964–1971 was indeed impressive. Yet when viewed in terms of their broad obligation to help the individual adjust to the changing society he or she is about to enter, the accomplishments of few institutions are impressive, and few instances can be noted when, in the absence of a student confrontation, the trustees, academic staff, and faculty have aided student personnel officers and participated actively in efforts to achieve these ends.

COUNSELING ACTIVITIES

Before World War II, the college experience was viewed as a *rite de passage*. The student lived in a sheltered environment while passing from the world of childhood to that of adulthood.[12] During the decades

---

[12] Some foreign educators, when contrasting the prevailing practices in their universities with the practices of American institutions, have contended that we are overly solicitous of our students and that we tend to develop in them a sense of continuing dependence (John S. Brubacher and Willis Rudy, *Higher Education in Transition*, New York: Harper & Row Publishers, Incorporated, 1958, pp. 35–51).

following World War II, the greater variety of individuals that made up student bodies were required to spend an even longer period in this "in-between world," and under increasing pressure as the essentiality of college education was more clearly recognized.[13]

For many, the conventional education period was prolonged by acceptance of the notions that all or most individuals should continue their education beyond the high school and that the undergraduate degree was not enough but should be supplemented by graduate study. For others this period was extended by the lack of opportunities for employment or the desire to avoid being drafted by the military.

As the education period was elongated, the progressive integration of the college and the university with the off-campus world created a set of pressures that bore on individual students. Pressure to obtain high grades commenced even before college entry as high school students competed for a limited number of places in the colleges or universities. It continued throughout the college years as continued avoidance of military service required "keeping up," and as it became clear that chances for the best jobs were related, in substantial measure, to the record of educational achievement.

Financial pressures loomed larger as an increasing number of young men and women from lower-income families were enrolled. Social pressures were generated by the enrollment of more blacks and intensified by the racial revolution raging in the society. Conflict was engendered among students, and between students and the institutions, by the emergence of liberalized attitudes toward personal conduct, the use of alcohol and drugs, sexual relations, and religious and political matters.

These conditions created tensions and frustrations among a substantial proportion of all students at a time when most institutions by virtue of their large size could not provide a sheltered and relatively individualized environment. The institutional response was to establish an array of counseling and guidance services that could aid the student to better cope with his problems. This array comprehended the services of:

- Financial aid counselors who help students find work, obtain grants and loans, and budget their resources

- Guidance counselors who help students assess their own talents and interests and relate them to educational programming and to occupational alternatives

---

[13] The nature and significance of this pressure are ably discussed by the Scranton Commission in *The President's Commission on Campus Unrest* (Washington: U.S. Government Printing Office, 1970), chap. 2.

- Psychological counselors who talk out with students the stresses they are undergoing and help them to reason out courses of action in the face of liberalizing attitudes prevalent in the society

- Psychiatric counselors who counsel those individuals who, in some measure, have been overwhelmed by the stresses that make difficult the adjustments involved in entering the adult world

- Health care counselors—physicians and nurses—who, in addition to meeting immediate health care needs, are called upon to help the individual cope with stresses that induce physical problems

These several services were introduced gradually, even as the institution of higher education was abandoning its role as surrogate parent.[14] Each service was essentially an extension of the role once performed by a fatherly dean[15] and subsequently by the deans of students. The introduction of each successive service involved a decision which, in retrospect, has significantly influenced the capacity of the institution to facilitate its students' development. In most institutions these services were accreted. They seldom resulted from the deliberate establishment of an institutional objective (i.e., to develop the whole student) and a considered decision that a particular service would be a further achievement of that objective. They were established to relieve an over-worked dean of students. Their creation was impelled by student demands manifested in various ways. Their need was pointed to by particularly sensitive faculty members who were beset by "problem cases." They were established to match what was offered by competing institutions. Or, perhaps most often, they were founded in response to the persuasive arguments of a progressive dean of students.

Many institutions—business enterprises, government bureaus, churches—grow by accretion. Decision making by accretion is not bad, per se. It can be effective if guided by clearly stated objectives and if periodically the array of products being sold or services offered are appraised in the light of objectives.

But most colleges and universities lack clearly stated objectives as to

---

[14] Some observers have contended that counseling "couched in the language of psychology rather than religion" is as paternalistic a form of control as obtained earlier (Nicholas von Hoffman, *The Multiversity,* New York: Holt, Rinehart and Winston, Inc., 1966, pp. 134–136). On many campuses religious counselors, sometimes compensated by the institution and often supplied by the churches proximate to the campus, supplement the activities of the several student personnel workers listed above.

[15] In my own experience as an undergraduate the role was performed by a "motherly" secretary to the dean!

what they propose to do to equip the individual student to function as "an emancipated, truly free individual" in an increasingly complex world. Few institutions periodically subject the array of counseling activities carried on to the appraisal of faculty representatives, students, academic administrators, and financial officers. Even fewer institutions confront their trustees with the basic question: Is this array of services what should be provided in the light of the students' needs and the institution's available resources?

LIVING FACILITIES

As enrollments grew, the task of providing essential supportive services —housing, food, the student "union" or "center" where students could meet and find recreational facilities, the book store, and others—grew proportionately. Simultaneously, the changed attitudes of students (e.g., their claim to a greater right of self-determination) and the consequent alteration of the relationship between the student and the institution have posed new questions as to the provision of these services.

The first of these questions is: Should the college or university any longer provide these facilities? Conversely, should the students be free and expected to make whatever arrangements they might deem desirable for housing, food services, and social relationships? These are not unprecedented questions; during the late nineteenth century there were attempts by students to force institutions to allow them to provide for their own housing, social activities, and in a few instances even libraries. In the 1970s this question was prompted by the fact that the students' complaints often focused on their dissatisfaction with food services or the physical conditions and parietal rules associated with institutionally operated dormitories and student unions.

Decisions to alter existing arrangements—to abandon the operation of dining halls, dormitories, and student unions, for example—were complicated by the large investments of many institutions in such facilities, by rising operating costs at a time when more students were being enrolled from low-income families, and by the growing proportion of commuting students whose need for services differed from the needs of an earlier generation of students. These decisions were further complicated on some campuses by the introduction of coeducation and on other campuses by liberalized views as to arrangements for the housing of students of both sexes.

On a number of campuses decisions were impelled, however, by the spread of the new culture among students: they insisted upon a relaxation of controls and the right to determine where they would live and where they would eat. Two trends can be distinguished in the decisions that have resulted from these forces. Students have been granted greater freedom in making their own arrangements for their housing, food, and recreation. This has resulted (when coupled with the lessened growth in enrollments) in the curtailment of dormitory construction, in the conversion of dormitories on some campuses into offices or apartments for married students, and in the development of new patterns of living for male and female students on campuses where coeducation prevails and residential students form a substantial portion of the student body.

The second discernible trend is the greater dependence on others outside of the university for the provision of housing and food services ("book store services" had been a private, for-profit operation on most campuses for some time). The trend toward nonuniversity operation is particularly noticeable in the provision of food services. Perhaps 30 to 40 percent of all colleges and universities now "contract out" for the operation of dining halls, cafeterias, and snack bars. Such decisions have been prompted by a desire on the part of institutional business officers to divert the responsibility for meeting student complaints to others and by the growing unionization of food service employees. And this trend has been facilitated by the development of "food service companies" to meet a contemporaneous demand for the provision of food service in industrial plants, in hospitals, and on airlines. The contracting out for the construction and operation of dormitories[16] or student recreational facilities is less extensive, but is being experimented with on a number of campuses.

The second question posed for those responsible for governance is: Should the students be given a larger voice (*a*) in determining what living facilities (housing, feeding, recreational, and "book store") should be provided by the institution and what facilities by nonuniversity operatives, (*b*) in formulating the rules that will govern the use of such facilities, and (*c*) in operating the facilities?

The answer to this question has generally been affirmative. This is exemplified on a number of campuses by the entrustment of the operation of the student union (or "center") to students. In these instances customarily a board headed by students, all or most of whose members are elected by students, is authorized to establish rules as to how and for what the student union shall be used and is charged with the responsibility for the financial results of the operation. On a greater number of campuses students have participated in the formulation of rules as to

---

[16] Where community mores and student mores differ sharply, the management of living facilities by commercial real estate managers may provide better "counseling" than do student personnel workers.

the use of dormitories and the kinds and cost of food services to be provided. On fewer campuses students have been consulted as to whether dormitories should be built and by whom (the institution or by private operators), and as to whether food service should be contracted out.

THE WARD'S RIGHTS

This trend toward granting the students (long dealt with as wards) a greater right to voice their views as to matters affecting them is also apparent in the functioning of student publications and radio stations, in the alteration of the structure and scope of student governments, and in the participation by students in a growing number of decisions as to the governance of the entire institution.[17]

The concern of students, as citizens who now have the right to vote, with such issues as this country's participation in the Vietnam war and racial integration has been described in Chapter 2. Once aroused, the students on a number of campuses manifested their concern as to issues on or close to the campus. That concern was expressed in student-operated publications or on student-operated radio, through the functioning of mechanisms of student government (e.g., the election of student officers committed to "eliminate racism from the institution's admissions practices") and through demands for the replacement of what some described as "Mickey Mouse" or "sand-box" mechanisms of student government by direct student participation in the decision-making councils of the institution.

Evidences of institutional racism were attacked; at a large mid-Western university a sit-in was staged to call attention to alleged discrimination against Negroes in the rental of university-owned housing. At a prominent Southern university, students held a week-long "silent vigil" in support of nonacademic Negro workers seeking to organize a union and continued the protest until the university agreed to set up procedures for arbitrating disputes between the employees and the university. The expansion of urban campuses at the expense of the surrounding community, often a ghetto area, was another student issue.

---

[17] In *Should Students Share the Power?* (Philadelphia: Temple University Press, 1970), Earl J. McGrath reported the results of a survey of student participation in college and university governance: "The findings reveal that in the fall of 1969, 88.3 percent of the 875 institutions that supplied usable information had admitted students to membership in at least one policy-making body. It is, therefore, the atypical institution which has not moved in this direction, and such institutions are now for the most part actively considering doing so" (p. 38).

The Students for a Democratic Society (SDS) accused Columbia University of dislodging thousands of minority families in order to build a gymnasium on Morningside Heights in Harlem (although informed observers suggest that SDS would have espoused any of numerous other causes to bring about the confrontation that they sought). With this issue Columbia's activist students forced trustees and presidents to grapple with new issues: What is the university's responsibility to the community in which it resides? Should the community have a voice in university decisions that affect it?

Turning inward, students on a number of campuses criticized the administrations for being "too conservative and tradition-bound" and as not genuinely interested in educational innovation and institutional reform. SDS leaders, running on a platform of "student power," were successful in spearheading campaigns to gain greater student participation in the governance of the institutions they attended. They claimed the right to join with faculty and administration representatives in formulating decisions as to the curricula to be offered, the size of classes, the hiring of faculty, the granting of tenure, and as to the rights and responsibilities of students.

Here is seen again the impact on institutional governance of social trends operating in the larger society. Issues posed by the functioning of student media of communication were, in most instances, a reflection (and oftentimes extreme extension) of opposition to war and to racial prejudice, and of liberalized views as to sex apparent in the society. Issues raised as to the student's right to determine rules governing student life and as to various aspects of the governance of the institution reflected (*a*) the general assertion by subordinate groups in the society— blacks, workers, females—for a larger voice in decisions affecting them and (*b*) the tendency of youth to discount the wisdom of their elders and the willingness of the adult society to live by the values they professed.

By extreme actions, induced in substantial part by these social trends, the students, on perhaps a third of all campuses, forced the trustees and administrations of most colleges and universities to become aware of students' views and to grant students substantially greater freedom in the expression of their views and greater voice in the governance both of student life and of the entire institution. In addition, the tactics the students used in a number of instances forced trustees and presidents to make decisions on such new issues as: When students engage in demonstrations that disrupt educational activities and result in violence, should the local police or the National Guard be called in and what risks accompany such a decision? What liabilities attend a decision to suspend classes? To close the campus? To withhold grades? What steps should be taken to safeguard student rights to due process when institutional discipline is imposed?

ROLE OF STUDENT PERSONNEL WORKERS

As the number of professional student personnel workers has grown (between 1957 and 1972 this number grew twice as rapidly as did aggregate enrollments) and expenditures for a broadened range of activities have increased,[18] the status of the dean of students (or vice president for student affairs) and his staff has not grown proportionately. "Many undergraduates look upon the dean of students as a symbol of authority and control over their activities or their personal behavior . . . at the very time they are rebelling against parental authority and, possibly, institutional authority as well."[19] Faculty members, whose respect is reserved for the scholar's life, look down on the student personnel worker as a "doer" rather than a "thinker," as one more interested in helping others than in ideas. Presidents tend to look ambiguously at the dean of students and his staff: at times they are regarded as instruments for communicating with, manipulating, and keeping under control the students, and at other times they are thought of as oriented toward being the spokesmen for or advocates of students. Trustees tend to discount the professional knowledge trained student personnel workers bring to their jobs and are prone to substitute their own judgments for the recommendations offered by the deans of students.

If student personnel administrators work closely with students and voice the students' viewpoint, they are sometimes accused of "going native," and their views tend to be discounted by their academic colleagues—administrators and faculty both. Moreover neither faculties nor presidents generally credit student personnel work with having a

---

18 W. H. Cowley in his notable essay "Student Personnel Work in Retrospect and Prospect," op. cit., identifies three periods in the evolution of student personnel work: during the years 1900–1919 student personnel work was performed largely by workers interested in helping youth—"humanists," Cowley calls them; in the 1920s the field of student personnel work was invaded by the "psychologists," who, with the old tests and methodology developed in the Army during World War I, concentrated on one-to-one counseling; 1937 marked the third era in the development of student personnel work during which the student personnel worker has become an administrator supervising a number of specialists with supplementary skills.

19 T. R. McConnell, "Student Personnel Services—Central or Peripheral?" *NASPA Journal*, July 1970, pp. 55–63. See also Marie Louise Vergata, *Prestige Rankings of Student Personnel Occupations in Higher Education*, a thesis submitted at the University of Arizona, 1970, order no. 70–19, 961.

philosophical base or an analytical approach. They tend, hence, to regard it as peripheral rather than central to the educational function.[20]

Further, during the late 1960s and 1970s, the legislatures and the courts made decisions (e.g., as to whether students might be required to live in dormitories, as to the nature of disciplinary actions, as to surveillance that might be exercised over student newspapers, and as to whether applicants once convicted of a felony might or should be admitted as students) which circumscribed the freedom of the institution to make its own determinations. These decisions and the circumstances listed earlier have caused the dean of students and his colleagues to play a lesser role in the formulation of decisions than their professional competence and their awareness of the immediate problem warranted. In a few institutions they were supplemented by "ombudsmen" appointed to hear students' grievances, and in a few other institutions the deans of students were drawn from individuals trained in the law, reflecting the greater emphasis on the students' insistence upon due process.

The students claimed a greater voice in decision making. Faculties often supported students' contentions, but countered students' petitions for a voice in educational decisions and (in those relatively few instances when students sought) the right to participate in decisions as to faculty hiring and promotions. Presidents were forced to decide many more student-related issues than in the decades of the 1940s and 1950s, and trustees were confronted with a variety of unprecedented questions for the answering of which they had little factual information and little relevant experience. Both presidents and trustees were in many instances forced to decide such issues under crisis conditions.

During the early 1970s a number of colleges and universities, under the pressure of enrollment declines and financial crises, made cuts in their student personnel staffs and their programs. But the effective performance of their missions during the late 1970s and 1980s will require that colleges and universities provide an adequate and well thought-out program of student personnel services if their students—confronted with the pressures of an urban, industrialized society—are to become emancipated, self-sustaining, and truly free, as well as informed, individuals.[21] The making of those decisions that will be involved in devel-

---

[20] McConnell, op. cit., pp. 55–56.

[21] A useful summary of the "benefits" that will be derived by students, by faculty members, and by the institution from effective student-personnel services is provided by Paul Dressel in the article previously cited, "Measuring the Benefits of Student Personnel Work," *Journal of Higher Education*, January 1973, pp. 24–26.

oping the student-oriented processes requires first and foremost the establishment by trustees, upon recommendation by the faculty and president, of a clear-cut statement as to what is to be accomplished by these several services and how it is related to the educational objectives of the institution. It requires, secondly, the formulation by vice presidents for student affairs and their staffs of a reasoned explanation, founded on continuing analysis of student interests, life, and behavior, as to how particular services and the complex of services provided can be expected to accomplish the objectives established by trustees. If the vice president for student affairs enlists the full participation of representatives of the faculty and of students in the formulation of that rationale, he can gain the status in the structure of the institution which the student personnel function warrants.

Decisions in Response
to Social Demands

All the noise and argument of last year about whether a university should be "involved" in the affairs of the world or "detached" seems to have settled down to the common sense conclusion that it must be both. James Reston[1]

American higher education has never faced seriously the question of purpose. If one asked, "What are you trying to do?", the answer was, "anything we can get anybody to pay for." The purposes of higher education were not its own, but those of individuals, groups, sections of the population, who wanted something from it and from whom it can get something. Robert Hutchins[2]

7 The need for a considered philosophy as to its own role when the college or university responds to the voices of "outsiders" was demonstrated in Chapter 2. That need was underlined by the depiction in Chapter 3 of the pressures by federal and state governments on the institution. The institution cannot meet the needs of all who seek its assistance, for these several pressures are antithetical and disintegrating. It must—and does—choose, and the decisions it makes from day to day in response to various pressures determine whether the college or university accepts the predominant values of the society, rejects the society's values and withdraws into the ivory tower, or establishes a relationship that serves the society while benefitting the institution.[3]

Such day-by-day choices are reflected in decisions as to curricula, as to the environment it maintains for and its relations with students, in its choices of faculty members, and particularly in decisions as to the circumstances under which its staffs will carry on research and provide

---

[1] *The New York Times*, Nov. 25, 1970.

[2] "An Appraisal of Higher Education," 1962.

[3] S. E. and Zella Luria, "The Role of the University: Ivory Tower, Service Station or Frontier Post?" *Daedalus*, Winter 1970, pp. 75–83: "the key question for any institution and for the university in particular, is its ethical interaction with the society in which it operates. This interaction may result in acceptance of the predominant values which become identified as the university's own; or it may lead to a rejection of society's values and a withdrawal into the ivory tower; or it may generate a critical, creative relation between society and university . . . the latter kind of interaction both benefits the university and ultimately benefits the society most."

services for others in the society. The purpose of this chapter is to illuminate such decisions, to picture the factors that must be weighed, the development of staffs to formulate policies to guide such decisions, and the influence of various participants in the making of such decisions.

THE NATURE OF SOCIETY'S NEEDS

Decisions as to standards that will govern admissions, as to the introduction of career-oriented programs in fire science, in nursing, or in merchandising, and as to the establishment of additional schools of law or medicine constitute, whether or not recognized as such, responses to society's needs. Decisions as to the fullness of the student personnel services an institution offers are determinations as to whether the college or university will accept the obligation to develop self-sustaining adults or leave that obligation to the family and to civic authorities. Its choices of faculty members implement decisions as to curricula, as to the relationship maintained with students, and determine the extent to which the institution will emphasize teaching or research.

World War II illuminated an additional need of the society that universities (and some colleges) could help to meet. Higher education and scholarship had long been regarded as inseparable activities. The good teacher was persistently involved in research, that is, in the search for more and new knoweldge. It was wholly logical, hence, that as business and government leaders learned that they could benefit by focusing the minds of scholars on the problems that beset the society, the university should be called upon to undertake a vast variety of research projects and to provide various services.

The rapidity with which this demand of the society for help by the universities is suggested by the growth in federal financing of university research. In 1940–41 federal expenditures approximated $4 million. By 1945–46 this aggregate had grown to about $225 million. A quarter of a century later, in 1970–71, the federal expenditure had increased almost fifteenfold. The volume of research carried on by university faculty members and the scope of their inquiries grew in unprecedented fashion.[4] By 1973, despite some leveling off of federal expenditures, the faculties of some universities were at work on a broad assortment of research projects supported by the federal government and other agencies outside the university. In many instances these projects had

---

4 This growth in the volume of research carried on by university faculty members occurred in a sharply limited number of universities. Little research is done by faculty members in most liberal arts colleges or in many of the state colleges.

little direct relationship to the university's teaching program and particularly to its undergraduate teaching.

The growth of the service function[5] of the university is apparent on many campuses. The land-grant colleges commenced to provide through their extension divisions in the late 1800s services that have contributed greatly to the development of American agriculture. Many other institutions have rendered various services to other segments of the society. On one the faculty of physical education works continually with the Bureau of Alcoholism in a state department of mental health. On another courses are offered to equip young people for employment in the local glass industry. A distinguished Harvard professor designed a garbage disposal ship for the City of Boston. A professor, on leave from Michigan State University, under contract with the U.S. Department of State, aids the faculty of the University of Lagos in establishing a school of business administration.[6] At the request of a large private employer, the faculty of a liberal arts college trains foremen in the employer's plant. A school of education faculty, at the behest of the U.S. Office of Education, develops programs for the rehabilitation of unemployed persons, and supplies experienced advisors to help local school systems cope with problems of racial integration. A medical school faculty contracts to provide medical care for the poor, and the same university's law school provides legal assistance for residents of a neighborhood wracked by race riots.

This list of illustrations could be lengthened. It suffices to make clear the range of activities carried on in response to the needs of society. It does not indicate the operational implications of the growth of this function. A major benefit of the growth of this function is seen in the growth of graduate education: graduate students have been involved in many of the research and service projects, and funds have gone to support a substantial proportion of all graduate students. Some additional faculty positions have been created to provide individuals capable of carrying on research projects or foreign service projects. A class of professional personnel, not a part of the faculty, has come into existence at least in those universities with major research and service programs. A variety of institutes and laboratories, independent of the traditional

---

[5] By the term "service function," I mean those activities carried on by university faculty members that are supported, in whole or in part, by agencies other than the university.

[6] In the late 1960s more than sixty universities were rendering services in 40 or more developing countries under contracts with the U.S. Department of State. For a discussion of the nature and significance of such services see *The University Looks Abroad: Approaches to World Affairs at Six American Universities* (New York: Education and World Affairs, 1965).

departmental structure, has been established. And the project method of financing research and service projects, i.e., by grants to or contracts for particular activities to be carried out by specific individuals or departments, has tended to fragment the university and undermine the authority of academic officers.[7]

These expansions and modifications of the university structure were threatened when the support made available by the federal government for research was leveled off in the early 1970s. Simultaneously, largely as a consequence of the uncertainty of economic conditions, the support from private industry declined. For example in 1969, Procter and Gamble, Inc., Shell Oil Company, and the Standard Oil Company of New Jersey (now Exxon) supported research projects at more than fifty universities; these encompassed explorations of basic physical and chemical processes, the study of product applications, evaluation of the effect of various materials on the environment, and clinical verification of the companies' own research findings. By 1974 such support for universities had declined.

In summary, this country's major universities (for the bulk of all sponsored research was performed by the one hundred largest and most prestigious institutions) wrestled in the early 1970s with two unresolved problems. The first—and major—problem was how to absorb within the structure and operations of the university a function that had grown large and in some instances almost overwhelmed the conduct of research and the provision of services. The companion and presumably temporary problem was how to finance this function when the primary source of support that had kindled the expansion of these activities was reduced.

The major problem—how to absorb and control these activities as a part of the university—poses two precedental questions: Why has society turned to the university? Why should a university carry on research or provide services that exceed the minimum needed to provide students with requisite experience and to enable faculty members to learn and to grow?

WHY THE UNIVERSITY?

Why did not private business or private individuals satisfy these new needs as, historically, they had built railroads, invented the gadgets that made life simpler, discovered new life-saving drugs, and created better

---

[7] Joseph W. Garbarino, "Managing University Research," *California Management Review,* Spring 1970, pp. 71–75.

textbooks? Why did not government expand its own staff and gear itself to handle the new facets of international relations, or to invent and develop new fighting weapons, or to provide the medical and social services needed to combat racial tensions? Answers to these questions are found in five reasons why the American society increasingly turned to the universities for aid with the vitally important problems of building a great society.

First, the university provides unique institutional strengths. It has a staff, buildings and grounds, an endowment, and—most important—a climate within and a prestige without that provide unique institutional leverage for resolving the problems of a society.

A panel, created and supported by the U.S. Office of Education to diagnose the ills of elementary and secondary schools and to conduct the research that may produce solutions, recognized this lack of institutional strength, in reviewing the accomplishments of one of the regional educational laboratories. The laboratory under review was a new, independent, nonprofit institution. It lacked the libraries, laboratories, and administrative structure found in a typical university. It could not attract the ablest of researchers; it did not offer the collegial-interdisciplinary approach to inquiry that makes some universities truly great; and it lacked the reputation for objective, independent fact finding that the term "university" carries with it. Its accomplishments, the panel found, had been achieved in spite of the lack of institutional advantages that a good university could have provided.

Second, the universities, as they grew, acquired a substantial monopoly of the particular kind of human talent required for dealing with some problems of the society,[8] as distinguished from the problems of an enterprise. It is not that the universities have a corner on superior intellects. Indeed, there is substantial evidence that neither government nor the universities attract and hold their share of truly superior intellects. The rewards offered by the profit-making world, whether in business or the professions, are so much greater that government and the universities suffer. But when engaged in private enterprise, many of our ablest minds are focused on the problems of making, selling, promoting, and accounting for products (from diapers to tombstones) and services (from nursing to hairstyling, selling insurance, and preparing income tax forms). The business world seldom focuses its attention and energy

---

[8] The universities' record in research has not been uniformly outstanding. In medicine and earlier in agriculture, the universities have made many and notable contributions through research. In education, in contrast, the universities have contributed less through research; greater contributions in this field have been made, for example, by the Educational Testing Service in Princeton, New Jersey, than by any one of the universities.

on the formulation of foreign policy,[9] the design of educational programs, space exploration, or the eradication of urban blight, be it slums
or smog. The university, however, has a small but growing proportion
of men and women who are capable of and concerned with concentrat-
ing informed intelligence on such problems.

Third, the universities emphasize a discipline of objectivity, an asset
that is scarce and infinitely valuable in a competitive, tension-packed
society. The sales manager, Negro leader, union leader, corporate labor-
relations negotiator, or political executive in government cannot afford
objectivity, nor has he time for it. Moreover, the organization itself—
corporation, union, government department, political party, or even the
Church—demands or perhaps even requires for its survival acceptance
and conformity with its policies. After a decade or two spent plying
their trades, most businessmen, public officials, union leaders, and
preachers are so habituated to one way of thought that they cannot
attack a problem with the fresh, detached objectivity that is required.
William James was surely right when he wrote of the scarcity and
"infinite value" of the capacity for "nonhabitual perception."

Society needs objective questioning and criticism. It needs clear-
headed and courageous questioning of obsolete dogmas (e.g., the infalli-
bility of pure and unadulterated "free enterprise"), the challenging of
political demagogues, and the continual analysis of social trends (e.g.,
population control) and the posing of alternatives (e.g., the provision of
publicly supported health care). To perform these tasks faculty members must not only be objective but well informed; continual involvement in research provides the knowledge on which questioning and
challenging can be founded.

Fourth, the universities are committed to the search for new knowledge. The product of that search, i.e., of basic research, constitutes the
foundation for later practical applications. We live in what Robert Solo
has dubbed "the science-based society."[10] This means that advance in
many, or most, fields depends upon the creation of new knowledge.

To paraphrase Emerson, in a science-based society he who would
have the world beat a path to his door will find the idea for his improved mousetrap in a university laboratory. The day when progress
was based on tinkering and improvisation has passed. Solutions not

---

9 The revelation in 1973 of the International Telephone and Telegraph Corporation's activities in Chile, and the activities of the major oil companies in the
   Middle East obviously were designed to influence the country's policy, but do
   not constitute assumption of like responsibility for formulating foreign policy
   in the national interest.

10 "The University in a Science-Based Society," an unpublished paper.

only for our physical ills (cancer and heart disease, for example) and scientific problems (like those involved in the elimination of air and water pollution), but also for international problems and racial difficulties will most likely be found in the minds of those who have the capacity, time, and inclination for rigorous, detached, creative thought.

Fifth, a university possesses values; it stands for something. It stands, indeed, for some of the most civilizing values we know—freedom, for example. Thus, Merrimon Cuniggim aptly suggests that university people must "say their piece . . . must proclaim their values, that by their very nature they believe and accept not for society's salvation alone but for their own."[11]

His advice poses conscience-shaking questions: Can a university be true to itself, let alone to the society that supports it, if with the knowledge at its command or within its reach, it does not, for instance, accept responsibility for administering, through its medical school, programs that would alter the lives of crippled children? Or can a university, which has access to or can create knowledge that might lighten the social problems of our cities, be true to its purported beliefs if it does not collaborate with regional and municipal authorities in efforts to combat juvenile delinquency, reduce racial conflict, or renovate obsolete forms of local government? Or can a university stand by when it has the know-how to "make the world safe for democracy," in 1975 terms, by undertaking the responsibility for building educational, governmental, agricultural, or health institutions of less developed countries? Or can a university choose to have no part in the national struggle for stable economic growth? Can it refuse to heed the request it receives to investigate surging prices or rising unemployment, even though its findings may well create enemies while they contribute to the identification of solutions?

These five reasons indicate not only why society has turned to the university but why the university strives to absorb within its structure and functioning more than that minimum of research or service effort needed to provide needed experience for students and the opportunity to grow for faculty members.[12] They indicate that the university has a public duty. The conduct of research also serves the university's self-interest; research and services bring financial support

---

[11] "A Campus without Limit," talk delivered to the Danforth Associates Conference, Camp Minniwanca, Aug. 29, 1966.

[12] Carl Kaysen (*The Higher Learning, the Universities and the Public*, Princeton, N.J.: Princeton University Press, 1969, pp. 33–55) has contended that the university needs a politically persuasive and intellectually honest rationale for its activities. That rationale is found in these five reasons.

that has been particularly useful in supporting the graduate and medical schools, and bring the moral and political support (of agricultural interests, for example) that enhances the institution's reputation and increases its appropriations.

WHERE DECISIONS ARE MADE

The answers to these questions are, in considerable part, being made by the individual faculty member. More often than not the demand from the government, a business enterprise, or a foundation is for the services of a particular individual; often because the individual has especial talent or capabilities, but in many instances because the individual has kindled or sought the interest of a sponsor or "sold the idea" to a funding agency.

Indeed, the availability of funds for research and services has created within the academic realm a substantial number of academic entrepreneurs. For the most part these academic entrepreneurs are not found among the most respected scholars. They have distinguished themselves largely by their ability not to acquire or to preserve knowledge but to apply it, and particularly to apply it to the material, political, industrial, military, and economic issues of the times. The role they play is atypical of the conventional view of the university. They acquire resources to support the research or services in which they find opportunity; they may assemble a following of younger students whom they support from the grants they acquire; and they establish a substantial reputation within and for the department, the college, and the university.

There is a substantial argument to be made that decisions as to what research shall be done or what services shall be rendered should be made by the individual. The individual teacher, if he is a good teacher, must pursue his intellectual interests. The discipline he underwent in preparation for academic life created an insatiable and persisting desire to learn more about, and to grow in the command of, his field. Thus research and services offer him opportunities he needs for his personal fulfillment.

Not all faculty members, even in our most prestigious universities, are engaged in research or the provision of services. Indeed, perhaps one-half to three-fourths of all individuals holding professional rank are content to teach. They do not have the intellectual curiosity, the imagination, or the essential skills that are required to do research or to provide services. Many who do carry on research or provide services do so not as an intellectual exercise or for the development of understanding and skill, but, pragmatically, for the supplementation of income.

Nevertheless the opportunity to engage in these activities offers the encouragement that is needed to motivate many to continue to grow.

There is a further and similarly substantial argument that decisions as to what research shall be done or what services rendered should be participated in or controlled by academic administrators and trustees. The educational character and climate of the institution is influenced by such decisions. Questions as to the appropriateness of certain kinds of research (e.g., the development of bacteriological weapons) or services (e.g., the support of covert intelligence activities) are involved. And, in substantial measure, as has been indicated, such decisions involve evaluation of the society's needs and determination of the institution's *social* obligations.

THE UNIVERSITY AND THE RESEARCHER

Most universities, hence, have established some machinery for the review of the individual professor's decisions. Usually, the professor is obligated, first, to carry a basic teaching load of six or nine hours and to carry on research and service activities only in such time as is available after he has met this commitment. It is the department chairman and the dean who are expected to see to it that the faculty member lives by this rule.

In addition, an increasing number of universities have established additional machinery for the development of policies and the review of requests for funds via contracts, grants, or other means. This machinery may consist of an assistant to the president, a vice president or an assistant vice president for research, a faculty research committee aided by one or more staff members, or of a more extensively staffed "development office."[13]

As such machinery evolved over the decade of the 1960s, its function has grown. At the start, the function was substantially limited to ensuring conformity with certain financial and contracting rules laid down by the universities. Those rules were designed to ensure that the extent of commitment the university was assuming—at a faculty member's behest —was fully recognized, for example, that space and equipment could be provided for the activity to be carried on. Particularly, those rules were designed to ensure that through the contracts or grants the sponsor would fairly provide for the indirect costs borne by the university— i.e., the cost of maintaining accounts, paying salaries, and operating the

---

[13] For an excellent discussion of the role and function of such a central research agency, see J. Douglas Brown, *The Liberal University* (New York: McGraw-Hill Book Company, 1969), pp. 185–188.

library upon which the researchers would rely—and the basic costs of maintaining the infrastructure of the university.

Gradually, experience on project after project in university after university dictated the necessity for other rules. These rules, it became clear, were essential if the university were to maintain those five qualities (enumerated above) that identify the university as *the* institution in society that should assume responsibility for research and services that serve the public interest. As a minimum, such rules provide that:

1. The research or services to be undertaken shall not encroach on the primary teaching obligations of the university faculty.

2. The individuals that are expected to carry out the research or perform services are qualified and enthusiastic.

3. Sponsoring agencies should not be permitted to maintain any continuing control over the nature or direction of the research once the objectives are agreed upon.

4. The activity to be carried on has been soundly thought out and offers reasonable assurance of a significant contribution to knowledge or to the public welfare.

5. The investigator shall be free to reveal the purpose, scope, and results of his investigations so that they may contribute to the expansion of human knowledge.

6. The research or services to be carried on are consistent with the objectives, beliefs, and capabilities of the institution.

As the decade of the 1960s posed new problems, the universities (sometimes prodded by students and sometimes by faculty members) have given increased meaning to such rules. Perhaps the last of these rules (6) provoked the greatest concern and resulted in the most striking modifications of existing practices. In summary, it brought about the substantial limitation or phasing out of research designed to develop weapons for the Department of Defense or the Atomic Energy Commission,[14] insistence on greater educational interaction between the governmentally supported university-operated laboratories and instructional activities, the placement of greater relative emphasis on basic research as distinguished from applied research and development, and recognition

---

[14] See, for example, Massachusetts Institute of Technology, "First Report of Review Panel on Special Laboratories," May 31, 1969.

that the university is not effectively structured to carry on large projects involving multidisciplinary research.[15]

Gradually the rules controlling sponsored research in many universities came to reflect, in substantial measure, the philosophical debates of the era, as interchanges between students, faculty members, administrators, and trustees, sometimes through formal committees and studies, distilled new consensuses. Rules formulated by one university illustrate this development:

> Although it is recognized that it is impossible to maintain effective control over application of the results of research once those results are published, it is believed that the university should support no research the immediate and obvious implications of which would facilitate the destruction of human life or the impairment of human capacities.

> Since the explicit purpose of research within a university is the expansion of the corpus of human knowledge . . . the university would not take part in a project the existence of which or the identity of whose principal or subsidiary sponsors could not be revealed.

> . . . only when the urgent needs of the nation, such as in a time of national emergency proclaimed by the President of the United States or when urgent problems of local, national, or international community may uniquely call for a university research project whose primary aim is service rather than contribution to general knowledge [will the university] on the approval of the President of the University after consultation with the departments involved and with the consent of the committee on research . . . [accept responsibility for such a project].

THE GOVERNANCE PROBLEM

The expansion of the demands of society on the university for the undertaking of research and the provision of services has posed in aggravated terms two central issues of modern-day governance. The first has been aptly stated in these words: "Is the university basically a loosely knit

---

15 Alvin Weinberg explains why in these words: "In the individualistic, competitive university environment, genius flourishes; but things go slowly because each genius works by himself with his own small group of students and assistants. In the less individualistic, cooperative institute environment, genius probably does not flourish as well, but things go very fast because so many different talents can be brought to bear on a given problem" (*Reflections on Big Science*, Cambridge, Mass.: The M.I.T. Press, 1967, p. 110). See also "Interdisciplinary Problem-Oriented Research in the University," *Science*, Mar. 12, 1971, p. 3.

company of scholars, each with his individual conscience, or is it an institutional entity with a conscience and direction of its own?"[16] The second is: Can the university, while involved in the affairs of the society through the provision of a broadening range of services, in addition to its involvement through its students and as a citizen of a community, maintain on its campus a climate that encourages rational, detached objective reasoning?

ENTITY OR ?

The first issue was posed during the late 1960s when several score universities were heavily involved in conducting research for the U.S. Department of Defense and the Atomic Energy Commission, and some in providing services for the Central Intelligence Agency. The national revulsion against the Vietnam war, coupled with the evolving new youth culture, stimulated protest by students and others, and posed such questions as: How free shall the teacher be to undertake rsearch the objective of which runs counter to the prevailing thought of the university community? How far can the teacher go in asserting his personal views on social issues, e.g., in challenging speakers invited to the campus, without destroying his capacity to lead his colleagues and students in rational, objective learning? How free shall the student be to assert his views on social issues and to demand that the institution or its president publicly voice supporting views? And, relatedly, how free shall the student be in the choice of what he shall study, what class rules (e.g., attendance), and what personal conduct rules (e.g., association of the sexes in dormitories) he shall follow?

The developments, on several score campuses, during the traumatic years 1969–1972, provided a clear answer. That answer is that the university is an institutional entity; and if it is to survive, it must have a conscience guide it. This means that the university as an institution, in responding as it must to society's demand for research and services, "should take more responsibility than it has in the past for the overall size and for the distribution of its research effort."[17] That has already meant some encroachment on the historic right of the individual investigator to determine what research he shall carry on (e.g., he shall not carry on research for a secret sponsor—the Central Intelligence Agency —or research the results of which cannot be disseminated among his

---

16 Robert S. Morison, "Some Aspects of Policy Making in the American University," *Daedalus*, Summer 1970, p. 612.

17 Ibid., p. 639.

professional colleagues). It will likely mean some further encroachment, and it presages the prospect of some limitation of the freedom of both faculty and students in other areas of academic life.

RATIONALITY DESPITE POLITICIZATION

Because it accepted opportunities for the conduct of research that served the interests of governments, business firms, foundations, and others, the university has been criticized. It is contended that it has lost sight of its central purposes, that it has become "all things to all people," and that by association, through research or services, with various governmental or private programs or interest groups (e.g., organized farmers or organized educators), it has lost the detachment and neutrality that gives credibility to its objectivity and is essential to the maintenance of a climate for rational learning.[18]

But in a society in which knowledge is of increasing and greater importance than at any previous moment in history, the university needs involvement—for the education of students and for the continual updating and sharpening of the capabilities of faculty members. It has an obligation to contribute to the resolution of those problems for which it has unique capabilities.[19] And it is responsible for serving as the critic of social actions, for challenging trends, for posing alternatives—for serving as an "agent of change." Thus, the university, and to a lesser but substantial degree the college, is destined to be more involved, not less.

Decisions, hence, as to what research shall be undertaken and what services provided, under what conditions, and how these activities shall be related to and contribute to the instructional process are of large importance to the governance of colleges and universities. Such decisions will shape the character of the institution and determine whether it is a center for rationality and the pursuit of truth. A thesis of this book is that it can maintain that character if it develops those institu-

---

[18] "As Yale University Professor Kenneth Keniston has stated: 'The main task of the university is to maintain a climate in which, among other things, the critical spirit can flourish. If individual universities as organizations were to align themselves officially with specifically political positions, their ability to defend the critical function would be undermined' " (quoted by the Scranton Commission in *The President's Commission on Campus Unrest*, 1970, chap. 6, p. 9).

[19] The President's Committee on the Future University of Massachusetts, after cautioning that this institution is and should be a university and not "another kind of higher education facility," "a community-action agency, a housing authority, or a pollution abatement agency," outlined an extensive array of "public services" that it believed the university should perform ("Report of the Presidents' Committee on the Future of the University of Massachusetts," December 1971, pp. 90–106).

tions of governance that assure that all members of the community who are responsibly concerned with knowledge—its development, dissemination, and application—shall have a voice in the formulation of the policies they live and work by.

IMPLICATIONS OF PRESENT NEEDS

The land-grant college accepted an obligation for the development and dissemination of new knowledge among farmers a century ago. What is new is simply this: The American society in the 1970s avidly and hungrily seeks solutions for many more problems than those of the farm and rural population that the land-grant colleges have been concerned with for decades. It seeks persons with the knowledge, specialized skills, and capacity for objectivity required for the resolution of health and of racial, economic, international, and other problems. The universities, encompassing a large proportion of all persons possessing the knowledge, skills, and objectivity required, face the prospect of still greater demands in the future than they have been confronted with to date.

These demands are reflected in pleas for assistance from scores of urban centers; in the seduction by business firms (through consulting contracts) of the mobile members of university faculties; in the provisions of Titles I and III of the Higher Education Act of 1965, of Title II of the Economic Opportunity Act of 1964, of the State Technical Service Act of 1965, the Law Enforcement Assistance Act of 1965, and the Cancer, Heart, and Stroke Program enacted by Congress in 1965. It is manifest in the National Association of State Universities and Land-Grant Colleges' study "The State University and Public Affairs."

The university has accepted these added responsibilities and the central role of knowledge in the advance of civilization in the future forecasts that the university will be expected to assume still additional responsibilities. The conventional plaint will be voiced repeatedly: the university's responsibilities are, first and foremost, the discovery of knowledge (or research) and, second, the transmission of knowledge (or teaching). Those who emphasize this view will rightfully inquire: Who is going to do the teaching?[20] Will faculty members who become involved in projects outside the university maintain their detachment?

---

[20] That is a task for which the university has a substantial responsibility. James A. Perkins has asserted that ". . . the university can never again run on the assumption that it commands or can command the full time interest and attention of all its faculty," *The University of Transition* (Princeton, N.J.: Princeton University Press, 1966, p. 55).

Can the institution accept such responsibilities and maintain its autonomy? And where is the money coming from?

During the years since 1960, the universities have developed certain structural arrangements, policies, and procedures for the control of these activities and the minimization of their disintegrating effect on the governance of the institution. The answers to the questions just stated remain quite unclear. But this much is clear. American society in the 1960s was desperately seeking the means to better the cities, improve schools, lengthen lives, overcome racial tensions, and find solutions to international ills. And this society is plagued by the fact that most of those able to help on such problems "are simply tending the machinery of that part of the society to which they belong. The machinery may be a great corporation or a great law practice or a great university. These people tend it very well indeed, but they are not pursuing a vision of what the total society needs."[21]

---

[21] John Gardner, "The Anti-Leadership Vaccine," in an essay included in the annual report of the Carnegie Corporation of New York, 1965.

PART THREE
SUPPORT ACTIVITIES

Applying What Is Known
of Management

*By at least 1984, if we work hard we can make education
supremely efficient and accountable. Efficiency is what we
render unto Caesar, and we hardly need reminding that
Caesar has his legions. But the very awesomeness of the
powers and principalities of the cult of efficiency compels
me to argue with some fervor that there are limits to
accountability, limits to efficiency, limits to slide rule
definitions of educational productivity. Surely the ultimate
philistinism of our culture would be to impose management
science upon the educational process.* Stephen K. Bailey[1]

8 "Management," "efficiency," and "productivity" are for most
academicians ugly words.[2] Yet the demands upon colleges and
universities for an accounting of what they are accomplishing, the
competition for resources among institutions and between higher education and other functions of government, and the internal need for
means to ensure that limited resources are utilized to achieve desired
educational ends force each institution to seek more efficient and more
economic management processes.

Many institutions have experimented with the application of management techniques used by business firms and governmental agencies,
e.g., program budgeting, operations research, management by objectives, and systems analysis.[3] The purpose of such techniques, viewed
collectively—it is essential to recognize—is to assemble information as
to each aspect of an overall operation and to place that information (in
the form of studies, budgets, analyses, and plans) in the hands of those
individuals responsible for making decisions. The assembly of that
information, its distribution to and its use by decision makers, and the
implementation of decisions taken comprise the substance of "management."

---

[1] "Combatting the Efficiency Cultists," *Change*, June 1973, p. 8.

[2] For illustrative explanations of the reaction of academics to "management" see
David C. Knapp, "Management Intruder in the Academic Dust," *Educational
Record*, Winter 1969, pp. 58–59; and Simon Marcson, "Decision Making in a
University Physics Department," *American Behavioral Scientist*, December
1962, p. 37.

[3] Francis E. Rourke and Glenn E. Brooks, *The Managerial Revolution to Higher
Education* (Baltimore: The Johns Hopkins Press, 1966).

The application of management techniques to the academic activities of colleges and universities has proven difficult, or at least unacceptable. Why? First, in the college and the university the assembly of evaluative information about each of the processes described in Chapters 5–7 is made difficult by two facts. While teachers, department chairpersons, deans, and others do judge, rate, grade, or otherwise evaluate change in knowledge, skills, educational products and even attitudes, the core activities involved in the instructional, the student-oriented, and the research and service processes are relatively unquantifiable. Moreover, there is much disagreement as to what changes in knowledge, skills, and attitudes are desirable, and hence how change is to be evaluated.

One can categorize admittees and count students, courses, credit hours, counseling hours, and other facets of those activities, but one encounters less satisfying ways of measuring the wisdom, values, or self-reliance developed in students of varying natural endowments, experience, skills, interests, and educability. Nor can one measure the benefits that flow from the research and services faculty members perform, particularly those benefits that students derive from the enthusiasm of an instructor stimulated by research, nor the neglect students suffer from professors who slight their teaching responsibilities in favor of research or consulting services.

Second, the process of communicating such information as can be assembled to many decision makers—trustees, the president and his staff, department chairpersons, faculty members, and in some instances, students—who have markedly varying comprehensions of the institution and its objectives is difficult. It is made difficult by the differing degrees of affiliation each has with the institution. It is made difficult, also, by the different educational and philosophical orientations which teachers, department chairpersons, and deans bring to bear on the data on which decisions are based.

Two additional characteristics of the college or university make difficult the exercise of controls. The first is the diffusion of authority that obtains within most colleges and universities.[4] The second is the creative nature of the educational and the research tasks. Of these tasks it may be said: One should control those engaged in teaching and in research as one would cook a small fish—gently. Too much cooking, too much interference with the natural process make it fall apart or

---

4 Kenneth D. Benne in an article entitled "Authority in Education" (*Harvard Educational Review*, August 1970, pp. 385–410) describes the authority relations that obtain among students, teachers, and institutions and describes this set of relations as "anthropological authority," a relationship that invokes "the collaboration of equals in a creative task."

destroy its flavor. So the "controls" management science enthusiasts would apply may be counterproductive.

These factors have contributed to the prevalence of the idea that academic activities cannot be "managed" and that efficiency is to be expected only in the business affairs of the institution.[5] They are responsible also for the existence in most institutions of higher education of an organizational dualism: the simultaneous existence of two separate and relatively little-related organizations—the academic organization governed by the faculty and the business affairs organization governed by administrators and the trustees.

PLANNING AND MANAGEMENT

The need is for the adaptation of management techniques (such as program budgeting, operations research, management by objectives, and systems analysis) to the particular character and the climate of the college or the university. This is feasible *if* attention is concentrated on the fundamental objective of management—the mobilization of the collaborative zeal of associated individuals in the pursuit of agreed-upon ends. Overly simple? Yes. But this brief statement offers a guide to the adaptation needed to make techniques, the efficacy of which has been demonstrated elsewhere, usable in the academic enterprise.

First, agreement on ends must be continually strived for. Colleges and universities (as was pointed out in Chapter 4) seldom have "explicit and understood objectives . . . to guide management," and the achievement of agreement on objectives is difficult. Yet if the management of a college or university is to be effective, there must be a continual effort to plan for the future, for in that planning lies the prospect of approximate agreement on ends. Mark you, the need is for "planning," not "a plan."

Second, a continual and carefully designed flow of information must be available to those involved in planning and to those responsible for making decisions in accordance with such proscriptions as are agreed upon by the planners. The design of this flow, i.e., the determination of just what information is needed and justifies the cost of gathering and processing, is also difficult. The installation of "management information systems" in many institutions has floundered on this determination.

Third, the authority for decision making must be clarified. As a

---

[5] Robert D. Clark, president, University of Oregon, *AGB Reports*, November–December 1972, p. 15.

common framework of agreed-upon ends is hammered out by the planners, the feasibility of as decentralized decision making as exists in the college or university will be increased, *if* simultaneously there is a common understanding of who is authorized to make what decisions.

"Agreed-upon ends" or "objectives" will have been determined when some degree of consensus has been reached through a process that is democratic and participatory. This means that planning must be done by a body that includes representatives of each of the groups (other than trustees) that are authorized to formulate or to make decisions.[6] Three models illustrate the kind of planning structure needed.

At Princeton University two committees are responsible essentially for long-range and short-range planning, respectively, and are made up of the principal academic officers, faculty members, graduate students, undergraduate students, and other groups included on the university staff, e.g., the library staff and the professional research staff. At Furman University, there is a Committee on Institutional Planning, which is chaired by the president and includes three vice presidents, two deans, the business manager, the heads of three major academic and administrative committees, seven faculty members, and two students. The system for planning proposed by the National Association of College and University Business Officers (NACUBO) provides for an Analytical Studies Group to be composed of administrators, faculty members, and students.

Planning has two functions: to enhance agreement on explicit long-run objectives for the institution and to advise the president and trustees as to what activities should be given priority in annual budgets.[7] Long-run objectives will necessarily be stated in general terms.[8] But they still

---

6 The nature of the planning process in academic institutions is described, appraised, and prescribed for in a suggestive article by Alvin Eurich, "Plan or Perish," *College and University Journal*, Summer 1970, pp. 18–22; a brochure by John G. Bolin, *Institutional Long-Range Planning*, Institute of Higher Education (Athens, Ga.: University of Georgia, 1969); and in several "how-to-do-it" publications of the Western Interstate Commission on Higher Education, e.g., *Implementation of NCHEMS Planning and Management Tools at California State University, Fullerton*, August 1972.

7 It is not proposed here to prescribe *how* the planning for a college or university should be carried on. The purpose of this section is to indicate the role of planning in governance and to suggest how planning is related to the achievement of better academic management by techniques utilized in business and government.

8 Long-run objectives usually will be concerned with such ends as the intellectual and personal development of financial viability, the establishment of participative governance, and the cultivation of an image of intellectual achievement. See Norman P. Uhl, *Identifying Institutional Goals*, NLHE Research Monograph Number Two (Durham, N.C.: National Laboratory for Higher Education, 1971).

must be stated with sufficient specificity to guide deans in determining whether to emphasize the liberal arts or career preparation in shaping the curricula to guide department chairmen and professors in framing course objectives and in selecting new faculty members; to guide student personnel workers in shaping the student environment, in selecting students for admission, and in allocating financial aid; and to provide general direction for administrative officers, technical staffs, and students. Such general guidance will be made more meaningful over time as the planning body considers and suggests courses of action on such matters as the introduction of new programs, coeducation, or student participation in governance, and as it offers its recommendations as to what activities should be given priority in each successive annual budget.

The prospect of arriving at agreed-upon ends will be enhanced by looking outward, as well as inward. To "look outward" is to think deeply and to strive to appraise the institution's outputs.[9] What is the intellectual quality of the graduates? How and to what extent have the values of students been affected? In comparison with competing institutions what degree of academic excellence can be claimed and what shortcomings must be admitted? What is the image of the institution, not alone in the eyes of peers in the academic world, but in the eyes of legislators, prospective donors, secondary school guidance counselors, and prospective students?

To look inward is to translate generally stated objectives into answers to questions such as these: Why does the institution emphasize general education, or preparation for graduate study, or career-oriented education? What kinds of students are to be admitted and how are they to be recruited and selected? What enrollment goals shall be set for the institution as a whole, the various programs (e.g., the school of education versus the college of arts and sciences versus the graduate school)? How will the performance of faculty members be evaluated? What standards for faculty workloads and compensation will be maintained?

If some consensus as to the answers to both sets of questions—those focused on outputs and those focused on internal decision making—is continually sought through a participatory planning process, the first and basic adaptation of management techniques used in business and government will have been achieved. Techniques used in organizational environments in which authority is more centralized and controls are

---

[9] The identification of "outputs" and their measurement is helpfully discussed in *The Outputs of Higher Education: Their Identification, Measurement, and Evaluation*, a brochure that includes the papers presented at a seminar held in Washington, D.C., May 3–5, 1970, by the Western Interstate Commission for Higher Education in cooperation with the American Council on Education and the Center for Research and Development in Higher Education, Berkeley, California.

more acceptable will have been adapted to the more decentralized and less controllable organizational environment of the college and university.[10]

ORGANIZING FACT FLOWS

The process of planning—the work of whatever broadly constituted body is assigned this responsibility—is an intellectual task. It is the continual reexamination of the institution's functioning in terms of agreed-upon ends or objectives. The task involves the examination of operations and of proposals in the light of a body of facts that has several components:

- *Academic facts*, which describe the institution as it now exists, e.g., the characteristics of the student population, the makeup of the faculty and evidences of its performance, the distribution of enrollment among programs, the balance of income and resources, and the adequacy of physical facilities.

- *Financial facts*, on which assumptions as to the future can be founded, e.g., prospective income from each major source, prospective enrollments, the competition for students by institutions offering various types of educational programs, and trends in faculty salaries and in other elements of costs.

- *Operational facts*, which must come in principal part from the harnessing of three flows of information. The first of these informational flows has to do with the number of students, classes, majors, degrees, and other quantitative measures of the institution's instructional operations; the second has to do with dollars —with revenues, expenditures, investments, and their yields; the third has to do with operations—space available and utilized, meals served, dormitory operations, items purchased, buildings maintained, and the like.[11]

The first two categories of facts must be assembled for the planning body by a central staff agency, presumably a part of the president's staff. This assembly is performed in many smaller institutions by an

---

10 Essentially, the foundation will have been laid for the use of the popular technique described as "management by objectives." That is, the basic information that enables each decision maker, e.g., the department chairman, to set for his department, in collaboration with his colleagues, objectives consonant with those of the whole, will have been made available to him.

11 In the jargon of management science, the "harnessing" of these flows is described as the development of a "management information system."

assistant or assistants to the president. In larger institutions, it is usually performed by an office of planning, by the budget staff, or an office of institutional research. The third category of needed facts flows from the continuing operations of various organizational units. The need in all three areas is to identify the information that is required and provide for its reporting and usage.

The organizational units that produce these several flows of information perform many tasks in addition to "serving up" the data required for planning. For example, they prepare payrolls, maintain personnel records, keep accounts, control inventories, prepare class rolls, record grades, and write out transcripts. Here we are concerned with the analyses distilled from the basic data they record and store, which provide the information required by those who are responsible for governance. For example, decision makers need as a basis for recurrent decisions answers to such questions as these: What would be the various impacts of an increase in enrollment? Or, as at the University of Virginia in mid-1972, a limitation of enrollment? And what would be the various impacts of an increase in tuition costs? What do federal agencies need to know? And what do the university systems, of which the institution is a part, need to know?

"It is almost axiomatic," in the opinion of one well-known student of higher education, "that decision making has been overly simplified and based on dreadfully inadequate information organized in dreadfully unsystematic ways."[12] But, as this observer also points out, there are now management information systems, similar to those developed in business, tailored specifically to serve the needs of academic institutions.

Obviously, the three informational flows that have been identified must be interrelated. Decision making by faculties, presidents, and trustees will often involve the integration of data from each of these flows and from each organizational unit of the university.[13] All three informational systems will likely converge in one computer center. The remainder of this chapter deals in turn with each of these three informational systems. It pictures summarily the functions of the organiza-

---

[12] Lewis B. Mayhew, in "Jottings," a column of commentary published regularly in *Change*, July–August 1972, p. 70.

[13] A study made in 1970 indicated that of a large sample of colleges and universities less than one-quarter reported a full-time office for institutional research, slightly more than one-eighth had established computerized management information systems, and approximately one-third used some form of planning, programming, and budgeting system (Lawrence Bogard, "Management in Institutions of Higher Education," chap. 1 in *Papers on Efficiency in the Management of Higher Education*, by Alexander M. Mood, Colin Bell, Lawrence Bogard, Helen Brownlee, and Joseph McCloskey, Carnegie Commission on Higher Education, Berkeley, Calif., 1972).

tional units that assemble and analyze the data included in each system. More important, it indicates the kinds of questions that can be resolved by analysis of such data. And it describes methods being utilized in some institutions to enable trustees, presidents, and deans to make more and better decisions of the sort that affect the character and quality of the college or university as an educational institution.

THE ACADEMIC INFORMATION SYSTEM

Decision making as to the central issues in a college or university should be based on analyses of data on applicants, students, professors, classes, classrooms, majors, degrees, library books, and other units that can be used to measure aspects of instructional operations. Much of these data are regularly assembled by the registrar and by the director of admissions, and—in an increasing number of institutions—are analyzed by a relatively new unit, the office of institutional research. Hence, this section depicts the functions of these organizational units, the data they generate, and the kinds of issues arising in the governance of colleges and universities the resolution of which requires such data, e.g., which applicants for admission have the best prospect of graduation? Why do some students—and which ones—drop out? What proportion of a faculty member's time is devoted to teaching, preparation, research, serving on faculty committees?

OFFICE OF THE REGISTRAR

The office of the registrar is one of the oldest organizational units within the university structure. The incumbent has been known as the "official custodian and historian of educational records." Decades ago, the registrar's function was as limited as this summary statement suggests. But, as colleges and universities have grown, the range and importance of the registrar's function have expanded. The office of the registrar has become a major source of the information that can and should provide the raw material for effective academic management; in some institutions it does.

The office of the registrar usually is responsible for following five operating functions.

REGISTRATION The registrar derives his title from his central function of making a record (usually just prior to the beginning of classes) of each student's vital statistics, previous academic record, and classes in which he is enrolled.

SCHEDULING CLASSES   After assembling from departmental chairpersons or the academic dean a list of all classes to be offered, the registrar relates these classes to the space that is available. He is responsible for scheduling each class (and each section of a class) in a particular classroom at a specific time. He is responsible for promulgating information as to the times, places, and names of instructors for each class. And, at those fateful seasons of the year, he similarly schedules examinations.

RECORDING AND STORING DATA   The assembly of the foregoing and related data is an ongoing process. Students earn grades that must be recorded; they enroll in additional courses and drop others; they transfer in and out of the institution. This record of what he has accomplished has always been of substantial value to the student; as the value of college attendance, and especially graduation, has grown, the significance to the individual of this record (and its confidentiality) has become markedly greater. Thus, the registrar is responsible for the continuing job of compiling each student's record—the courses taken and the grades earned.

PRODUCTION OF REPORTS   For the student, the end product of the registrar's work—and a valuable product, indeed—is the transcript certifying his record of accomplishment. Throughout a lifetime, he may have need to request an official record of his studies. And for a like span of years the registrar must preserve that record. Consider the magnitude of this recording, filing, and record-maintenance task in any institution with thousands, or tens of thousands, of students.

For those who govern the institution, the student's records have other values. These records represent the analogue of the automobile manufacturer's work-production record—just as the latter form records the work done on each auto frame that traverses the assembly line so the student's academic record indicates what courses were "hung on" the human frame that passed through the institution. And from those records can be distilled much of the intelligence required for effective academic management; that intelligence goes into reports as to number of enrollees, classes, space requirements, and grades granted.

ACADEMIC ANALYSIS   Generally, registrars have been and are record keepers, not analysts. Indeed, it has been suggested that registrars throw away more data every day than many offices of institutional research are able to get their hands on. Many registrars have been content to devise and apply the forms, the machines, and the processes which assure that students are enrolled, classes scheduled, grades collected and recorded, and transcripts issued. Fewer registrars have recognized how much their records, when imaginatively analyzed, can contribute to the institution's policy making and to research into the academic process. If trustees, presidents, and deans conclude that financial pressures necessitate reduction of the proliferation of courses, the basic information as to number of courses by department and by size of enrollment is found in the registrar's records. If deans want to assess the extent to which faculty-approved regulations are being conformed with, the evidence is reflected in these records. If a harassed president, besieged by faculty complaints as to inconvenient scheduling of classes, strives to formulate alternative arrangements, it is the registrar's assistance he needs. If deans, confronted with a rising proportion of failures among students, look for the cause, the records of the registrar may not supply definitive answers as to *why*, but those records will supply invaluable materials for those who must formulate remedies.

Yet the registrar is more often an automaton than a supplier of needed intelligence. He prides himself on the accuracy, the thoroughness, and the currency of his records. As enrollments have grown, the maintenance of these records has required the introduction of automatic processing equipment and the development of microfilm filing systems that conserve space and expedite the retrieval of individual records. And the more the registrar has been consumed with the problems of large-scale record processing, the less concern he has manifested for the meaning of the flow of data for which he is responsible.

OFFICE OF ADMISSIONS

Originally, the actual handling of applications for admission was a responsibility of the registrar, and in some institutions that office was known as the "office of admissions and records." But, as the admissions function has been broadened and professionalized and as the function has increasingly been entrusted to personnel trained in the techniques of psychological measurement, the office of admissions has been separated from that of the registrar. The admissions office customarily is responsible not only for the actual appraisal of applicants' qualifications, but also for maintaining relations with the secondary schools from whence applicants come (and particularly with the counselors in those schools) and for counseling those who apply not only as to their applications, but also as to their choice of courses and other matters.

Organizationally, offices of admissions are found in three principal locations.[14] A minority of such offices (10 to 15 percent) are immediately responsible to the president or chancellor, and those usually in institutions that are substantially reliant on tuition income. Approximately half of all such offices report to an academic vice president or dean. And 15 to 18 percent report to the vice president or dean responsible for student affairs. The balance (approximately a third) have various other reporting relationships. In any of these organizational locations, the office of admissions is customarily aided by the guidance of a faculty "committee on admissions," which establishes standards and guidelines for the appraisal of applicants for admission and exercises continuing surveillance over the functioning of the admissions office.

Successive changes in the prevailing philosophy as to who shall attend college have given increased importance to an understanding of the admissions process and have tended to bring about changes in the organization of this function within the college or university. A century ago, all who sought admission and could meet the costs of higher education were generally admitted. A half century ago, the beginnings of a selective process were initiated; in successive decades, as enrollments grew, that process became increasingly more exacting. Limited facilities necessitated some screening, and the techniques of psychological measurement—of intelligence, aptitude, and motivation testing—permitted more informed choices among the many applicants seeking a limited number of places in many institutions. Then, after 1965, the social pressures demanding equality resulted in the development in some institutions (particularly, public institutions) of what has become known as an "open admissions" policy—a substantial abandonment of the selectivity that did obtain.

These changes in prevailing philosophy suggest the intimate relation between the admissions process and the social-political issues of the day. As the institution of higher education has provided an increasingly valuable means of equipping the individual for a job, and an avenue toward higher social status, a social philosophy that permitted only a minority to have access to such education became increasingly unacceptable. But, simultaneously, the larger and larger expenditures made each year for higher education made desirable for the society, the institution, as well as the prospective student, some means of assessing the individual's capabilities, of facilitating his choice of a junior college, college,

---

[14] Harry Gibson and James E. Thomas, "Doing Your Own Thing: A Study of Offices of Admissions and Records," *College and University*, Winter 1971, pp. 139–147.

or university suitable to his needs, and of forecasting the likelihood of his eventual graduation.

Both the importance of the admissions process to the quality of the institution and the increased social and political importance of decisions as to who shall be admitted make manifest the significance of the decisions made by the admissions office. It is the admissions office that is responsible for the quality of the student body and is influential in communicating an image of the institution to prospective students and to counselors on the staffs of the secondary schools. It is the admissions office that supplies in the spring the critical data as to prospective enrollments on which financial and operating plans are founded. It is the admissions office that can supply the basic intelligence to facilitate the articulation of secondary schools, two-year colleges, and the four-year institutions. It is the admissions office that can supply knowledge of student wants and that can guide the faculty in formulating programs of study. In considerable part, it is the admissions office that determines, and could forecast, the proportion of students that will drop out before graduation.

OFFICE OF INSTITUTIONAL RESEARCH

"Sound governance and good learning are what make a good university."[15] This is a capsule-like statement of the need for interrelation of what are in many colleges and institutions quite separate bodies and it is illusory to think that a college or university can function effectively when responsibilities are split down the middle with the faculty in charge of academic affairs and the president and trustees responsible for business and financial affairs. A half century ago the president of an American college or university was expected to, and could, interrelate these separate bodies and processes. In the 1970s, the president needs competent staffs capable of assembling information from each functioning part of the institution—from the schools, colleges, and institutes, as well as from the registrar, the admissions office, the financial officers (comptroller and/or treasurer), and the business affairs officers (those responsible for dormitories, buildings and grounds, dining halls, supplies and equipment, and the bookstores and other "auxiliary enterprises"). Of late, such staffs have been added to the institution's organization in what has become known as the office of institutional research (OIR).

In general terms, the office of institutional research is responsible for continually studying how instruction throughout the institution can be

---

15 F. deW. Bolman, "University Reform and Institutional Research," *The Journal of Higher Education*, February 1970, p. 89.

made more effective and how the management can be made more efficient. Unfortunately, as offices of institutional research have come into being (and most are less than six or eight years old), they have concerned themselves with particular problems (e.g., faculty salaries, student dropouts). In general, they have focused their attention on the following five categories of studies.

Student studies, e.g., prediction of student success on the basis of high school origins, test results, and other criteria; the distribution of scholarships, loans, and work opportunities among students; the evaluation of practices used in the reinstatement of students after periods of absence from the campus; analysis of grades given by departments or to various categories of students under varying admissions policies.

Faculty studies such as analyses of the distribution of faculty members' time among teaching, preparation, student advising, research, public service, and committee assignments; the publications and other professional accomplishments of faculty members; and problems encountered in the recruitment and retention of faculty members.

Curricular studies consist of two separable types of curricular studies. The first type produces evaluation data on which plans for improvement can be based. This type includes analyses of the proliferation of courses and of course duplication; student evaluations of courses taken; alumni retrospective evaluations of courses and programs; and analyses of professional programs by practitioners (e.g., nurses) in the field. The second type may be described as educational research and includes the evaluation of alternative methods of instruction—lectures, seminars, tutorials, independent study—and the appraisal of new technological aids (television, cassettes, etc.).

Operational analyses, such as appraisals of space utilization; of the library, learning laboratory, and the bookstore; studies of facility needs; projections of prospective needs for both academic and non-academic personnel; and analyses of the data needed for effective operation of the whole institution.

Financial studies are generally of two sorts: budget analyses and cross analyses of educational data and cost data. Typical of the first of these two sorts of studies are analyses of trends in categories of costs, in income by sources, faculty salaries, and in equipment costs, and those studies incident to the development of program budgeting. Typical of the significant cross analyses of educational and cost data are those that reveal per student costs by programs (e.g., business administration versus liberal arts), by majors in various disciplines, and by student class hour and student credit hour.

"If the university is to be capable of responding to changing public and educational needs, it is essential that sustained self-study and evaluation become permanent parts of the academic and administrative process. . . ."[16] In these words, the President's Committee on the Future of the University of Massachusetts (December 1971) stated an additional (and urgent) objective for the office of institutional research: the continual provision of those analyses that will enable deans, presidents, and trustees to guide those changes in programs, curricula, and practices needed to serve better the society's evolving needs. This requires the asking of questions and the challenging of assumptions that are rooted in long-standing practices and revered characteristics of the institution.[17] Such questions might include: How does one justify the absence of change? Is there an awareness of options—in curriculum, in finance, in philosophy, or in forms of governance? Do prevailing institutional rewards and sanctions tend to perpetuate the status quo or to encourage change? Are the principles of the institution provisional without being merely opportunistic? What evidence is there of broad and continuous support for the institution and the characteristics and qualities that identify it?

The maintenance of a focus on the institution as a whole and on its managerial efficiency and educational effectiveness is difficult. The offices of institutional research may be called upon to serve many constituencies both internal (the president, the financial officers, the faculty, and the students) and external (federal-aid granting agencies; the state coordinating agencies; professional accrediting agencies; budgeting, civil service, purchasing, and other offices of the state government; the alumni; the community in which it is located). The demands of each are parochial; they are reflected in a virtually continuous flow of questionnaires to be answered. Besieged by these and like demands from all other "customers," the OIR too often becomes a compiler of facts, does little to evaluate institutionwide problems, and never gains the role of consultant to the president and trustees, a role which is vigorously advocated by those who conceive of what the analyses of this office can provide for those responsible for governance.

THE FINANCIAL-INFORMATION SYSTEM

At the heart of the effective management and the efficient operation of any enterprise is the allocation of resources. This requires accounting

---

16 "Report of the President's Committee on the Future of the University of Massachusetts," Boston, December 1971, p. 112.

17 Ideas stated here are adapted from Warren Bryan Martin, "Thoughts on Institutional Research as Gate-Tending, Book-keeping, and Goal Mining," *Liberal Education*, May 1971, pp. 224–235.

and budgeting procedures that will provide the information required by decision makers. In the college or university this means that those who have decision-making responsibility require information with which to answer such questions as: What educational programs (perhaps even courses) should be added, continued, or eliminated? For how large a student body should these programs be offered? When should tuition charges and fees be raised and by how much? What kinds of research should be supported? What public services should be rendered and at what "prices"? What mix of instructional programs, research, and public services can be afforded? What resources should be allocated to the support of such auxiliary services as dormitories, dining halls, athletics, the library, a computer center, and other "common-use" facilities? How much should faculty salaries, administrative salaries, and staff salaries and wages be increased and when? What resources should be sought for investment in buildings and grounds and how rapidly will the institution's current resources permit the absorption of the costs of operating and maintaining new facilities? How should endowments be invested in the light of the institution's need for current income?

The accounting systems utilized by most colleges and universities do not provide the information required for such decisions. Generally, those systems are concerned primarily with recording the receipt of funds by source and their expenditure by purpose. For many public institutions, systems of accounting are prescribed by state authority— and are designed to provide for the uniform recording of receipts and expenditures by all agencies (e.g., the prisons, hospitals, and executive departments) to facilitate control by the governor and his staff. Such accounting systems do not provide trustees and presidents with the cost data needed for effective management of the institution.

Usually, responsibility for maintaining the college or university's books of accounts is assigned to a financial officer, variously titled "treasurer," "comptroller," "director of finance," or "chief accountant," and sometimes still by the older title, "bursar." The individuals who occupy these positions seldom come from the academic ranks: they are recruited from a variety of sources—frequently from among retired military officers. They often bring to their assignments a limited understanding of, and often limited curiosity as to, academic objectives. Hence, the creation of a flow of financial information that will facilitate governance by departmental chairpersons, deans, the faculties, presidents, and trustees suffers. The academic minds are usually not equipped to prescribe what combinations of financial and academic information are needed, and financial officers are often not sufficiently aware of academic objectives to conceptualize that data which would aid evaluation of accomplishment.

Responsibility for the budgeting function, once generally entrusted to the finance officer, has generally been shifted in recent years to an officer more closely related to the president or his chief academic officers, i.e., the provost or vice president for academic affairs. This responsibility should be closely associated with the office for planning and with the office for institutional research—where such an office exists though unfortunately often does not. Such associations would reflect recognition of the need for the consideration of academic as well as financial viewpoints in the budget process.

Approximately a third of all colleges and universities experimented, during recent years (1966–1973), with a system of budgeting that was developed in the Department of Defense—and more recently has been widely used within the federal government.[18] This system known as PPBS (planning, programming, and budgeting system) gained a considerable mystique, and its adoption was equated in the minds of some academic administrators with progressive management. While adoption of PPBS led to costly floundering in some institutions, experimentation with this system by a few has led to the identification of the essential elements in an improved budgeting system for a college or university.[19] These elements are illustrated by conclusions reached at Princeton University. There it was concluded that the budget process must:

1. Make it possible for those responsible for drafting the budget to view *all* the institution's needs and *all* its resources at the same time, e.g., the research programs and sources of research support as well as instructional programs and funds available for their support

2. Be related to the institution's basic programs (e.g., undergraduate instruction, graduate instruction, research, public services) and

---

18 Lawrence Bogard, "Management in Institutions of Higher Education," *Papers on Efficiency in the Management of Higher Education,* op. cit., p. 3.

19 Alice Rivlin has stated the essentials well in her *Systematic Thinking for Social Action* (Washington: The Brookings Institution, 1971), p. 3: "Anyone faced with the problem of running a government program, or, indeed, any large organization would want to take these steps to assure a good job: (1) Define the objectives of the organization as clearly as possible; (2) find out what the money was being spent for and what was being accomplished; (3) define alternative policies for the future and collect as much information as possible about what each would cost and what it would do; (4) set up a systematic procedure bringing the relevant information together at the time the decisions were to be made. PPBS was simply an attempt to institutionalize this common-sense approach in the government budgeting process." Contrast her enumeration of the essentials with the steps involved in the planning process described earlier in this chapter, pp. 147–149.

facilitate the viewing of all elements of expense in relation to these programs

3. Provide a projection of income and cost beyond a single year enabling decision makers to view the consequences of current budgeting upon resources likely to be available in subsequent years

4. Involve representatives from each segment of the college or university community—administrators, faculty, students, alumni, and the adjacent community—in the preparation of the budget

These conclusions reflect principles of large significance both for the making of budgets and for the processes of governance. They affirm our earlier observations that the achievement of effective management in institutions of higher education requires:

1. Processes that identify the institution's objectives (agreed-upon ends) and the programs it will carry on to achieve those objectives

2. A continual flow of information for decision makers, and particularly accounting records which generate information that enables decision makers to view all costs and resources in relation to the institution's programs and at appropriate times

3. The existence of structural arrangements (e.g., a broadly constituted planning committee) that permit representatives of each constituency within the institution to view all resources available and all claims on those resources and to voice their views as to the allocation of resources among programs[20]

THE OPERATIONAL INFORMATION SYSTEM

Experience has demonstrated that the management techniques developed in business and government during the 1960s, particularly operations research, management by objectives, and systems analysis, can contribute significantly to the efficiency with which a college's or university's large and numerous business-like activities are run. These

---

[20] At Princeton this structural arrangement is known as the Priorities Committee of the Council of the Princeton University Community. It is made up of the provost as ex officio chairman; the dean of the faculty; the financial vice president and treasurer; six members of the faculty including one nontenured member; four undergraduate students and two graduate students; and one member each from the alumni, the library staff, and other groups. The president, the director of the budget, and the vice president for development are invited to all meetings. This committee is empowered only to make recommendations to the president, who may accept, reject, or modify them (*Budgeting and Resource Allocation at Princeton University*, a report of a demonstration project supported by the Ford Foundation, June 1972).

include dormitories, dining facilities, student health care facilities, fleets of cars, bookstores, computer centers, and the allocation of the costs for providing classroom and laboratory space. Together these operations claim from 16 to 20 percent of the budgeted cost of the college with an enrollment of 1,000 to 5,000. In the larger university, they include also such separate operations as hospitals, presses, and research laboratories.

By the application of management techniques—plus imaginative curiosity—in making decisions as to such activities trustees and presidents of colleges and universities cannot only increase the efficiency with which these activities are carried on and control costs, but can also influence significantly the character of the institution. The physical nature of dormitories, dining halls, health care facilities, book shops and like facilities, and the character of their operations are substantial determinants of the quality of life on the campus.[21] The allocation of funds for the support of such facilities reflects also the relative emphasis placed on the institution's various programs, i.e., undergraduate versus graduate or professional programs and daytime undergraduate programs versus evening programs in continuing education. The character of the facilities provided and the services offered on the campus, and decisions that trustees and presidents authorize as to charges for dormitory rooms and "meal tickets," will influence the extent to which the institution attracts residential versus commuting students. The formulation of models by operations researchers and studies by systems analysts can provide materials that will enable trustees and presidents to make decisions that will further objectives that have been agreed upon.

The information required to make decisions on such questions must be drawn, on the typical campus, from a variety of sources. Dormitories are operated on most campuses by a housing division usually associated with the dean of students. The dining facilities usually are the responsibility of the chief operational officer, variously titled "vice president for business affairs," "vice president for administrative operations," or "vice president for administration and finance." The computer center is found in a variety of organizational locations, sometimes under the vice president for finance, sometimes in an office for planning, and sometimes in an independent unit directly responsible to the president or to one of his senior associates, e.g., the provost or executive vice president.

---

21 Harold Hodgkinson cited (in a talk before the annual Institute for Presidents, Lake Placid, N.Y., June 26, 1973) as one of a number of "unobtrusive measures" of the character of a college or university, the relative number of books and classical records in the bookshop as compared with sweat shirts and cans of beer! Another such measure, he cites, is the proportion of students that check out of the dormitories each weekend.

Effective management dictates that the president (or in a large institution his principal aides) should have regularly available integrated analyses of relevant data that reflect the accomplishments and costs of each of these auxiliary activities. Effective management also dictates that information be available as to the proportion of classroom, laboratory, and recreational spaces utilized by time periods and by programs, the unit costs of unoccupied space, the cost per hour of services provided by the computer center, and the utilization of these services by each program, institute, or department. Such information in the hands of decision makers throughout the institution makes for more efficient and economical operation by subjecting those responsible for day-by-day decisions as to educational and research programs to self-determining controls rather than to the direction of a hierarchical superior.

COORDINATION AND COMMUNICATION

The effectiveness of the management of a college or university is determined by the imagination with which information is assembled and analyzed, and the skill, candor, and subtlety with which it is communicated throughout these highly decentralized organizations. The size of the institution will dictate the assistance the president will require to enable him to assemble, analyze, and make use of the intelligence that is imbedded in the academic, financial, and operational data generated throughout the institution. In the typical institution of 10,000 students that assistance needed will likely include:

- A staff that is concerned with institutional planning and that is capable of formulating and interpreting academic objectives

- An individual or small staff skilled in systems analysis and operations research and sufficiently imaginative to apply those techniques to academic activities

- A staff capable not only of formulating traditional budgets but of visualizing academic objectives and relating costs to such objectives

Finally, if the president's leadership is to be effective and if the activities throughout the institution are to be coordinated toward agreed-upon ends and to elicit the zeal of department chairpersons, faculty members, and students, the president needs staff assistants skilled in communication. He must devote as much care and attention to interpreting and explaining why he does what he does as he invests in gathering the facts for decision making. The functioning "of a University government in which many participate and in which participants

have a maximum opportunity to arrive at mutually acceptable decisions
. . . requires a wide distribution of knowledge about how to influence
decisions, about current issues, and about what is said on the various
sides of current issues."[22]

---

22 *The Governing of Princeton University,* final report of the Special Committee
on the Structure of the University, April 1970, p. 94.

Decision Making:
Finance

The financial situation of universities can only be ambiguous. It has many rich friends who pour money into it—and manage thereby to add to its costs. It raises great sums from powerful foundations and draws on the public purse at all three levels of government—and even this fails to fill the void. It charges high tuition fees that pay less and less of the cost of education—and thus the increased enrollments that all desire further impoverish the institution. Jacques Barzun[1]

9 The bankruptcy of some colleges and universities was predicted by Beardsley Ruml as early as 1958. It was declared imminent by the Ford Foundation in 1967 and became a tragic fact when, in 1970–71, 40 private institutions closed their doors, a score of colleges merged with other institutions, and over 70 percent of a group of "illustrative" institutions studied were found to be either "headed for trouble" or "in financial difficulty."[2] It was further affirmed in mid-1971 when 61 of the nation's 103 medical schools requested "special distress grants" from the National Institute of Health; in 32 cases "the continued operation or accreditation of the schools was threatened."[3]

After more than a decade of expanding enrollments and growing revenues, many colleges and universities (and particularly the private institutions) were faced in the early 1970s with costs that rose more rapidly than revenues and with deficits that grew alarmingly.

This chapter considers the processes by which the individual college or university governs its financial affairs. This is not to say that it will provide a manual of approved accounting, budgeting, or investment practices. Rather, it is concerned with governance—"the expression of value judgments about what kinds of action . . . are necessary, good

---

[1] *The American University* (New York: Harper & Row, Publishers, Incorporated, 1968), p. 17.

[2] Earl F. Cheit, *The New Depression in Higher Education,* a report prepared for the Carnegie Commission on Higher Education (New York: McGraw-Hill Book Company, 1970).

[3] Dean Russell Nelson of Johns Hopkins University Medical School in *The Washington Post,* May 5, 1971. As a result, some schools have been forced to consume endowment funds (e.g., George Washington Medical School had substantially used up its entire endowment fund by July 1972).

and just,"[4] and the fixing of responsibility for arriving at such judgments. Hence, this chapter examines by whom and how decisions are made as to:

- Future revenue needs and how those revenues shall be obtained

- The allocation of available funds among the institution's current activities and new construction needs

- The investment of endowment funds

- The making of ends meet when revenues are limited

DECISIONS AS TO REVENUE GETTING

As long as rising enrollments and increasing governmental appropriations provided revenues that exceeded rising costs, there was little quibbling as to where the authority to make decisions as to revenue getting should reside. That responsibility fell, in both public and private institutions, primarily on the president and secondarily on the trustees. But, as in other areas of governance, in the last ten years other constituencies have claimed a share in the making of decisions as to from whence revenues shall be obtained and in what proportions.

This country's colleges and universities generally operated on a narrow excess of income over outgo during the 1920s, the depression 1930s, and the years of World War II. Enrollment of federally supported GIs during the late 1940s brought increased revenues, but during the early 1950s, after the wave of GIs had graduated, many institutions experienced difficulties in making ends meet.

Between about 1957 and 1969, a substantial and seemingly inexorable rise in educational costs was accompanied by an equal or greater expansion of revenues. Thus, presidents and trustees were able to meet their responsibilities for revenue getting with relatively little difficulty. The principal sources from which they obtained needed revenue and the relative contribution of each are indicated in the table on page 167.

These several sources of revenue are susceptible to markedly varying degrees of control by those responsible for seeing to it that adequate resources are available. Let us consider separately (a) those sources of revenue over which presidents and trustees have substantial independent power and with respect to which they can effectively determine the amounts that will be derived and (b) those revenues derived from

---

[4] John D. Millett, *Governance, Management and Leadership in Higher Education,* a paper circulated privately by the Academy for Educational Development, 1973.

REVENUE SOURCES, INSTITUTIONS OF HIGHER EDUCATION (by type of institution and source of revenue, in percents)

	All Institutions		Public Institutions		Private Institutions	
	1959–60	1968–69	1959–60	1968–69	1959–60	1968–69
Tuition and fees	20.0	20.2	10.1	11.8	32.7	34.1
Federal government (research)	17.9	17.1	16.7	15.7	19.5	19.3
	(14.3)	(10.9)	(12.1)	(8.8)	(18.3)	(15.7)
State government	23.9	25.6	41.3	42.0	1.4	3.7
Local government	2.6	3.2	4.5	4.9	0.2	0.5
Private gifts	6.6	3.2	2.6	0.4	11.7	7.8
Endowment	3.6	2.2	0.6	0.4	7.4	5.1
Other	6.5	11.3	6.3	9.1	6.8	9.7
Auxiliary enterprises	17.3	14.2	16.6	13.2	18.2	15.9
Student-aid grants	1.6	3.0	1.3	2.5	2.1	3.9
TOTAL	100.0	100.0	100.0	100.0	100.0	100.0

SOURCES: *Toward a Long-Range Plan for Federal Financial Support for Higher Education, A Report to the President, January 1969,* HEW, pp. 43–44; *Digest of Education Statistics, 1970,* T.123; OE, unpublished figures for 1968–69; *Fact Book,* ACE.

government, which are susceptible only to such persuasive influence as they can exercise. In the first category are the revenues obtained from tuition and fees, private gifts, endowments, and auxiliary enterprises. In the second category are those revenues supplied by the federal, state, and local governments.

STUDENT TUITION CHARGES

Student tuition charges are the principal source of revenue over which presidents and trustees have effective control. Tuition provides about one-third of all revenue obtained by the private institutions and about one-eighth of the total revenue of public institutions. Between September 1961 and September 1974, tuition rates almost doubled at private institutions and increased more than 50 percent at public institutions. This means that tuition rates rose more rapidly than did per capita personal disposable income during the same period.

In the early 1970s, when the increase in costs outran, for many institutions and particularly the private ones, the growth in revenues, two constraints on the raising of tuition charges and the obtaining of the needed revenue from this source also loomed up. While presidents and trustees considered increasing revenues by raising tuition charges they were confronted from without by social pressures to make access feasible for students from low-income families and by the market fact that a large proportion of prospective students from middle-income ($12,500 to $25,000) as well as low-income (under $12,500) families were unable to meet the prevailing rate of tuition charges. The presidents and trustees of private institutions were confronted by the additional fact that the differential between public and private institutions was widening at a time when relative "quality" was narrowing.[5] From within they were confronted by pressure from students to keep charges down; this pressure was reinforced by parents and, at times, supported on ideological grounds by faculty members. The second constraint upon the further raising of tuition charges was provided by competition; the lower-tuition charges of the public institutions limited the extent to which private institutions could raise their rates, and the lower-tuition charges of the public community colleges limited the extent to which public four-year colleges and universities found it desirable to raise rates.

Yet the prospect is that the inability to obtain increased revenue from other sources will force those responsible for the financial affairs of both public and private institutions to strive to raise tuition charges.[6] This may be made the more feasible by increased utilization of borrowing by students to finance their education. Yet, the economics of family life and the social philosophy that holds that every young person should be given the opportunity to continue his or her education beyond the high school suggest that tuition charges will not likely provide a substantially greater portion of the revenues needed.

INCOME FROM ENDOWMENTS, PRIVATE GIFTS, AND GRANTS

Income from endowments, private gifts, and grants supplies a minor but significant source of revenue for private institutions and an insignifi-

---

5 In late 1973 proposals were advanced by the Carnegie Commission on Higher Education and by the Committee on Economic Development that the tuition charges of public institutions be raised and that the differential between the tuition charges of private and public institutions be narrowed. These proposals were vigorously opposed by spokesmen for public institutions, applauded by spokesmen for private colleges and universities, and roundly criticized in a number of newspapers and magazines on the grounds that increased tuitions would unduly burden middle- and low-income families.

6 This prospect implies a conclusion of questionable validity, i.e., that the benefits to individuals who pursue a college education are so relatively greater than the societal benefits for which society should pay (as it pays for elementary and secondary education) that the individual should pay a greater portion of the total cost. Are the processes of institutional decision making capable of taking these relative benefits into account?

cant source for public institutions. The amounts derived from this source are largely dependent on the efforts of presidents and particularly (with the exception of grants) trustees. The procurement of endowment and the stimulation of annual giving have been a prime responsibility of trustees. They have led the "campaigns" to raise funds for endowments, to finance new buildings, and to encourage annual giving by alumni and corporations, and they have in most institutions been responsible for maximizing the income from invested endowments. For some of the more prestigious institutions, and those with large bodies of relatively well-to-do alumni, the efforts of trustees in raising money by these means have been notably successful.

But the needs of many colleges and universities, particularly the private institutions, prompted reexamination, during the late 1960s, of prevailing investment and fund-raising practices. This reexamination gave rise to two developments that led to the involvement of those other than presidents and trustees in decisions as to the investment of endowment funds.

The first, and more influential development was the exposure of the relatively low return earned by most endowments at a time when the need for revenue was urgent. This disclosure prompted a recommendation that "trustees should not themselves attempt to manage their investment portfolios. The decision-making responsibility should be clearly and fully delegated to an able professional portfolio manager with a capable group of fellow professionals around him."[7] Encouragement for institutions to follow this advice was subsequently provided when the Ford Foundation granted $2.8 million to cover the costs of organizing and operating a nonprofit corporation (the Common Fund) designed to "enable colleges, universities and independent schools to join together in obtaining professional management of their endowments and other long-term investment funds." As a result of these stimuli, a number of institutions have contracted with investment management companies for the handling of their portfolios;[8] more than 200 colleges and universities had entrusted some portion of their resources to the Common Fund for investment within its first six months of operation;[9] and a few institutions gave consideration to the utilization

[7] *Report to the Ford Foundation of the Advisory Committee on Endowment Management*, Educational Endowment Series, August 1969. This report written by a committee of university officials and investment men dealt in considerable depth and simplicity with modern-day principles and practices of investment and their application to college and university portfolios. For appraisal of this 64-page report see "The Ford Foundation Firecracker," September 1969.

[8] *The New York Times*, May 19, 1968, pp. 1, 83.

[9] COMPACT, monthly publication of the Education Commission of the States, October 1971, p. 36.

of some portion of the gains in the capital value of investments as current income. Generally, however, the earnings from endowments were not substantially increased. State laws prescribing kinds of investments for charitable trusts, as well as the lethargy of institutional officials, limited change.

The second development, one that influenced decision making as to the investment of endowments less, is the emergence of the idea that colleges and universities should weigh the social, political, and moral behavior of the corporations in which they invest as well as the prospective return on the investment. After about 1968, universities, along with churches, foundations, and charitable and other nonprofit institutions, were pressed to accept "some moral responsibility for the social conduct of corporations in which [they] hold stock"[10] and "to consider how [they] can discharge that responsibility."[11] This pressure came from within and without the institution and made university portfolio managers realize that the masters they served were no longer limited to the president, his financial vice president, and the trustees, but included also faculty members, students, and some alumni.

Simultaneous reexamination of the organization for, and the practices used in, raising funds in the form of gifts and grants resulted in some institutions in improvements in what is generally described as the "development function." Yet, despite these improvements, and despite the growth in numbers of alumni and of corporate givers, the proportion of all revenues derived from "giving" remained small (from 4 percent in public institutions to 8 percent in private institutions), and the rate of increase of private giving to all 2,600 United States colleges and universities increased modestly during the years 1970–71 (4 percent over 1969–70) and 1971–72 (3 percent over 1970–71) when institutional needs were urgent.[12]

---

10 Burton G. Malkiel and Richard E. Quant, "Moral Issues in Investment Policy," *Harvard Business Review*, March–April 1971; see also *Harvard and Money: A Memorandum on Issues and Choices* (Cambridge, Mass.: The University Committee on Governance, November 1970); Brian H. Smith, "Physicians, Heal Yourselves . . . ," *America*, Oct. 17, 1970; and John G. Simon, Charles W. Powers, and Jon P. Gunneman, *The Ethical Investor: Universities and Corporate Responsibilities* (New Haven, Conn.: Yale University Press, 1972).

11 To aid institution portfolio managers "consider how [they] can discharge that responsibility," a group of foundations and universities established in 1972 the Investor Responsibility Research Center, Inc., to provide college and university portfolio managers who subscribe for its services a continuing series of reports describing the social, political, and moral behavior of corporations on which they may base decisions to invest, or how to vote the shares their institution now holds.

12 William G. Bowen has reasoned persuasively in his *The Economics of the Major Private Universities* (Carnegie Commission on Higher Education, New York: McGraw-Hill Book Company, 1968, pp. 46–50) that past rates of growth in private giving will not be maintained.

Private giving is a vital source of revenue for many private institutions. Yet despite the urgent need of these institutions and the lesser but not inconsequential need of many other institutions, public as well as private, this source of revenue has not been made to yield more than 5 or 6 percent of the aggregate revenue needed by all save a few prestigious institutions.

Why? Generally colleges and universities are engaged in a continual fund-raising effort. That effort in a minority of all institutions is well organized and publicized; is planned and directed by efficient, trained development officers; and enlists the zeal of presidents, trustees, and faculty members. In a larger proportion of all institutions, development officers are inexperienced, faculties assume "fund raising is not our job," presidents manifest little appetite for the task of fund raising, and trustees demonstrate limited commitment. In addition, the limited amount of private giving to colleges and universities during the late 1960s and the early 1970s must be attributed in part to the modification of federal tax laws, which reduced the incentives that had encouraged individuals to give annually or to make large individual gifts.

GOVERNMENTAL APPROPRIATIONS, GRANTS, AND LOANS

Within the 1960s, the proportion of the annual operating budget provided by federal and state governments increased in more than half of all institutions.[13] The federal government's support of higher education increased from $1.3 billion in 1960 to $3.48 billion in 1972, much of this in the form of research contracts and increasingly in the form of student aid. In 1973, the further concentration of federal support in the form of grants and loans made directly to students provoked complaints from many institutions that this method of providing financial support for higher education did not meet total institutional costs, and fears that students would use aid available to them to purchase narrow, abbreviated, vocationally oriented educational programs. "The classics and the arts will suffer and the profit-making institutions offering short courses in the trades and business administration will prosper," it was prophesied.

State and local governments also appropriated substantially increasing amounts for the support of colleges and universities during the 1960s; state appropriations have not increased as rapidly as have state revenues since 1968, however, and the states have provided a smaller

---

[13] Harold L. Hodgkinson, *Institutions in Transition*, Carnegie Commission on Higher Education (New York: McGraw-Hill Book Company, 1971), p. 59.

portion of total revenues in the early 1970s than in the early 1960s.[14] Private schools, because of their inability to raise revenues, have pressed their claims for public support on the grounds that (a) diversity among institutions is needed and (b) it is cheaper to provide higher education by supplementing the incomes of private institutions than to establish new and additional public institutions.

Government has simultaneously provided increasing amounts to help colleges and universities finance the construction of new buildings needed to house rapidly growing enrollments. Public institutions obtain most of the funds needed to expand their facilities—classrooms, dormitories, laboratories, libraries, etc.—by state appropriations, by the sale of revenue bonds, and by borrowing or obtaining grants from the federal government; private institutions obtain needed funds for new facilities largely from private gifts and federal loans.

Decisions as to such capital investments have been of substantial importance throughout the past decade. The more venturesome and more enterprising institutions of the expansionary 1960s found funds to provide for the needed expansion of facilities—and, in the early 1970s, found themselves in financial trouble. They were confronted with substantial annual charges for interest and amortization payments on debts incurred to finance new buildings while enrollments slackened off in 1972 and 1973, leaving dormitories, classrooms, and libraries partially unoccupied or underutilized. This sequence of events has been described as a "financial paradox"; "the greater the performance of the university [in the expansionary 1960s] the greater its deficit today."[15]

The reason for this financial paradox is revealed by contrasting the business enterprise's process of deciding that a building shall be built with that of the college or university. The business decision requires that the building be functional, demonstrably needed, and cost justified. It must be clear that the use of this money for the construction of the building will result in savings or profits in greater measure than would the use of the money for other purposes, e.g., expanding inventories.

Four factors often prevent such logical cost-function decisions as to college and university buildings. First, the donor of a building may want to suit his objectives or his assessment of the institution's needs

---

14 Lyman A. Glenny and James R. Kidder, *Trends in State Funding in Higher Education,* a preliminary report, Education Commission of the States, report no. 33, January 1973.

15 James A. Perkins, "A Comparison of the University with the Corporation," *The University as an Organization,* a report for the Carnegie Commission on Higher Education (New York: McGraw-Hill Book Company, 1973), chap. 6, p. 117.

rather than the institution's own calculation (e.g., he may choose to provide funds for the construction of a stadium in honor of his son, a distinguished athlete, rather than a much needed library—where perchance the son spent little of his undergraduate time). Or the donor may choose to construct a monumental edifice, leaving the institution to worry about future costs of operation or maintenance.[16] Still more influential in decisions as to what buildings will be built are agencies of the federal and particularly the state governments that provide the bulk of all funds for buildings at publicly supported institutions. A large voice in decisions as to what buildings shall be built and in what form is claimed by state coordinating boards, state architects, public works departments, and budget officials. The federal government, in assisting institutions in financing the construction of buildings, has stipulated the kind of building for which its low-interest loan funds shall be available, and has specified aspects of the construction to limit future operational and maintenance costs.

Second, there is an apparent tendency to make of many campuses architectural showplaces. Thus buildings are designed to conform with a style of architecture established decades ago rather than to serve essential educational functions.

Third, the increasing public-utility nature of the college and, particularly, the public university means that the public institution must be "ready to serve," to provide an education for all who can benefit by education beyond the high school. They must build ahead of the demand. Thus, despite record-breaking expenditures for construction during the 1960s, some universities—particularly some urban universities—have been unable to keep up with the demand for classroom space and have been forced to use various makeshift facilities, e.g., erstwhile apartment houses, residences, factory and office buildings, and mobile housing units. Moreover, they have been forced to provide housing with little assurance of the needed income to operate and maintain such structures in the future.

The fourth factor is the increasing desire of faculty members and students to participate in determinations as to priorities among building needs. On one large university campus a vigorous struggle was waged between the science faculty and the business school faculty as to whose needs should be met first. On another large public university campus several little-utilized buildings are a monument to the unrestrained demands of the faculty. In a private southern university students pro-

---

[16] In one instance, now legendary, a foundation grant of $34,000 cost the recipient university nearly a half a million dollars over eight years ("Financial Stress in Academe," *Morgan Guaranty Survey*, June 1971).

tested the acceptance of a gift of more than $1 million for a new law school building, claiming that a student center and an extension of the library were more needed.

The substantial and increased dependence upon government revenues assumes even greater significance as one looks into the future. Between 1959–60 and 1969–70, the annual revenue available to institutions of higher education (including capital funds, income from auxiliary enterprises, and funds made available for student aid) increased nearly $8 billion. Over the decade 1970–1980, it is forecast that $20 billion more revenue will be needed annually. Hence, the total required in 1980, about $28 billion over and above the revenue available in 1960, will likely be derived from the following sources in these amounts:[17]

- $6.7 billion from state and local governments

- $12.2 billion from the federal government

- $6.8 billion from student fees and charges

- $0.9 billion from private gifts and grants

- $1.7 billion from earnings on endowments and other sources

This forecasts a substantial and increasing dependence by this country's colleges and universities on governmentally supplied revenue. The students in some institutions have opposed the increase of tuition charges and have voiced concern over some other revenue matters. But the prime consequence that flows from the greater dependence on government for financial support is the marked delimitation of the influence the president and trustees can exercise over the revenue-getting function. The president, with three or four of the most influential board members, must go for the bulk of all revenues, hat-in-hand, to state and federal authorities.

Before the state legislatures, the public institution's representatives are confronted with judgments of representatives of the state budget office or the board of higher education as to what funds should be appropriated,[18] and by substantially increased competition from other

---

17 Figures derived from Howard R. Bowen, "An Eclectic Approach," in M. D. Orwig, ed., *Financing Higher Education: Alternatives for the Federal Government* (Iowa City: American College Testing Program, 1971), p. 294; and "Financial Needs of the Campus," Robert H. Connery, ed., in *The Corporation and the Campus* (New York: Frederick A. Praeger, 1970), p. 92.

18 "The fact is," John D. Millett has written, "that today the expense of public higher education has become too great to permit the luxury of institutional autonomy in academic decision making" ("The Impact of a State Board of Higher Education Upon College Management and Finance," a research paper prepared for the Committee on Economic Development, November 1971).

functional departments, e.g., the state highway, health, welfare, and correctional departments.[19] In seeking federal funds, the representatives of both public and private institutions encounter an intention to channel much of all federal support into the hands of students, as student aid, rather than to institutions. Determinations as to what revenues shall be made available, and—as the next section will reveal—for what purposes they may be expended, in substantial measure are no longer within the power of those charged with responsibility for the character and performance of the institution—its president and trustees.

ALLOCATIVE DECISIONS

Much of the revenue available to colleges and universities from government (and some from private sources), as mentioned earlier, is made available for particular purposes and under specified conditions. Consider the constraints that this tying of revenues and expenditures for each major function imposes on those responsible for governance.

INSTRUCTION

In public institutions the sums needed to meet faculty salaries and other instructional costs (which represent 50 to 60 percent of all expenditures in most institutions) are provided largely by state appropriations. The amounts are determined in an increasing proportion of all states by formulas.[20] For example, in Connecticut, the number of faculty members for which salaries will be provided is determined by this calculation:

---

[19] State appropriations for higher education increased nearly fivefold between 1950 and 1970 and now claim in most states 15 to 20 percent of all general revenue funds, ranking third among purposes of expenditure, after elementary and secondary education and welfare.

[20] Malcolm Moos and Francis R. Rourke (in *The Campus and the State*, Baltimore, Md.: The John Hopkins Press, 1959) cite the formula adopted by Oklahoma: "The number of faculty members to be supported at the University of Oklahoma and at Oklahoma State University is determined as follows:

For the first 6,800 students: a base faculty of 453 (15-to-1 base).

For all additional students: one additional faculty member for every 25 students.

Thus, for an enrollment of 11,000 students, a faculty of 621 (453 plus 168) would be needed. This would result in a student-teacher ratio of 17.7 to 1 (11,000/621)."

A similar formula is used in determining the number of faculty members at the state's four-year colleges.

	Faculty-Student Ratio		Credit Hrs. Per F.T.C. Student		Student Credit Hrs. 1 Faculty Position			Faculty Position
Lower division	19.35	×	15.5	=	300	=	1	Assistant Professor
Upper division	11.60	×	15.5	=	180	=	1	Average Assistant-Associate
Master's degree	7.5	×	12.0	=	90	=	1	Associate Professor
Doctoral degree	7.5	×	8.0	=	60	=	1	Full Professor
Thesis supervision and independent study					25	=	1	Full Professor

NOTE: The salary levels for professors are determined in relation to annual analyses made by the American Association of University Professors. The nonfaculty support staff is determined in this manner: 2 clerical positions for 1 dean; 1 clerical position for 1 department chairman; 1 clerical position for 4 faculty; 1 lab assistant for 50 stations.

SOURCE: Robert O. Berdahl, *Statewide Coordination of Higher Education* (Washington: American Council on Education, 1971, p. 271).

Having determined the numbers to be allowed, the dollars to be appropriated are arrived at by multiplying numbers by fixed salary rates for each grade of professors, clerks, and others. Then—typically, by varying formulas—the states determine the amounts to be made available for other noninstructional purposes. In Oklahoma, for instance, 30 percent is added to the sum calculated for faculty salaries to obtain the "budget base,"[21] and this aggregate is then apportioned as follows:

Organized activities related to instruction	3%
General administration	7%
General expenses	8%
Organized research	12%
Extension and public service	11 to 14%
Library	8%
Physical plant	16%

Such formulas do not control the selection, promotion, assignment, or tenure of individual faculty members. They provide norms that presumably reflect the experience of well-managed institutions, and give academic and financial administrators useful tools for the appraisal of the claims of departments and schools. But they also establish relatively rigid frameworks into which new appointees must be fitted and which determine when and how many faculty members can be promoted. In view of the prospect that a majority of all institutions will be continu-

21 Ronald M. Brown, "Formula Budgeting for Higher Education" (Ann Arbor Center for Higher Education, University of Michigan, 1968), cited in R. O. Berdahl, op. cit., p. 271.

ally dependent on state support,[22] such formulas promise to be a continuing limitation upon the freedom of institutional trustees and administrators to allocate resources as they deem best.

The private institution meets the bulk of its instructional costs from student fees, private gifts and grants, and the earnings from endowments. In their use of funds derived from these sources, the presidents and trustees of private institutions enjoy much greater, though not unlimited, freedom. Private gift and grant money and endowment earnings are often designated for particular uses.[23] But monies from student fees, despite an increased but still minor effort by students to have a part in the budgeting of institutional funds, are relatively unconstrained.

RESEARCH

Research is an activity that is indigenous to and essential for a university. Spurred by the demand for and the expansion of knowledge, the annual cost of this activity has approximated 7 to 10 percent. In both public and private institutions, research is supported in principal part (i.e., three-fourths or more) by the federal government. Lucky indeed is the institution that has money from gifts or endowment earnings that is available for the support of research without any proscription.

During the 1950s and much of the 1960s, federal support for research produced noteworthy scientific achievements and advances in the teaching of sciences and engineering and was the main vehicle of support for higher education. Simultaneously it had a disintegrating influence on the recipient institutions. By tying their support to individual research projects, the federal agencies caused some faculty members to focus attention on research, to the detriment of their teaching, and to magnify their concern with their discipline rather than the institution that employed them. It was difficult or pragmatically impossible for the president and trustees to reject available federal funds for research that faculty members wanted to undertake. Moreover, the prestige as well as the resources that federal grants brought constituted a further pressure to accept such grants. Yet, having approved acceptance of such funds, the president and trustees would often learn that they had dimin-

---

[22] The aggregate annual support provided by state and local governments will have grown from about $5 billion in 1968–1969 to $8 billion or $9 billion in 1980–81 according to an estimate of Howard R. Bowen, "Financial Needs of the Campus," op. cit., p. 92.

[23] For instance, two-thirds of Columbia University's endowment funds are restricted and cannot be used for general operations (M. M. Chambers, *Higher Education: Who Pays? Who Gains?* Danville, Ill., Interstate Printers and Publishers, 1968, pp. 82–83).

ished significantly their power and influence over particular schools, departments, or faculty members that tended to transfer allegiance to the federal funding authority.

The magnitude of support for research gave rise to a dependence by some institutions, particularly those with substantial graduate and medical school enrollments, on federal funds for a major portion of their budgets. The availability of those funds tended to create an imbalance in institutional programs (e.g., the emphasis on the sciences as distinguished from the humanities), and, as was subsequently demonstrated when federal research funds were sharply reduced (1970 to 1972), made the institutional budget unstable.

AUXILIARY SERVICES

Auxiliary services (i.e., dining halls, dormitories, health, and other services for students) are supported in major part, in both public and private institutions, by funds derived from student fees. Such monies are in substantial measure dedicated to specific purposes. The president and trustees of many institutions have granted students a large voice in decisions as to their allocation.

STUDENT FINANCIAL AID

Student financial aid expenditures rose sharply during the ten-year period ending in 1974. Two forces underlay this increase. The first was the prevailing social pressure to provide educational opportunities for capable students from low-income families. The second was intensive competition for students when growth in enrollments slackened.

This substantial increase in expenditures for student aid was made possible by the provision of greatly increased funds for student aid by the federal government to make access to higher education feasible for more young people from low-income families. In 1973, probably 40 percent of all student-aid money was provided by the federal government through five kinds of programs.[24] An additional 20 percent was provided by the state governments.

The intensive competition for students in the early 1970s was impelled by the inability of some institutions to fill their dormitories and

---

[24] Categorical-aid programs (e.g., aid for students in the health professions, in nursing, in law enforcement); aid for veterans and for dependents of social security beneficiaries; in-service programs by the military, the CIA, and other federal agencies; manpower-training programs; and institutionally based programs, including "educational opportunity grants," work-study, National Defense student loans, and guaranteed student loans.

classrooms. Faced with financial deficits some institutions admitted students on the tacit understanding that they would pay what they could. In such instances the reported expenditure for student aid was in reality the difference between the aggregate of sums collected and stated tuition rates and charges. Federal aid was not sufficient to meet the total need and the institution's funds were drawn on.[25]

Those students that were enabled to attend by the availability of federal aid (and in some instances scholarships provided by the foundations and others) brought funds to the institution that were relatively "free monies."[26] Their availability to students may be limited to those having a particular status (e.g., veterans or social security beneficiaries), or studying in particular fields (e.g., nursing), or may be provided in return for hours worked, but when used by students to pay tuition charges, they become substantially free money in the hands of the institution.

CONSTRUCTION

Public institutions have substantial freedom in proposing what construction is needed, within guidelines set for the state's colleges and universities, but they are subjected to an arduous and time-consuming regulation of how construction shall be carried out. Private institutions must develop their campuses within the limits of their abilities to raise funds for what they determine is needed rather than what a donor may wish to give, or within the specifications that federal agencies fix to ensure economical construction.

In summary, the governance of the financial affairs of most institutions is markedly affected by the particular mix of revenue sources on which each depends. In general, private institutions, which derive almost three-fourths of their current budgets from tuition charges and fees, private gifts and grants, endowment earnings, and "other sources," enjoy relatively greater freedom to allocate available resources as their trustees, administrators, and faculties deem best. But these sources of revenue are likely to provide a lesser proportion of all revenues for private as well as public institutions in the future. That prospect fore-

---

[25] For an excellent analysis of the problems involved in budgeting for student-aid expenditures see *Budgeting and Resource Allocation at Princeton University*, a report of a demonstration project supported by the Ford Foundation, by William G. Bowen et al. (Princeton, N.J.: Princeton University, 1972).

[26] Public universities (with some exceptions, e.g., the University of Michigan) have to have tuition income appropriated for their use. In this sense, it is not "free" for institutional use.

casts less freedom for these institutions in making the financial decisions involved in governance.

CAPACITY FOR ADJUSTMENT

The time has passed when the president could (and did) assess the financial needs of each school, department, and office; prepare the annual budget; and subsequently control expenditures in most, if not all, institutions. As institutions grew larger during the 1960s, as has been shown, the governmental suppliers of resources, the faculties, and to a lesser degree, the students claimed a share in financial decision making. Thus, when between 1968 and 1974, this country's colleges and universities were confronted with the essentiality of making painful decisions "to adjust limited financial resources to expanding demands" those decisions had to be made "within an increasingly consultative system of decision making."[27] Within such a context these institutions faced, in the early 1970s, deficits, near deficits, or, at the least, revenues that were increasing less rapidly than operating costs. What could and what did these institutions do to gain control of their financial situations?

"SCRAMBLING FOR FUNDS"[28]

A primary effort, and one on which all parties to decision making usually agreed, was to enroll more students. A secondary effort—to raise tuition charges—often met the objections of students and exposed the institution to competition with other institutions for needed additional students. But necessity often dictated that both public and private institutions would raise tuition charges. A third effort was to raise additional funds from donors and particularly corporations; this customarily evoked general agreement within the institution, but yielded little additional revenue. Thus, the fourth and principal effort institutions made in seeking revenues to enable them to gain control of their financial situations was to seek additional support from the federal and state governments. This effort, too, attracted general agreement within the institution—but it affirmed the institution's dependence on governmental support and highlighted the influence of state authorities on the governance of public institutions.

---

[27] "Report of the President's Task Force on Higher Education," *Priorities in Higher Education,* August 1970, p. 17.

[28] This term was used by Earl F. Cheit, op. cit., to describe the efforts of institutions he studied to increase income.

CUTTING COSTS

The financial problem faced by colleges and universities is highlighted by the fact that the cost of education per full-time-equivalent student has been rising more than the consumer price index.[29] The relationship between these factors makes it essential that, to gain control of their financial situations, institutions reduce costs.

Typically, the first response to the need to cut costs that prospective or actual deficits impose is to cut administrative expenses. This has meant the postponement of expenditures that can be deferred, for example, the maintenance or renovation of buildings. It has resulted in the trimming or elimination of expenditures for supplies, equipment, and travel by administrative staff, and even reducing the number of athletic scholarships. Food-service costs have been reduced by more careful menu planning. Library expenditures have been reduced by such steps as cutting the number of subscriptions to periodicals, postponing the binding of periodicals, and reducing multiple-copy book acquisitions. Personnel costs have been cut by curtailing the number of secretaries serving faculty members and the staffs of administrative offices and by reducing the number of support personnel (e.g., guidance counselors, testing personnel, and library assistants). And expenditures have been reduced by eliminating reimbursement for travel of faculty members to conferences and professional meetings and for costs incurred for association memberships.

The curtailment of administrative expenses, in most instances, meets little objection from within. The curtailment of expenditures for support services—the library, counseling, testing—provoked reactions, and the curtailment of secretaries and amenities for faculty members, more critical objections from those affected. But the inelasticity of a college or university becomes apparent when to meet the need for reducing costs it is necessary to reduce instructional costs. Efforts to reduce or limit expenditures for the instructional function expose three types of rigidities unique to the institution of higher education.

The great bulk of instructional costs, up to 80 percent, consists of faculty salaries. This element of cost, unlike the cost of labor in most business and governmental enterprises, cannot be reduced by increasing productivity. The factors primarily responsible for productivity gains in industry—new technology, an increasing investment in machinery and

---

[29] June O'Neil in *Resource Use in Higher Education* (Berkeley, Calif.: Carnegie Commission on Higher Education, 1971), presents evidence that the costs of higher education rise on the average 2.5 percent faster than the increase in the consumer price index.

equipment, improved human skills, and economies of large-scale production—have had little effect on productivity in higher education. There is some evidence that the introduction of films, television, computers, learning laboratories, and similar proposed substitutes for teachers can reduce instructional costs slightly in a few fields, but the prospect for substantial cost reductions is dim. Productivity of teachers cannot be measured because learning cannot be measured, and students cannot be taught by assembly-line techniques. As Sir Eric Ashby has analogized, ". . . . it still takes 3 man-hours to play a 45-minute Schubert quartet. Technology enables more people to hear the quartet but technology never will improve the productivity of the performers."[30]

Reducing instructional costs requires gaining the understanding, if not the concurrence, of the faculty that the number of faculty members or the level of salaries must be reduced. But reduction in the number of faculty members other than by attrition is made difficult by prevailing proscriptions guaranteeing faculty security: proscriptions requiring extended notice for nontenured teaching assistant professors, and effectively guaranteed continued employment for tenured associate and full professors.[31] The effecting of savings by manipulating the proportion of teachers in each rank is limited by the relatively large proportion on many campuses that have attained tenure status and the prospect that relatively few replacements are to be made during the 1970s. Salary costs are destined to rise as present tenured salary members advance in rank and in salary. The perennial focusing of attention on salary levels by the American Association of University Professors (AAUP) and the prospects of unionization and continuing inflation suggest that while salary increases may be granted less frequently and in smaller increments, salary levels will rise.

The reduction of instructional costs is made difficult as well by the prevalence of fixed notions as to academic organization to which most faculties are firmly committed. The basic unit of academic organization —the department—represents a discipline of thought, and the elimination or merger of departments is usually resisted. The number of courses

---

30 *The Structure of Higher Education: A World View* (New York: International Council for Educational Development, January 1973), occasional paper no. 6, pp. 16–17. A fuller description of the basic character of the problem of increasing educational productivity is presented by William G. Bowen in *The Economics of the Major Private Universities* (New York: McGraw-Hill Book Company, 1968), pp. 12–16; out of print but available from University Microfilms.

31 Columbia, Dartmouth, and Princeton each announced during 1972 the reduction of faculty size—by attrition—slowly over forthcoming years. The Pennsylvania State colleges announced the reduction of faculties by the elimination of a substantial proportion of all teachers with only one and two years service.

offered by each department reflects the specialized interests of faculty members as well as their beliefs as to the requisite offerings in their field of knowledge. That large savings can be effected and the quality of education likely bettered by a substantial paring down of the number of courses in each discipline, by substituting new modes of instruction for the conventional class-lecture method, and by increasing the ratio of students to faculty members slightly without unreasonably increasing faculty workloads has been brilliantly demonstrated by Howard R. Bowen and Lloyd T. Douglass[32]—but this approach has not gained acceptance on many campuses. If the number of courses, the number of faculty members in relation to students, and the number of departments are inflexibly insisted upon by faculties, the reduction of instructional costs is effectively blocked.

A final rigidity associated with instructional costs stems from the right of self-determination treasured by faculty members. They effectively determine, as individuals, how the most costly resource the college or university employs—their time—shall be utilized. Their determinations are reinforced by prevailing notions as to what teaching workloads they should carry, i.e., 6 to 9 class contact hours or 120 to 180 student contact hours a week, and as to the proportion of their time that should be available to them for preparation and scholarship or research. Their determinations are further affirmed by the high order of specialization obtaining among faculty members, and the consequent inability of administrators, in many instances, to reassign faculty members to offer needed courses.

FINANCIAL INSTABILITY

Despite the difficulties imposed by (a) the relative inelasticity of major sources of revenue, and the lessened rate of growth of the revenue provided by government; (b) the marked delimitation of the power of presidents and trustees to allocate available revenues while costs have grown substantially; and (c) the peculiar characteristics of the academic enterprise, which make the adjustment of costs difficult when retrenchment is the price of survival, some institutions, when faced with financial emergencies, during the early 1970s made the decisions needed to order their financial affairs. Yet many other institutions face a very uncertain future.

The shortage of money, and the harrowing experience it induced, have

---

[32] *Efficiency in Liberal Education,* a report issued by the Carnegie Commission on Higher Education (New York: McGraw-Hill Book Company, 1971).

shed light on the handicapping context within which decisions as to financial matters are made, and pointed to steps that are needed if colleges and universities are to be the masters of their own fate. These steps include:

- The establishment of methods of regularly informing the institution's constituencies, and particularly its faculty, of its financial status

- The gaining of consensus that the immediate meeting of the cost-income squeeze and the long-run governance of the institution's finances require the recurrent consideration of educational objectives, educational offerings, teaching methods, and academic organization

- The introduction—and adaptation to the unique characteristics of the academic enterprise—of the most advanced techniques of management utilized in business and government

- The establishment of new organizational structures which equip those responsible for the governance of colleges and universities—the presidents and trustees—with an understanding of the views of affected constituencies and the power to act promptly and decisively

Decision Making:
Personnel Management

The resources of a university are seven in number: men,
space, time, books, equipment, repute and money.

Jacques Barzun[1]

10 Not by chance, Barzun lists men first among a university's resources. The college or university is a "labor-intensive" enterprise.
Its accomplishments are dependent upon the caliber, the zeal,
and the effectiveness of the human beings that make it up, particularly
the faculty, but also the large numbers of nonfaculty personnel—those
who provide student counseling and health services; those who staff
libraries, laboratories, and computer centers; those who serve as
accountants, secretaries, procurement clerks, and physical planners;
and those who operate or maintain the dining halls, buildings, and
grounds.[2]

Decisions, hence, as to who shall be hired, who shall be promoted,
what faculty members shall be granted tenure, how faculty members,
administrators, and the technical and operational staffs shall be compensated and evaluated, who may retire and when, and who shall be
dismissed significantly influence not only the operating budget, but especially the quality of the institution. At least six factors have an impact
on the processes by which such decisions are made in colleges and
universities.

FACTORS ENGENDERING CHANGE

SIZE

In September 1974 approximately 60 percent of all individuals serving
on the faculties of the country's four-year colleges and universities were

---

[1] *The American University* (New York: Harper & Row, Publishers, Incorporated,
1968), p. 95. Presumably in 1974 he would have substituted "people" for
"men"!

[2] John Millett, in a brochure entitled, *Personnel Management in Higher Education*
(Washington: Academy for Educational Development, 1972), reports that a
study of the personnel employed by public colleges and universities in Ohio
revealed that, on the average, for every 1,000 students those institutions employed 55 faculty members, 11 administrative officers, and 43 classified personnel for instructional activities, exclusive of personnel devoting their energies
to research, public service, and auxiliary services.

in institutions with enrollments of 5,000 or more students. In these larger institutions, the processes of personnel administration (for faculties and for support staffs) have acquired a formality and impersonality that contrast sharply with the processes that obtained in the smaller institutions a quarter of a century ago—for example, the college with less than 750 students.

CONTROL

In 1973 likely two-thirds of all men and women employed as accountants to zoologists in this country's institutions of higher education were employed in publicly supported and controlled institutions.[3] In many public institutions, the processes of personnel administration are governed (in varying degrees) by state civil service systems,[4] and those systems tend to be markedly more inflexible than the personnel arrangements that prevail in private institutions. In all institutions, public and private, employment practices were affected in the early 1970s by the insistence of the federal government that additional job opportunities be opened up to women, blacks, and other minority-group members.

DEMAND

During the 1960s, the demand for faculty personnel grew steadily. It was magnified by the development, expansion, and persistent subdivision of knowledge. Faculty members had to be added in new areas of specialization, e.g., in nuclear physics, in the economics of developing countries, and in the history of Southeast Asia. These same factors— the growth and subdivision of knowledge—created a competing demand for these same personnel in business (e.g., in the research laboratories of industry) and in government (e.g., the Atomic Energy Commission, and in the Department of State and its often unruly nephew, the Agency for International Development).

In the years to 1985, it is probable that the number of faculty members added will in *no* year equal the number that swelled the academic

---

[3] U.S. Department of Health, Education and Welfare, Office of Education, National Center for Educational Statistics, *Digest of Educational Statistics, 1970.* OE-10024-70, September 1970, p. 79; and *Numbers and Characteristics of Employees in Institutions of Higher Education,* OE-50057-67, Fall 1967, p. 8.

[4] See Malcolm Moos and Francis E. Rourke, "The Academy under Civil Service," in *The Campus and the State* (Baltimore, Md.: The Johns Hopkins Press, 1959).

ranks in either 1968–69 or 1967–68.[5] Because of declining budgets, some faculties have been faced in the 1970s with the unpleasant necessity of deciding which of their fellows should be dismissed;[6] with the demise of additional institutions others face the loss of jobs. This lessened demand for academically trained men and women came at a time when increasing numbers of women and blacks sought positions on faculties (with the support of the federal government) and a customary number of young white males struggled to find positions.

SALARIES AND WORKLOADS

So long as enrollments and the demand for academic personnel were growing, the compensation of faculty members rose generously. From 1955 to 1970, faculty salaries increased at an average annual rate in excess of 5 percent;[7] during the 1960s the median salary increased by 75 percent.[8] Simultaneously, fringe benefits—pensions, health and hospital insurance, subsidized housing, and allowances for the education of children—were substantially improved and new forms of fringe benefits established. Perhaps of still greater consequence, workloads were reduced, thus granting the individual greater highly valued freedom.[9]

With the onset of the financial stringency that beset colleges and universities in the late 60s,[10] there began a marked slowing down in the increase in faculty incomes, which was coupled with pressures to raise workloads. In 1971–72 and 1972–73 faculty salaries rose less

---

5 Allan M. Cartter, "Faculty Needs and Resources in American Higher Education," *The Annals*, November 1972, pp. 71–87.

6 *The Chronicle of Higher Education* reported on Sept. 25, 1972, that New York University planned to drop 200 faculty positions as part of an effort to cut in half by the next year a $14 million deficit.

7 *At the Brink*, preliminary report on the Economic Status of the Profession. 1970–71, American Association of University Professors, April 1971, p. 4.

8 During the decade 1959-60–1969-70, the median annual salaries of instructors increased 65 percent; of assistant professors, 72 percent; of associate professors, 77 percent; and of full professors, 84 percent (Research Division, National Education Association).

9 During the sixties, there was a "steady reduction of teaching loads in American colleges and universities noted for the effectiveness of their faculties in teaching and scholarship" ("AAUP Statement on Faculty Workload," *AAUP Bulletin*, March 1970, p. 31).

10 Earl F. Cheit, *The New Depression in Higher Education*, Carnegie Commission on Higher Education (New York: McGraw-Hill Book Company, 1971).

than living costs. In many institutions workloads were increased,[11] and several state legislatures enacted laws specifying the number of hours faculty members at state colleges and universities would be expected to meet classes if they were to be paid the stipulated salaries for their posts.

ACCOUNTABILITY

A prime attraction of college teaching for the individual faculty member has been his freedom from control and direction. Indeed, a strong body of thought has held that evaluation of the performance of the college teacher-researcher is not feasible.[12]

The large increase in public expenditure for higher education during the 1960s, coupled with a variety of disturbances on many campuses, prompted legislators and citizens to demand an appraisal of the accomplishments of the faculty and the economy with which institutions are operated. State budget officers and executives of state coordinating boards designed yardsticks for such appraisals, and trustees of private institutions, beset by a shortage of funds, also sought ways of measuring performance. Simultaneously, the demand for evaluation welled up within the institutions: from academic administrators who sought means of making more effective decisions among large numbers of professors as to promotion in rank, increases in salary, and granting of tenure;[13]

---

[11] In April 1971, faculty members at The Johns Hopkins University were asked to double the number of undergraduate courses taught (*The Chronicle of Higher Education*, Apr. 26, 1971, p. 5). The student-faculty ratio at Northeast Missouri State College was increased from 1:23 to 1:26 (*College Management*, January 1971, p. 17).

Some professors at the University of Wisconsin have taken extra sections; and at Yeshiva University in New York City, some volunteered to teach extra courses without pay or volunteered for increased administrative duty. But, generally speaking there is a conspicuous lack of enthusiasm about increased teaching loads. "It's like a worker going back to the 10-hour day," commented one professor (*Business Week*, Nov. 21, 1970).

New York University's Commission on Effective Use of Resources (composed of both students and faculty) boosted teaching loads rather than hold up raises and cut its staff 5 percent (*Business Week*, Nov. 21, 1970).

[12] Talcott Parsons wrote, as was indicated earlier in this volume, that "in a sense probably not true of most bureaucratic organizations, it is not possible for academic men, competent as they may be in their own fields, to understand each other's specialties at a very high level" ("The Strange Case of Academic Organization," *Journal of Higher Education*, June 1971, p. 489). Kenneth E. Eble, director of the Project to Improve College Teaching, cosponsored by the Association of American Colleges and the American Association of University Professors voiced a contrary view (April 1971) that it does not make sense to keep insisting that it is impossible or improper to evaluate college teachers.

[13] John W. Gustad, "Evaluation of Teaching Performance," in *Improving College Teaching*, Annual Conference Papers (Washington: American Council on Education, 1966), pp. 265–281. Yet Gustad and others contend that despite the need, reliable and accepted methods of evaluation have not yet been developed; see, e.g., Arthur M. Cohen and Florence B. Brawer, *Measuring Faculty Performance* (Washington: American Association of Junior Colleges, 1969).

and from students who, in many institutions, developed rudimentary systems for the evaluation of their teachers.[14]

REDISTRIBUTION OF AUTHORITY

Authority for most personnel decisions had been lodged in the president and the deans, with allowance for a "rubber-stamp-like" approval by trustees. During the 1950s and 1960s, much authority for decisions as to academic personnel was shifted to the faculties, particularly the departmental faculties and their chairpersons. Since the late 1960s students have claimed a right to participate in such decisions. Simultaneously, decisions as to support personnel in many public institutions have been increasingly controlled by agencies of the state government.

These six factors have modified the processes of personnel administration used in relation to both academic and support personnel. The purpose of this chapter is to picture, first for academic personnel and subsequently for nonacademic personnel, the processes by which individuals are (*a*) recruited and placed, (*b*) compensated, (*c*) developed and evaluated, (*d*) promoted, including the granting of tenure, and (*e*) pacified in their grievances. It is particularly concerned with the relative responsibilities, now and in the future, of faculties, students, administrators, trustees, and public agencies for those decisions which, over the years, vitally influence the quality and enterprise of the institution's human resources.[15]

---

[14] As early as 1951, Francis J. Muller reported ("Trends in Student Ratings of Faculty," *AAUP Bulletin,* Spring, 1951) that close to 40 percent of the 840 institutions responding to an inquiry had witnessed some student rating. In May 1969, Max S. Marshall wrote that "over half the colleges and universities in the country now seek students' appraisals of their teachers in some form, and the practice is rapidly growing stronger" ("Academic Anomaly," *Liberal Education,* p. 279).

By 1974 the practice was even more extensive. "Some universities apparently have an official system of rating; others, such as Colorado State University, have student organizations that collect and publish ratings, ostensibly for the benefit of students selecting courses" (Richard G. Weigel, E. R. Oetting, and Donald L. Tasto, "Differences in Course Grades and Student Ratings of Teacher Performance," *School and Society,* January 1971, p. 60). For considered appraisal of the use and worth of student and other evaluations see Kenneth E. Eble, *The Recognition and Evaluation of Teaching* (Salt Lake City, Utah: Project to Improve College Teaching, 1970).

[15] An additional and subtle factor that has influenced these processes in some institutions is the ideological polarizations among faculty members which have engendered political struggles that found their expression in faculty personnel procedures and determinations.

PROCESSES GOVERNING ACADEMIC PERSONNEL

RECRUITMENT AND PLACEMENT

Decisions as to who shall be selected to serve on the faculty probably influence the caliber of an institution of higher education more, over the long run (see Chapter 5, pp. 101–102), than any other category of governing decisions. Generally, determination of the *number* of individuals that may be recruited and for *what positions* is the responsibility of the deans and the provost, academic vice presidents, or the president. The responsibility for the vital decisions as to who shall be hired has been delegated, in major part, especially in the larger and more prestigious institutions to the faculties and, within the faculties, to the academic departments subject in many institutions to the approval of the dean or deans.[16] Presidents and trustees cling to the formal authority to "approve" faculty appointments (if not all, at least tenure appointments), but that approval tends to become a mere formality as institutions grow in size or as a faculty grows in prestige.

Since the recruitment of academic personnel is extensively delegated to a large number of individual departments and schools, the ways in which new teachers are found and appointment decisions made are manifold.[17] To the extent that generalization is possible, these observations depict the prevailing process:

1. Most additions to university faculties are made at the teaching assistant or instructor level, i.e., from among young men and women in the 23-to-30 age group who have completed their master's degree and propose to continue their studies toward the Ph.D. degree.[18] Four-year colleges that do not offer graduate education, and especially those located in areas remote from centers of graduate study, cannot usually attract the better-qualified young

---

16 As has been pointed out earlier, there are at least three types of departments (see Paul L. Dressel, F. Craig Johnson, Philip M. Marcus, *The Confidence Crisis*, San Francisco: Jossey-Bass, Inc., Publishers, 1970, pp. 216–218), and the extent to which the dean participates varies according to type. Usually the dean's influence is greatest in the "university-oriented" department.

17 Recruitment and placement in any enterprise are guided by the prevailing table of organization, which identifies and defines the positions to be filled. Generally in the college or university the table of organization within which academic personnel serve consists of the traditional disciplinary departments, and positions within the departments are defined as instructor, assistant professor, associate professor, and professor.

18 David G. Brown, *The Mobile Professors* (Washington: American Council on Education, 1967), pp. 68–69. See also Howard D. Marshall, *The Mobility of College Faculties* (New York: Pageant Press, 1964).

people in this category suggested above. These institutions content themselves with a smaller number of secondary-level personnel and recruit a larger portion of those they add to their staffs from older age groups and into the ranks of associate and full professor.

2. Most faculty additions are chosen from within a narrowly circumscribed group of potential appointees. Selection is often made from among individuals who were awarded master's degrees by the appointing institution, or by institutions of a prestige superior to that enjoyed by the appointing institution, or by those institutions from whence came influential members of the selecting department.

3. Department chairpersons play a prominent role in the selection of new faculty members, subject to varying degrees of control by their departmental colleagues. The department chairperson's authority is limited by the budget authority and such review of the qualifications of new appointees as is exercised by the dean and, increasingly, in public institutions, by civil service regulations.

4. The "bait" dangled in front of sought-after applicants is not salary compensation alone.[19] Quite influential in enticing the ablest young graduate students are the prestige of the institution (and of the particular department within the institution) offering the position; a limited workload, or conversely the promise of free time (and sometimes financial support) for research; and in some instances the provision of housing, usually in the form of a rent subsidy.

5. The selection and recruitment decisions are made, in major part, by relatively senior professors for their respective departments. These men, competent as they may be in their fields, in many instances have had limited experience in recruitment. Their deci-

---

[19] For an impressive list of faculty benefits other than salary, retirement provisions, and insurance, see *The Outer Fringe,* by Mark H. Ingraham with Francis P. King (Madison: University of Wisconsin Press, 1965). Even more valuable is the discussion of this matter by Reece McGee in *Academic Janus* (San Francisco: Jossey-Bass, Inc., Publishers, 1971), pp. 135–148. See also J. F. Wellemeyer, Jr., ed., "Case Studies of College and University Faculty Compensation Practices," *Compensation on the Campus* (Washington: Association for Higher Education, National Education Association, 1961).

The AAUP estimates that fringe benefits amount to 10 or 12 percent of the total compensation (*At the Brink,* op. cit., p. 38). Jacques Barzun notes that the ratio of fringe benefits to salaries is as high as 18 or 22 percent for academic staff and 9 to 11 percent for clerical and manual staffs (*The American University,* op. cit., p. 180).

sions, however, are seldom overturned by either departmental colleagues, the dean, or the president.[20]

When compared with the processes obtaining in many business firms, government agencies, and professional enterprises, the prevailing process of hiring faculty is amateurish and marked by the use of overly subjective criteria by inexperienced department heads. The penalty for decentralization and amateurishness in hiring is chance: when the process works, it may work well; when it does not work, it subjects the department at least to mediocrity.

The processes that generally prevail for the recruitment of academic administrators—department chairpersons, deans, and presidents—grant to the faculty a lesser but significant role in decision making. Generally, department chairpersons and deans are chosen by the president but seldom without consultation with the faculty. The president's (or the dean's) decisions as to the selection of department chairpersons particularly are circumscribed by the essentiality of gaining the concurrence of faculty members, and in many institutions department chairmen are elected by departmental faculty members rather than appointed by the president or deans. The president is freer to make what are especially important decisions as to the choice of deans, but seldom without consulting the relevant faculty. And while the choice of the president is the responsibility of the trustees, it is seldom made without the collaboration of a committee of the faculty and, in many instances, the students.

COMPENSATION

Two kinds of decisions as to the compensation of faculty members are made: decisions as to the proportion of the institution's annual budget that will be devoted to faculty compensation and the level of salaries that will be maintained and decisions as to the compensation of the individual faculty member.

The first of these two kinds of decisions is made by the president and his staff and participated in by the trustees. The second—decisions as to hiring-in salaries and as to who shall be promoted or recommended for a salary increase—is effectively made by the department head. In some institutions, substantial authority over such decisions remains with the dean, and in the smaller institutions that authority will likely rest with the president. Seldom is any authority exercised by trustees.

---

20 For a confirming judgment see Caleb Foote, Henry Mayer, et al., *The Culture of the University Governance and Education,* Study Commission on University Governance, University of California, Berkeley (San Francisco: Jossey-Bass, Inc., Publishers, 1968), p. 30.

Academic man does not conform consistently with Adam Smith's concept of "the economic man." Compensation—salary, supplementary fringe benefits and perquisites (e.g., subsidized housing, free tuition for children, and the availability of a subsidized faculty club), and the prospect of salary increases are important to these individuals. But the availability of such compensation will not suffice to content many and retain them as growing members of an institution's faculty. Other, nonmonetary forms of compensation influence the job satisfaction of many academic men.

The typical young professor is especially concerned as to what courses he is to teach and *how much* teaching he will be expected to do. Given the opportunity to teach what he is primarily interested in, and the companion opportunity to pursue such research as is of concern to him, the prospect is that his morale will be high, his zeal keen, and his loyalty unflagging. By and large, most academics seek four additional and interrelated factors in the environment about them: competent and reputed colleagues, particularly in the department of which they are members; competent and sensitive administrators—department head, dean, provost, and president—upon whom in varying degrees their futures depend; able students in their classes; and prestige of the institution, again, particularly, in the department of which they are members.[21]

The responsibilities for the making of decisions that influence professorial satisfaction are diffused. The responsibility for decisions as to *what* the individual shall teach and *how much*, and what time and opportunities he will have for research, falls in major part on the department chairperson and, secondarily, on his colleagues. Similarly, the quality of his colleagues and his students and the prestige of the institution rest in major part on the decisions of his colleagues in the departmental faculty and the college faculty.

Clearly stated and generally promulgated compensation policies and logical, orderly procedures for their application are also important. Such policies make known the minimum-salary rates for each academic rank, the normal range of salaries within each rank, the frequency with which salaries will be reviewed, and the rules that will govern such

---

[21] For confirming evidence see David G. Brown, *The Mobile Professors,* pp. 150–167; and the studies of John E. Stecklein of the University of Minnesota with Ruth E. Eckert, *An Exploratory Study of Factors Influencing Choice of College Teaching as a Career* (Washington: U.S. Government Printing Office, 1961), and with Robert L. Lathrop, *Faculty Attraction and Retention: Factors Affecting Faculty Mobility at the University of Minnesota* (Minneapolis: Bureau of Institutional Research, University of Minnesota, 1960). See also Reece McGee, *Academic Janus,* pp. 177–188.

related matters as the granting of leave, the availability of housing, and health and retirement benefits. Awareness of each of these aspects of compensation contributes to the job satisfaction of most faculty members.

DEVELOPMENT AND EVALUATION

Most individuals destined for teaching careers receive little or no instruction in how to teach in the process of earning their doctorate. They are taught little or nothing of curriculum design, of the strategies of educational programming, or of institutional environment. In the words of one wise academic administrator: "They often learn only about the trees, nothing of the ecology of the educational forest."[22] They are given little counseling in most institutions before being assigned to their first classes[23] and, except in a few institutions, are provided little or no supervision. Yet few deans, department chairpersons, or professors would claim that most graduate assistants or even their more experienced colleagues who have attained professorial rank are capable teachers or are even gradually improving their ability to impart such knowledge as they have. Generally, it is agreed that young teachers could benefit from lessons on organizing the content of courses and of lectures, selecting reading materials, understanding the dynamics of reading, and conducting class and laboratory periods.

A few institutions do conduct seminars to provide each graduate student some understanding of the arts of lecturing, counseling, and examining, e.g., Harvard, the University of Michigan, and Oregon State University. At the University of Wisconsin at Green Bay each member of the faculty is offered the opportunity to have his teaching performance filmed, analyzed, and reviewed with him. But, by and large, such efforts are not made in most colleges and universities and, indeed, are frowned upon as unneeded or inconsistent with the academic tradition.[24]

Departmental chairpersons or deans must form judgments as to the accomplishments and worth of individual faculty members. They evaluate scholarship, some hold, by bulk rather than by quality[25] because

---

[22] Morris T. Keeton in a letter to the author dated Sept. 29, 1973.

[23] John L. Chase, *Graduate Teaching Assistants in American Universities,* U.S. Office of Education, May 1970, pp. 48–50.

[24] See Lewis B. Mayhew, "Preparing Teachers," *Colleges Today and Tomorrow* (San Francisco: Jossey-Bass, Inc., Publishers, 1969), chap. 11, pp. 162–178.

[25] John W. Gustad, *Policies and Practices in Faculty Evaluation* (Washington: American Council on Education, 1961). See also John O. Meany and Frank J. Ruetz, "A Probe into Faculty Evaluation," *Educational Record,* Fall 1972, pp. 300–307, for a summary review of methods of evaluation and the extent of their application.

they are incapable of evaluating research in specialties other than their own. They evaluate teaching, at the best, on the bases of "hearsay," principally the occasional comments of students. Some academic administrators hold that the informal evaluations made on many campuses by peers are more reliable than the foregoing comments imply. They fear the "standardization" that would accompany more formal evaluation processes. But a growing point of view is reflected by the conclusions stated in a study of the practices that obtain as to the evaluation of teachers' performance in 584 institutions. The author of that study concluded that "not even approximately effective methods of evaluating teaching ability" were in use.[26]

On an increasing number of campuses, often with faculty encouragement but frequently on their own initiative, students have developed methods of evaluating courses and instructors. Such evaluations are published annually, semiannually on some campuses, and are used by students in selecting courses and by departmental chairpersons and deans in evaluating their colleagues. As yet no comprehensive study of the worth and use of student evaluations is available.

For a labor-intensive enterprise, such absence of effort to supervise at least the beginners, to stimulate the development of all members of the group, and to evaluate individual performance makes it probable that the very substantial freedom faculty members have enjoyed will be diminished. Civil service systems, which in many states are peculiarly ill suited for academic personnel administration, will likely be developed and extended. Thus, responsibility that belonged to deans and presidents will be lost to them, and primarily because they (and particularly the presidents) failed to ensure that positive and effective processes obtained. This prospect is suggested by the practice already prevailing in some junior colleges—the certification and periodic examination and recertification of all teachers by a state educational agency.

PROMOTION AND TENURE

Rank is of consequence to the academic man, perhaps not much less so than for the military man. Decisions as to rank are also of two sorts: decisions as to promotion from instructor to assistant professor, from assistant professor to associate professor, from associate professor to full professor, and decisions as to the granting of tenure which are often made when the individual is promoted to associate professor or to full professor.

Decisions as to promotions at the teaching assistant, instructor, and

---

[26] Ibid.

assistant professor levels are customarily made within each academic department. Their review by the dean and higher officers will customarily be limited to the consideration of whether the individual has served a stipulated number of years in the lesser rank, has received his doctoral degree, and has published. As institutions grow larger, the relative finality accorded the recommendation of the department head increases substantially.

Decisions as to the granting of tenure are, in the life of the academic man and in the life of the institution he serves, of special importance. While such decisions are usually reviewed by deans and presidents and approved by trustees, in many institutions they are effectively made by departmental faculties. The suitability of having departmental faculties make the decisions as to which members of a faculty shall be given the assurance of employment for life has been sharply challenged. The argument against this process is essentially this: ". . . the decision as to whether or not to grant tenure is fundamentally and intrinsically different from that of promotion. . . . it involves the application of criteria which transcend those of scholarship and recognition in a specific field of knowledge by a small group of fellow specialists, and which extend into spheres that encompass wider concerns than merely those of a particular department."[27] Thus, in some institutions and typically in the more prestigious institutions, ad hoc committees composed of faculty members from several departments, and sometimes including respected scholars from other universities, are created to review departmental recommendations and to advise the dean, provost, or president.[28]

Tenure is usually defended on two grounds: it provides needed job security, and it assures the faculty member's freedom to speak and write as his intellect and conscience prompt him. Kingman Brewster and George J. Stigler have both stated a third defense: to underpin the courage of the individual scholar to voice and defend his beliefs even when they run counter to those of his colleagues, department chair-

---

[27] "Report of the Commission on University Governance," Vanderbilt University, October 1970, pp. 19–20.

[28] For a description of this process see Jacques Barzun, *The American University*, op. cit., p. 41. It should be noted that even this modification of who is involved in tenure decisions may not go far enough; it does not include individuals who may be expected to weigh the long-range financial implications of such decisions.

person, dean, or president.[29] Talcott Parsons and Gerald M. Platt justify tenure on still another basis. Both the educational and the socialization functions of the university, they contend, make necessary some "pattern of stratification" related to competence and experience. Tenure is one element of that "pattern of stratification."[30]

The continuance of the institution of tenure has been challenged by some presidents confronted with increasing numbers of their faculties lodged in positions for life (see table, page 198), some of whom have been made obsolete as a consequence of the rapid advance of technology in their fields.

It has been challenged also by spokesmen for graduate assistants and younger faculty members who see the large proportion of faculty members that are tenured (over 60 percent in all institutions of one state) as obstacles to their own advance. This challenge is reinforced by the severe tightening in the job market for college teachers. And tenure has been challenged by legislatures and members of the public who are critical of rising costs of instruction and of happenings on the campus.[31]

Trustees, presidents, and faculties must meet such challenges; they must ensure that practices with respect to evaluation, and policies with respect to promotion as well as tenure do not discourage high-level talent from entering the academic profession. Tenure has been established so long in so many institutions, public and private, that it will not likely be abandoned, and the arguments stated above justify its continuance. Proposals that quotas be established as to the proportion of the faculty that may enjoy tenure at any point in time, and the number that may be granted tenure each year, do not go to the heart of the problem. What is needed, and urgently, are more rigorous methods of sin-

---

[29] During 1971–72, at least five state legislatures and an equal number of universities were examining tenure. During 1970, three major study groups—of the American Council of Education's Commission on Campus Tensions, the President's Commission on Campus Unrest, and a federally initiated task force on higher education—all called for a reexamination of tenure. Subsequently, the American Association of University Professors and the Association of American College, codevelopers of the 1940 Statement of Principles on Academic Freedom and Tenure, convened a commission to reexamine the principle. A considered statement of the challenges to tenure is presented in Robert K. Carr, "The Uneasy Future of Academic Tenure," *Educational Record*, Spring 1972, pp. 119–127.

[30] Talcott Parsons and Gerald M. Platt, *The American University* (Cambridge, Mass.: Harvard University Press, 1973), pp. 364–365.

[31] "If a university is alive and productive it is a place where colleagues are in constant dispute; defending their latest intellectual enthusiasm, attacking the contrary views of others. From this trial by intellectual combat emerges a sharper insight, later to be blunted by other, sharper minds. It is vital that this contest be uninhibited by fear of reprisal" ("On Tenure," *AAUP Bulletin*, Winter 1972, pp. 382–383).

STUDIES OF PERCENTAGE OF FACULTY ON TENURE

Percentage Range	Michigan State 1962 Study[a]	Dennison Study[b]	Byse and Joughlin Study[c]	
			Total Faculty	Full-Time Faculty
	Number of Institutions in Each Percentage Rank			
25–29			10[d]	
35–39	4	2	58[e]	
50–54	8			10[f]
55–59	5	1		58[g]
60–64	4	3		
65–69	6			
70–74	3	2		
85–89	1			
TOTAL	31	8		

[a] Paul L. Dressel, "A Review of the Tenure Policies of Thirty-One Major Universities," *The Education Record*, July 1963, pp. 248–253. Based on total faculty.

[b] Charles P. Dennison, *Faculty Rights and Obligations*, TC, 1955.

[c] Clark Byse and Louis Joughlin, *Tenure in American Higher Education* (Ithaca, N.Y.: Cornell University Press, 1952).

[d] Average for the 10 institutions with more than 200 faculty was 28 percent.

[e] Average for the 58 institutions with less than 200 faculty was 44.6 percent.

[f] Average for the 10 institutions with more than 200 faculty was 52 percent.

[g] Average for the 58 institutions with less than 200 faculty was 55.9 percent.

SOURCE: Coordinating Council for Higher Education, *Academic Tenure in California Public Higher Education*, May 6, 1969.

gling out a smaller proportion of upcoming faculty members for election to tenure. Such methods will likely include (*a*) the lengthening of service prior to consideration for tenure, (*b*) the establishment of improved means of evaluating performance, (*c*) the regular utilization of review committees composed of faculty members from without the candidate's department, and perhaps from without the institution, to assess the individual's performance and his or her promise of continuing growth, (*d*) the lowering of the age for retirement with exceptions only for scholars of notable distinction, and (*e*) the meaningful review of recommendations by presidents and trustees.

UNIONIZATION OF FACULTIES

In the typically small college and university during the 1920s, compensation for the teacher was determined by a dean or president dealing with the individual. If a faculty member was aggrieved by what he believed to be a limitation of his academic freedom, by the assignment of classes he was to teach, by the hour or the room in which he was to teach, or by his failure to be promoted in salary or rank, he stated his grievance to a paternalistic dean or president or, in the largest institutions, to an equally paternalistic department chairperson.

In the 1970s, the annual-salary increments faculty members receive are of concern to all (even if of less concern than to workers in nonacademic fields). Hence, most faculty members serve under contracts that set forth explicit terms of compensation, and these contracts are supplemented by faculty bylaws that specify conditions of employment.[32] Some institutions also have established compensation policies and procedures that inform faculty members as to the salary ranges for each rank, the frequency with which salaries will be reviewed, and the rules governing the granting of leaves, the availability of housing, and related matters. In the bylaws of some institutions provision is made for the existence of a Grievance Committee or an ad hoc committee to discuss particular complaints and the procedure to be followed. That procedure often provides for a right of appeal by a faculty member from the committee's decision to a superior group from within the faculty, to the faculty senate, or to the trustees.

During recent years such arrangements for setting compensation and for resolving grievances have often involved participation by organizations representing some part of the institution's faculty members, such as the local chapter of the American Association of University Professors or a union of the faculty members. These organizations are usually responsible for stating and bargaining for salaries, for continually monitoring arrangements as to such matters as are listed above, and for representing individuals in presenting their grievances.

During the early 1970s three organizations—the American Association of University Professors, the American Federation of Teachers, and the National Society of Professors (a division of the National Education Association)—succeeded, in varying degrees, in organizing faculty members. The AAUP assumed the role of bargaining agent for its members in a small proportion of the institutions in which it had chapters. The American Federation of Teachers, affiliated with the AFL-CIO, became

---

[32] Most "teaching assistants," a segment of the instructional staff that grew large as graduate enrollments expanded, do not usually serve under contracts and do not enjoy, in many institutions, the protection of established policies as to compensation, leaves, promotion, or dismissal. For a discussion of the economic status of the teaching assistant, see Peggy Heim and Becky Bogard, "Compensation of Graduate Assistants, 1968–69," *AAUP Bulletin,* December 1969, pp. 483–488; and John L. Chase, *Graduate Teaching Assistants in American Universities,* op. cit.

the bargaining agent for a limited number of urban-oriented institutions, particularly the City University of New York. The NEA is the leader (as of December 1974) in terms of the number of institutions in which it represents faculty members, but these are predominantly two-year colleges and the former state teachers colleges. All in all, organizations claiming the right to bargain in behalf of the faculty existed in more than 200 institutions (or nearly 300 separate campuses, the bulk of which were two-year colleges), and administration-union agreements covering faculty members' compensation had been negotiated in a number of institutions.

The AAUP, despite persistent protestations that it is not a union and that it chooses to share authority with academic administrators, seems destined to assume increasingly the role of an association representing predominantly public employees before the federal and state legislatures and in negotiations with institutional administrators.[33] The National Education Association now represents some professors, but its long-time identification with elementary and secondary school teachers suggests that many faculty members of higher education will be loathe to affiliate. The American Federation of Teachers consists principally of elementary and secondary school teachers; its growth among professors, who are reluctantly abandoning their prestigious status, will likely be slower than its rivals in the forseeable future.

The impact of the organization of faculties upon the personnel processes of these institutions and on the role of faculties in the governance of institutions cannot yet be assessed.[34] Organization will strengthen the demands of faculty members (perhaps those of the junior and marginal faculty members more than the senior members) for the betterment of their compensation and working conditions at a time when the relationship of the demand for and the supply of teachers is running to their disadvantage. It is likely that the organization will also raise new challenges to the role of the faculty in governance. When

---

[33] For discussion of the likely future of the AAUP, see George Strauss, "The AAUP as a Professional Occupational Association," in *Readings in Collective Negotiations in Public Education* (Chicago: Rand McNally & Co., 1967); and Daniel R. Coleman, "The Evolution of Collective Bargaining as It Relates to Higher Education in America," *Journal of the College and University Personnel Association,* May 1972, pp. 4–8.

[34] The AAUP's Committee Z reported in the spring of 1971 that faculties could react to lessened demand and to the employing institution's reduced ability to pay in three ways: (1) passively, e.g., to rely on "other segments of the institutions or . . . outside agencies" to do right by them; (2) assertively, i.e., to hold to the principle of shared authority and to insist that the faculty must be effectively involved in all of the decision-making processes; (3) adversely, i.e., to operate "not as a partner but as a power"—to organize, to establish unions, and to be represented by union spokesmen (*At the Brink,* op. cit., p. 18).

the faculty organizes to advance its economic interests, it is questionable whether it can continue to claim the right to participate in decisions as to the allocation of resources as between faculty compensation and other purposes of expenditure, and in decisions as to the rank and compensation of individuals. In the words of the Carnegie Commission on Higher Education, ". . . it should be clearly understood that faculty members cannot have it both ways—they cannot engage in codetermination (e.g., of curriculum) and in collective bargaining on the same issues at the same time."[35]

That the faculty may lose its right in many institutions to elect departmental chairpersons or, as in other institutions, to influence their selection by the dean or the president is forecast by decisions of the National Labor Relations Board. In four cases[36]—decided during 1971–72—the board excluded department chairpersons from faculty bargaining units because of the supervisory nature of their jobs. In two other cases,[37] it ruled that department chairpersons were not supervisors and could be included in the bargaining units.

Two considerations obviously influenced these decisions: (a) the chairperson's accountability (i.e., to whom does he answer—the faculty with whom he serves or the dean by whom he is appointed) and (b) the scope of his influence over personnel decisions (i.e., is his voice one among many, or does he possess the primary responsibility for personnel decisions as to departmental faculty?). The board's findings make manifest the generally known fact that the chairperson's status varies from institution to institution. More significantly it suggests that as unioniza-

[35] *Governance of Higher Education* (New York: McGraw-Hill Book Company, 1973), p. 47. For an additional, supporting point of view see Joseph W. Garbarino, "Faculty Unions and University Management," an unpublished paper prepared for the Committee for Economic Development, Feb. 2, 1972, and Everett Carll Ladd, Jr., and Seymour Lipset, *Professors, Unions and American Higher Education* (Berkeley, Calif.: Carnegie Commission on Higher Education, 1973), pp. 81–88. Mr. Garbarino states his point of view in these words: "the leadership characteristics appropriate for the officers of a faculty union are likely to be different from those appropriate to the officers of a faculty senate. The political skills, for example, that lead to success in union politics are likely to be more oriented to the membership and less to the administration than was true in the senates."

[36] The four cases were C. W. Post Center of Long Island University, Brookville, N.Y. *v.* United Federation of College Teachers, 189 NLRB 109 (1971), 77 LRRM 1001; Brooklyn Center of Long Island University, Brooklyn, *v.* United Federation of College Teachers, 189 NLRB 110 (1971), 77 LRRM 1006; Manhattan College, New York, *v.* American Association of University Professors, 195 NLRB 23 (1972), 79 LRRM 1253; and the Rosary Hill case decided in May 1973.

[37] The two cases were Fordham University, New York, *v.* American Association of University Professors, 193 NLRB 23 (1971), 78 LRRM 1177; University of Detroit *v.* American Association of University Professors, 193 NLRB (1971), 78 LRRM 1273.

tion of faculties is extended, trustees and presidents will likely insist more often upon appointing department chairpersons.

THE PROSPECTIVE IMPACT ON GOVERNANCE If the unionization of faculties continues at the rate that obtained between 1969 and 1975, it is likely that by 1980 the faculties of as many as 1,000 institutions (including community colleges) will be organized, and up to 250,000 faculty members will belong to bargaining units.[38] That prospect warrants speculation as to the impacts unionization of that extent will likely have on the governance of institutions. Straws now in the wind suggest these eventualities:

- The faculties and the administrator-trustees will be polarized in firm, adversarial positions.

- The system of governance (as a consequence of judicial decisions as well as collective bargaining) will become more explicit, more uniform, more proceduralized, and more centralized.

- Greater power and authority will be concentrated in "the management" (an objectionable term now but one likely more aptly descriptive of what will obtain in 1980). Many matters such as teaching loads now determined by individual faculty members and departments will have been written into contracts, management will have bargained for standards that will ensure productivity, and management will be obligated to enforce contractural provisions.

- The autonomy of public institutions will be further reduced. Faculty unions will tend to seek the opportunity to bargain with the agency, the official, or the body—the governing board, the governor, or the legislature—that holds the decision-making power over resources. The legislature, for example, may claim control by specifying by line item, even more exactingly than is done through

---

38 In the opinion of one observer: "As long as the principal activity of senates was 'governance' in the academic sense, and as long as the goals of the institution were not in dispute, the system worked well. As the area of shared goals has narrowed and as economic issues have become more important, faculties are more interested in organizations that can effectively represent their interests as an occupational group. As to 'participation in governance,' the senate system's workability is called into question" (Joseph W. Garbarino, "Precarious Professors: New Patterns of Representation," *Industrial Relations*, vol. 10, no. 1, February 1971). This point of view was expressed earlier by John C. Livingston, "Academic Senate under Fire," in G. Kerry Smith, ed., *Agony and Promise* (San Francisco: Jossey-Bass, Inc., Publishers, 1969), pp. 161–172; he contended that recent events and new problems on the campus "intensify the adversary character of relations between academic senates and trustees and administrators, and generally ... accelerate a trend toward collective bargaining" (p. 163).

formula budgeting, what appropriated funds shall be spent for, to prevent negotiation on the campus, or with the governor.

- Statewide faculty unions, and possibly also statewide student organizations, will emerge. If the power of decision rests with a state governing board, the governor, or the legislature, the union will soon be so shaped as to bring pressure to bear on the agency where power resides. Students, seeing their recently gained voice in governance undermined by their exclusion from bargaining between the faculty union and the administrators or the governing board, will similarly organize on statewide bases.

- As members of bargaining units, faculty members will lose their individuality. The flexibility with which administrators have dealt with individual cases will be reduced; the relative importance of seniority versus merit in gaining advancement will be changed; the tone of relationships between individual faculty members and dean, academic vice president, president, and trustees will likely be changed.

- The kind of individual emerging to leadership of the faculty will likely be different. Younger, more militant, politically motivated individuals will likely gain leadership posts in the union and will replace more senior and often respected scholars that have served in the faculty senate and in key committee chairman posts on many campuses. The egalitarianism of unions will tend to wipe out the factors that have granted distinction and status to some teachers and some scholars in the past.

PROCESSES GOVERNING NONACADEMIC PERSONNEL

SUPPORT AND STAFF PERSONNEL

Many colleges and universities employ more men and women in professional support roles (i.e., admissions personnel, attorneys, or administrators) and in clerical, technical, and manual positions than in academic and academic-administrative positions. This large and growing body of workers claims from 40 to 66 percent of the average institution's budget for all personnel services and is expected to grow in number, cost, and relative influence in the institutional community.

The relationship of the activities for which the professional workers in this group are responsible—e.g., student discipline, library administration, computer operation—to the primary activities of the faculty—

teaching and research—and the increasing professionalization of many in this group pose little precedented problems of personnel administration. These include problems as to the status of the new categories of professionals[39] and problems as to the evaluation of their performance, their compensation, their tenure, and their unionization. And all such problems must be resolved with due recognition of the treatment accorded faculty members.

The even larger number of clerical, technical, and manual workers poses a continuing flow of more familiar problems of personnel administration. These include the problems involved in maximizing the productivity of any work force: the maintenance of effective recruitment, placement, training, and evaluation processes. They include, too, the maintenance of competitive compensation, including fringe benefit and retirement provisions. They include the problems created by federal requirements as to the hiring, training, and promoting of women and of members of minority groups. And they include, on perhaps a third of all campuses, the problems that arise from dealings with organized unions representing categories within this body of workers.

By and large, analysts of university governance have given little attention to the handling of these emerging problems. Little has been written that is helpful in guiding decisions as to the resolution of such problems. In the public institutions, state civil service law and regulations provide guides—often devised with little recognition of the particular characteristics of these categories of workers or of the academic institution in which they perform their duties. But clear, considered policies to guide the utilization of these workers are found in relatively few institutions.

NEW PROFESSIONAL WORKERS

Among the professional and quasi-professional workers (sometimes referred to as NTPs, i.e., nonteaching professionals) who support the academic staff, several relatively new groups are expanding in size and in importance. The members of these groups generally do not teach (e.g., librarians—probably the largest category within the group, the curator, specialists in audiovisual techniques, and the directors of institutional research and the computer center), but they are closely associated with faculty members in the performance of their functions. Members of the continuing education staffs, often part time and located

---

[39] For descriptions of such problems, see "Librarians Press Claims for Faculty Status," *Chronicle of Higher Education*, July 3, 1972, p. 5; and Jack N. Ray, "Coping with White Collar Demands to Participate," *Journal of the College and University Personnel Association*, August 1972, pp. 69–73.

away from the campus, do teach. A few others teach as well as perform their support role, for example, the psychological counselor who also teaches psychology and the comptroller who teaches accounting in the business administration program.

Generally, the incumbents of such support positions do not enjoy the rights, privileges, and status that faculty members do.[40] In terms of professional training and experience in their respective fields, many will match the faculty members with whom they deal from day to day. Their salaries, usually established on a twelve-month basis, will often equal and in some instances exceed those of faculty members. But they are usually denied membership in the faculty and such associated prerogatives as the right to sabbatical leave, to attend faculty meetings, or to serve on faculty committees, and, in some institutions, to belong to the faculty club and to use its dining room.

These professional and quasi-professional workers are found in various parts of the institution. The newer and more professional activities (e.g., the computer center, the office of institutional research, and the research administration staff) tend to be found close to the president or the provost–vice president for academic affairs. Thus, decisions as to the recruitment, compensation, and the status accorded personnel engaged in these activities are made by the president, usually after consultation with a relevant faculty committee.

STUDENT PERSONNEL WORKERS

A larger and longer established body of support personnel includes the registrar, the dean of students, health officers, the chaplain, counselors, placement officers, student housing officers, the manager of the student center, advisers to student organizations, and the administrators of financial aid. This group of workers has expanded in number and in role as larger enrollments have brought into the institution an increased proportion of students needing a broader range of services. For exam-

---

[40] "Some 5 or 10 percent of the leaders in each of these professional groups must have the same type of academic training as the members of a faculty . . . [and must be] able to perform all the other duties performed by a teacher except that of standing before a class of students. Unless this top scholarly group is given the same rights, privileges, and prerogatives as are given to faculty appointees on tenure, it will be exceedingly difficult to attract bright young men and women to these nonteaching professional groups. Furthermore, it will be almost impossible to induce a teacher-scholar from another university to accept a nonteaching position, unless some of these rights, privileges, and prerogatives are bestowed upon him in his new institution" (Robert L. Williams, *The Administration of Academic Affairs in Higher Education,* Ann Arbor: The University of Michigan Press, 1965, p. 53). Accordingly, the trend has been toward extending these privileges.

ple, the administrator of financial aid and the placement officer who finds part-time employment for those students attending college and jobs for those who graduate represent relatively new specialties.

The categories of workers in this group require varying degrees of professionalization. The health care staff includes men and women trained in medicine and in nursing, while those individuals serving as housing officers and as placement officers may have had little professional training for the function they perform. Some directors of admissions and a few of their assistants will likely have obtained specialized training, whereas the director of financial aid will more likely have learned his "trade" on the job. In selecting individuals for the more professionalized positions, the vice president for student affairs will be constrained to make his choices from among individuals with the prescribed training for the work programmed for these positions—which is usually agreed upon by relevant faculty committees. In selecting individuals to serve in less professionalized positions, his freedom to choose is usually greater.

The staffs headed by these officers are usually directed by a vice president for student affairs who, under the guidance of the president, administers a staff that consumes about 4 percent of the institution's annual budget (an amount about equal to that provided for the support of the library) in the typical four-year college.[41]

These staffs perform functions that grew out of efforts originally performed by faculty members. It is logically contended that:

> . . . the faculty must remain the integrating force in the total education of the young person. . . . The faculty must make sure that, apart from the onset of physical or mental disability—when the physician relieves the teacher—the total educational program has balance and coherence.
>
> In specific terms, the faculty through appropriate committees should help establish criteria for admission; help determine policies in student aid and employment; assure that counseling enhances independence and growing emotional and intellectual maturity; and make certain that discipline does not become sloppy and sentimental.[42]

But in practice, faculty participation (through the several committees suggested by the foregoing comment) seldom is an "integrating force," and if "balance and coherence" are achieved, it is through the innovation and uphill efforts of a dean of students or a vice president for stu-

---

41 Laurine E. Fitzgerald, Walter F. Johnson, and Willa Norris, eds., *College Student Personnel: Readings and Bibliographies* (Boston: Houghton Mifflin Company, 1970), pp. 144–145.

42 J. Douglas Brown, *The Liberal University: An Institutional Analysis* (New York: McGraw-Hill Book Company, 1969), p. 58.

dent affairs, not through the efforts of the faculty. Indeed, the faculty tends to "look down" on the student personnel officers, and the faculty's influence on the student personnel function is often negative or even disintegrating.

BUSINESS AFFAIRS PERSONNEL

A third subgroup of the support staff approximates in numbers two-thirds of the typical institution's total instructional and research staff. This subgroup includes those engaged in accounting, auditing, budgeting, and financial and investment activities; the design and development of systems and procedures; purchasing and inventory management; the design, planning, and supervision of construction of the physical plant; the maintenance and operation of buildings, equipment (e.g., the power plant and heating and air conditioning equipment), and grounds; and the management of auxiliary enterprises (e.g., parking, residence halls, dining rooms, and bookstores).

The bulk of the personnel engaged in these activities are hired from the same pool of manpower upon which the banks, stores, manufacturing plants, and other business enterprises and governmental agencies draw. Thus, the institution of higher education must maintain conditions of work and levels of compensation comparable with those of other enterprises in the surrounding geographical area if it is to staff these activities adequately. Many individuals (perhaps two-thirds) who head various business-like activities—when appointed—have little familiarity with higher education. Yet some of these individuals are engaged in performing tasks (e.g., budgeting and physical planning) that can vitally affect the instructional program and the climate that prevails in the institution. The aggregate expenditure they direct approximates 40 percent of the budgets of the colleges and universities they serve; the number of employees they supervise is large, perhaps one-third of the total number employed by these institutions. The long-term success of a college or university rests in part upon the understanding as well as the effectiveness with which these individuals administer its business and financial operations.

The mobilization of so large a technically qualified staff, and its subsequent development and utilization, involves the persistent seeking out of individuals qualified to perform the variety of tasks that make up an institution's business affairs (as well as secretaries and clerical assistants for the academic staff), the placement of individuals in appropriate positions in the operating divisions of the university, the formulation (when these employees are not included under state civil service provisions) of an orderly and equitable system for fixing salaries, wages, fringe benefits, vacations and leave, and the handling of the constant and large number of actions (e.g., the filing of a health insurance claim) that flow out of such a system.

Technically, these employees are subject to the direction and leadership of a vice president for business affairs, a vice president for finance, or a similarly titled officer. Pragmatically, some—particularly those employees in the financial, planning, building design, and construction offices—often communicate directly with the institution's president and sometimes with its trustees. Their activities will likely be under the continuing surveillance of trustee (or trustee-administration-faculty) committees which establish policies and approve plans and programs for the carrying out of these activities. Because many trustees claim greater familiarity with these "business-like" activities than they do with respect to academic matters, this line of communication often approximates direction. The president may—and a strong president does—involve himself in all business affairs and discourage such direct trustee intervention. He will seek to be "on top of" the institution's total operations and in a position to take firm and progressive action.

ORGANIZATION FOR PERSONNEL ADMINISTRATION

The distribution of responsibility for making major decisions relative to the promotion, evaluation, compensation, granting of leaves, eventual retirement, and related matters for faculty members, on the one hand, and nonacademic personnel, on the other, has just been depicted. To support these two separate decision-making processes, most colleges and universities have separate organizations for personnel administration: one supporting academic personnel decision making, which operates under the general direction of the vice president for academic affairs (or the provost) and his staff assistants and the department chairpersons, and one supporting nonacademic personnel decision making, which operates under the direction of the vice president for business affairs and his director of personnel.[43]

The separate personnel organizations are separately responsible for the formulation of personnel policies and the approval of personnel actions in their respective jurisdictions. In large multicampus univer-

---

[43] John D. Millett has written: "There is one personnel procedure for faculty, a different personnel procedure for administrative officers, however defined, a third personnel procedure for the non-academic or classified staff and possibly a fourth procedure for student employment" (*Personnel Management in Higher Education,* p. 3).

sities, both organizations are usually responsible, in consultation with relevant committees, for the establishment of policies governing their respective personnel matters in the branch institutions. But personnel administration involves additional activities requiring specialized skills (e.g., employee and union relations, the handling of insurance, unemployment compensation, retirement claims, and training of employees) and voluminous routine activities (the maintenance of personnel records and the processing of forms relative to sick leave, promotions, transfers, and other matters). These activities customarily are handled for both bodies of personnel by the institution's director of personnel and his staff.

The existence of separate organizations rests principally on the logic that the contrasting functions (e.g., those of the professor of physics and the purchasing agent), conditions of work (e.g., the conventional freedom of the professor and the discipline enforced on the accountant), terms of employment (e.g., the nine-month year of the professor versus the twelve-month year of the plant engineer), and statuses of the two groups necessitate different treatment. This logic has tended to disappear; the nonfaculty group has grown to include more professional and quasi-professional workers, and the intervention of federal and state governments and union organization have imposed new and similar requirements ("affirmative action" programs, civil service classification, and legal stipulations as to bargaining processes) for both groups of workers.

In a few institutions, generally those credited with having especially advanced personnel administration staffs,[44] the personnel director and his key aides have gradually proven their ability to assist in the handling of academic personnel matters. For example, at Pennsylvania State University the officer in charge of the "department of personnel relations" serves as secretary of a committee that reviews faculty recommendations for promotion to full professor, participates with faculty representatives in rewriting prevailing policy as to tenure and criteria for the academic ranks, and represents the University in negotiations with organized faculty members. This trend reflects the utility of trained and experienced professionals in personnel administration.

SUMMARY AND IMPLICATIONS

The foregoing descriptions of personnel processes that generally obtain within colleges and universities make patent that responsibility for per-

---

[44] For example, Pennsylvania State University, the University of Colorado, and the Massachusetts Institute of Technology.

sonnel decisions is widely diffused and that prevailing practices do not conform with standards for effective personnel administration.

Decisions as to how many faculty members may be employed and what they may be paid are made by the administrators and approved by trustees; decisions that bear more directly on the caliber of academic personnel and condition their zeal are made by the faculties. In public institutions, both types of decisions are made within constraints set by (and tending to be extended by) the state governments; that is, in a number of states, officials fix by budgetary decisions the numbers that may be employed and salary levels. Their decisions substantially influence the salary levels maintained by neighboring private institutions. Few institutions make continuing efforts either to train or to evaluate the performance of any or all faculty members. Students have undertaken the evaluation of teacher performance on some campuses, thus supplying a needed element of personnel administration and indirectly influencing decisions as to promotion and compensation.

Responsibility for decision making as to the nonacademic personnel within the typical college or university is more centralized.[45] For the public institutions, while practices vary, generally the state governments exercise substantial influence over the numbers that may be employed, salary and wage rates, and recruitment. In some states, state personnel agencies establish processes for the evaluation of the individual's performance, the amount of salary increases and the frequency with which promotions may be made, and the adjudication of grievances.[46] Within the institution, such decisions, within the constraints imposed by the state government, are concentrated in the vice president for business affairs (finance or administrative operations).

In both areas—academic personnel and nonacademic personnel— the influence of employee organizations is growing.[47] Nonacademic personnel, particularly those employees in the crafts and trades and in custodial jobs, have long been employed in accordance with union requirements. Unionization among these employees and among food

---

45 "The 1971 Personnel Practices Survey," conducted by the Research Committee of the College and University Personnel Association and published in the *CUPA Journal,* August 1971, provides a useful and informative depiction of the state of nonacademic personnel administration.

46 An inquiry as to the administration of nonfaculty personnel programs in 52 state-supported institutions in November 1969 indicated that more than two-thirds of these institutions were autonomous in all functions of their nonfaculty personnel programs (Andrew W. Campbell, "Autonomy in Nonfaculty Personnel Programs," *CUPA Journal,* vol. 2, no. 212, March 1971, pp. 79–85).

47 That prospect is heightened by the decision of the National Labor Relations Board to assert its jurisdiction over private nonprofit colleges and universities with gross revenues of $1 million (*Federal Register,* Dec. 3, 1970).

service and some other employees has tended to increase, and wage rates and grievance handling are effectively governed by local union practices. Academic personnel are, as yet, substantially unorganized, but the prospect is that unionization will spread; that prospect carries with it the likelihood of major changes in the authority of the faculty to make personnel decisions not now entrusted to them and to participate more generally in the governance of the institutions they serve.

The factors engendering change in college and university personnel administration (enumerated at the start of this chapter) illuminate the need for improved organization for personnel administration. The prototype for the effective organization of this function and improved practices of recruitment, evaluation, and development are emerging. The central importance of each institution's human resources—in terms of the quality of the education provided and its costs—lend crucial significance to these developments.

PART FOUR

ONGOING RESTRUCTURING

Evolving Structure and
Function of the
Higher Education Industry

*The problem of governance is tied up with the question—
increasingly an ambiguous one—of what a university is
and, more broadly, what a university system is in the
society.*
                                                    Daniel Bell[1]

11 Economists study industrial structure[2] to learn how individual firms may be expected to behave—e.g., how they will expand, alter, or limit their product lines; how they will price their product or service to consumers; what relative cost and efficiency each firm in each segment of the industry may be expected to achieve (e.g., large and small firms, firms in each geographical region); what consumers will be attracted by each; and what shifts in structure would (or in their opinion should) provoke governmental intervention.

Students of governance have given little explicit attention to the structure of this country's higher education industry. Yet the structure of the higher education industry substantially affects the range, variety, and nature (perhaps as well, quality) of educational services that are made available. Change in the structure of the higher education industry also influences the related services (e.g., research, housing, feeding, etc.) offered, and, hence, the number and kinds of students that will be enrolled in various kinds of institutions. And changes in the structure of this industry are influences in the extent to which government intervenes in the functioning of individual institutions.

The purpose of the concluding part of this volume is to assess the "ongoing restructuring" of (a) the higher education industry within the United States and (b) the impact of this restructuring on the forms and processes of governance within individual colleges and universities. This chapter focuses on the higher education industry—the forces that

---

[1] "Quo Warranto, Notes on the Governance of Universities in the 1970's," *Public Interest*, Spring 1970, p. 61.

[2] By "industrial structure" the economist comprehends the number, size, and concentration of firms in an industry and in each identifiable subdivision of the industry. See the foreword by Richard E. Caves to Joe S. Bain, *Essays on Price Theory and Industrial Organization* (Boston: Little, Brown and Company, 1972).

are bringing about change in the types and size of institutions and the functions expected of them as a group and of each principal type of institution. Succeeding chapters deal in turn with the roles in governance of students, faculty members, presidents, and trustees; the need for strengthening leadership; and the evolution of organizational forms in the individual college or university.

FORMS AND PROCESSES ARE CHANGING

Much that has been written as to the governance of institutions of higher education is founded on the assumption that what was will be, that the forms and processes of governance that have existed will persist. It is generally assumed that the mix of institutions that will exist in 1980 will be substantially the same as the mix that makes up the more than 2,900[3] postsecondary educational institutions that existed in 1973. It is presumed that these colleges and universities will perform traditional functions in traditional ways, and in a familiar social context.

These assertions do not gainsay that the institutions existing in 1980 will be called upon to serve more and different students than in the past. Nor do they overlook the possibility that these institutions may assume additional functions that cannot now be foreseen. They simply assume that added functions will be integral to the institution's prime responsibilities for the discovery, transmission, and application of knowledge, and that these functions can be added while preserving the structure and processes that their schools, colleges, and departments inherited from prior decades.

That this assumption is not tenable becomes clear when one observes the extent to which what society expects of the higher education industry has been and is being altered. That changing expectation is forcing adaptation of the colleges and universities that make up this "industry," and of the forms and processes these institutions use, or will use, to meet their evolving obligations.

FORCES AT WORK

A quarter of a century ago when I was learning the arts of a management consultant, our managing partner bought, and hung in the room in which our partners met, an abstract oil painting entitled *Forces at Work.* I recall it as an unintelligible assortment of shades of blue. His purpose was not to further the art appreciation of his colleagues but to

---

[3] *The Campus Resources of Higher Education in the United States of America* (Academy for Educational Development, November 1973), pp. 16–17.

emphasize our obligation, in studying the organizational and management problems of corporate clients, to look beyond conventional measures of sales volume, net profit, operating ratios, and return on investment to the "forces at work" in and around the industry in which the client company operated and to which its organization and processes would have to adapt.

In appraising the governance of colleges and universities, it is equally relevant to consider the forces at work with which the organization and processes of governance must cope. The title of a popular musical comedy held that "on a clear day you can see forever." The day is not sufficiently clear to permit one to foresee the structure and functions of higher education in 1980 which will have an impact on individual institutions. But one can see forces that are altering what society will expect of the colleges and universities in 1980 and the changes in the structure of the higher education industry that are taking place to enable institutions to meet those expectations.

THE EXPANSION OF KNOWLEDGE

The expansion of knowledge—the very stock-in-trade of institutions of higher education—is restructuring the work force of the nation, the job opportunities to which students aspire and for which they seek "certification," and, hence, the courses and programs in which they enroll. In the decades that have elapsed since 1900, the body of knowledge (as was earlier pointed out in Chapter 5) has greatly expanded in volume and become infinitely more specialized. A consequence of this expansion of knowledge has been a substantial increase in the demand for professional, technical, managerial, and service (e.g., paraprofessional health technicians) workers. In 1970 these groups made up about 35 percent of the national work force;[4] it is likely that by 1980 they may constitute 44 to 45 percent of the work force.

To develop the manpower required has necessitated the addition of many specialists to the faculties of colleges and universities. Knowledge has grown by the identification of new subdivisions of old fields of knowledge, i.e., econometrics, urban sociology, and polymer science, and by the regrouping of newly identified subbodies of knowledge, i.e., biochemistry, social psychology, and geopolitics. Teachers of these new specialties had to be recruited and, in the future, additional specialists in presently unrecognized fields will be sought.

---

[4] For discussion of "The Impact of Technological Change upon Employment" see *Technology and the American Economy*, Report of the National Commission on Technology, Automation and Economic Progress, vol. 1, February 1966.

To develop the manpower the society has increasingly sought required also the development of those new courses and programs that will equip individuals to serve in the plants, laboratories, and factories of a technological society.[5] The institutions of higher education have become the gatekeepers to those job opportunities that require possession of knowledge; in this sense they have become public utilities, i.e., the providers of a service that is essential to a substantial portion of the population.

Finally, the expansion of knowledge and its consequences have reemployed the need for a persisting search for still further knowledge. The meeting of this obligation is reflected in the research done for the health care, the military, and the industrial segments of the society, and in the general recognition that economic and social advance rests on the continuing discovery of new knowledge. The expansion of knowledge and the university's central role in the discovery, codification, conservation, and transmission of knowledge has brought it uncomfortably close, at times, to the centers of economic, political, and military decision making. For in a "knowledge society," as Bell and Galbraith contend,[6] knowledge gives power to its possessors. That closeness and that power have caused some to challenge the objective detachment of the universities engaged in some researches. But this intermeshing of the college and university with other institutions—business enterprises, the professions, the government—has brought the benefits of a vastly broadened experience, involvement in a reality difficult to simulate on the campus, and the support of groups and agencies throughout the society.

The growth in numbers and the change in character of the total of students enrolled is steadily increasing the size of many institutions and forcing modification of educational programs and of relationships between the institution and the student. The rate of increase in enrollees will be less rapid in the future than during the years from 1960 to 1972, but by 1980 the mix of students (and the prospective mix of institutions) will be significantly different than in 1970. Of the institutions that survive the economic travail of the mid-1970s, more will have enrollments of 20,000 or more students, and those enrollments will include relatively more graduate and relatively fewer undergraduate students.

Approximately 65 percent of all students will be attending part time.

---

5 Eric Ashby, *The Structure of Higher Education: A World View*, occasional paper no. 6 (New York: International Council for Educational Development, 1973), pp. 9–11.

6 Daniel Bell, "Notes on the Post-Industrial Society," *Public Interest*, Spring 1967, p. 102; J. K. Galbraith, *The New Industrial State* (Boston: Houghton Mifflin Company, 1967), pp. 372–376.

Up to two-thirds will be attending an institution located within commuting distance of their homes (perhaps a "learning center" removed from any campus), and most students will be living at home—their own or their parents' home—or with relatives. The college or university will in most instances no longer be the "total institution" (see discussion in Chapter 4) within which students and faculty members spend their working, social, and recreational lives.

The shift in demand from courses in the liberal arts to vocationally oriented courses and career-preparatory, credential-providing programs will force further modification of curricula, require the reconstitution of faculties, and materially alter the mix of institutions.

The change in academic demand (i.e., "the student focus on practicality") will result in the institutions' granting degree-seeking students an even greater freedom of course choice in meeting degree requirements. It will cause the introduction of many new courses and programs for both degree-seeking and non-degree-seeking students. It will necessitate a marked reduction in the number of teachers in the classics, the humanities, and languages, and a shift of enrollments from liberal arts colleges to the comprehensive colleges and universities to the proprietary schools.

The shift in control of many colleges and universities will reduce the college and the university (as it is reducing other business, governmental, and social institutions) to the status of a unit within an increasingly compact, centralized system.

The proportion of all institutions and of the total number of enrollees in public, as distinguished from private, institutions will increase. The proportion of all institutions and of the aggregate enrollment in private (nonprofit) colleges and universities will have decreased significantly further by 1980, as will the number of institutions and the proportion of enrollees in institutions serving a single sex or a single race. Simultaneously, the proportion of all students enrolled in proprietary institutions will likely have grown substantially; their concentration on vocational education at the postsecondary level, especially designed to meet the credential-seeking desires of many students within minimum time periods, seems destined to drain students from institutions offering broader educational programs.

Pressures for homogenization will reduce further such diversity among institutions as has existed.[7] Three kinds of pressures are combining to bring about greater similarity among colleges and universities.

---

[7] Harold Enarson, "University or Knowledge Factory," *The Chronicle of Higher Education*, June 18, 1973.

The oldest of these pressures is that of the accrediting associations, which despite efforts to encourage innovation, by enforcing the judgments of peers, limits the willingness of administrators to propose unprecedented ventures, and encourages them to stick to accepted patterns. The professions exercise a similar influence over curriculum development. So too the state coordinating agencies that exist (and are needed) to disapprove proposals that make for duplicative costs—even though the proposed, duplicative program offers a novel, and seemingly worthy, approach.

In a society characterized by more pervasive means of communication than the world has previously known (e.g., the communication among peers in education, among members of each profession, and between governmental authorities and the institutions they control), it has to be proven that pluralism can flourish. Leaders who challenge traditional ideas and practices, be they individuals, groups, or institutions, are vulnerable to destruction by the bright light such communication sheds on them even as they might be by a searing desert sun.

The impact of control and of the pressures toward homogenization are matched in the "compact society" of the 1970s by similar forces that limit the "autonomy" of other social institutions. The "compact society" is one in which the number of institutions, as well as the number of people, is large in relation to geographical and social space, and in which all are interrelated by an unprecedented system of communication and increasingly controlled by extensive government. In such a society every institution bears the impact of social harness.[8]

Business firms, for example, are pressed to measure up to imprecisely defined, but ever more exacting, "social responsibilities." Their actions in relation to consumers, investors, and employees are exposed to the public gaze by the press, the radio, and television. The society, through numerous governmental agencies, imposes its standards on business operations. These agencies require more revealing accountability, e.g., through the examination of labeling and advertising, through more detailed annual reporting to stockholders, and through regular reports as to accidents suffered by employees and as to the number of minority groups employed.

So it is with the private philanthropic foundation. Foundation activities have received greater attention in the press, on the radio, and on

---

8 William E. Chamberlain, territorial commander for the Salvation Army in the Southern States, told Blue Ridge Institute for Southern Community Service executives that private social agencies under government guidelines are becoming like grade A milk—homogenized and pasteurized (*Asheville Citizen,* July 23, 1973, p. 8).

television as their resources have been used to ameliorate racial tensions, to shed light on civil rights, to facilitate the decentralization of the public schools, or to stimulate the development of public television. Foundation activities have been subjected to congressional investigations on three occasions within the period since 1950. The Tax Reform Act of 1969 imposed new standards as to activities in which foundations may engage and the rate at which they must expend their resources. They were subjected by this legislation to more frequent auditing and to the obligation of fuller annual reporting.

What colleges and universities point to as the "loss of autonomy" is a similar public exposure, a comparable imposition of externally determined standards, and similar requirements for fuller accountability. Yet the pressures to make the college and the university "accountable" pose an especially pregnant question. Will this society manifest the greatness that is required not only to grant substantial freedom to but as well to subsidize an institution responsible for continual inquiry, appraisal, and criticism of the society itself?

REDEFINING MISSION

Of the aggregate of all postsecondary educational institutions,[9] as of business enterprises and of foundations, the society is expecting more than in the past. Yet simultaneously colleges and particularly universities "have a bad case of organizational indigestion because they have swallowed multiple and conflicting missions."[10] What missions will the four-year colleges and universities be performing in 1980 as a consequence of readjustment to these conflicting forces during the intervening years?

1. THE TRANSMISSION OF KNOWLEDGE

During the late 1970s from 6.75 to 7.70 million students will be enrolled in institutions of higher education each year. This demand ensures that teaching will continue to be their central and justifying function. As the volume of knowledge in every field expands and as the capabilities and

---

[9] The report of the National Commission on the Financing of Postsecondary Education defines this group to include (*a*) the "Collegiate sector" including 2,948 public and private institutions of higher education; (*b*) the "Non-collegiate sector" comprising 7,016 occupational schools; (*c*) "Other Post-secondary institutions," i.e., about 3,500 vocational and recreational schools; and (*d*) "Other Learning Opportunities," i.e., formal and informal learning programs offered by civic organizations (pp. 14–18).

[10] James A. Perkins, "Missions and Organization: A Redefinition," an essay included in *The University as an Organization* (New York: McGraw-Hill Book Company, 1973), p. 247.

diversity of students increase, teaching becomes a more demanding activity. Thus this basic activity will require of an aging and relatively stable body of teachers (see Chapter 10) expanding comprehension, increased ability to select and emphasize the relevant, and the capacity to inculcate in students a sense of values as well as knowledge.

Teachers will be pressed to increase their productivity and their reach—to aid more students to learn more, despite the intangibility of learning and the varying educability of students, and to provide instruction for many students, not in the classroom but in learning centers remote from the campus, in their homes, and at work. Financial stringencies make likely attempts to replace live teachers by the further development of television, computers, cassettes, and other teaching aids.[11] But the prospect is that, in the future as in the past, teachers will form the core and teaching will be the preeminent function of higher education.

In the aggregate the society will rely on the teachers in this country's four-year colleges and universities to achieve the following four distinguishable and important tasks.

(*a.*) The development of scientists and scholars to serve on the faculties of the various institutions of higher education, and the development of men and women of especial talent who must be equipped to serve as the leaders of business, government, education, the church, and other segments of national life. The first of these responsibilities is to develop individuals capable and willing to concentrate on teaching and on research appropriate to the institution of higher education—not to develop scientists to solve applied problems for business and government. The second of these responsibilities is to discover, to raise the sights of, to broaden the horizons and to hone the intellects of those few endowed young men and women who form an invaluable national resource, and without whom a society can "run down" within a generation. In 1974 it appears that the demand for the development of such scientists and scholars will be less than the probable supply, and the demand for men and women with capacity for broad-gauged leadership will, as in the past, exceed the supply that is developed.

(*b.*) The development of professionals and technicians to serve in agriculture, industry, government, and education. This task is essentially one of vocational education, ranging from the paraprofessional

---

11 For a description of prospective technological developments and their probable impact on the instructional process, on faculties, on students, and on institutional costs, see *The Fourth Revolution, Instructional Technology in Higher Education,* a report and recommendations by the Carnegie Commission on Higher Education (New York: McGraw-Hill Book Company, June 1972).

who is equipped to serve after training of a year or two years to the fully qualified professional agronomist, architect, chemist, forester, lawyer, physician, physicist, social worker, or zoologist. The growth of the national economy, the advance of technology, and the persisting trend toward specialization forecast an enlarged demand for such professionals and technicians.

(*c.*) The provision of basic postsecondary education leading to the baccalaureate degree for all who are capable of meeting a broad admission standard equivalent to graduation from a fully qualified high school. Such a standard college program will comprehend a broadening mixture of general education, vocational education, and content providing a foundation for professional education. The aggregate demand for education in the liberal arts has tended to decrease during the early 1970s but the demand for vocationally oriented programs (e.g., in business administration, in a widening variety of health activities, in law enforcement, in social work, and in education) and for programs that lead to professional training in law and medicine have increased. The aggregate demand will be diminished if programs that permit completion of the baccalaureate-degree program in less than the conventional four years are established and flourish.

(*d.*) The provision of a wide range of postsecondary educational and training programs of both a vocational and cultural character. This task involves serving those who are not able to meet the requirements for admission to the "standard college program" and those adults who seek education to serve particular developmental, recreational, professional, or cultural objectives. The demand for such education will grow because many secondary school graduates now (and an even larger proportion in the future) need further preparation for the world of work. It will grow also because more adults will seek assistance in adapting to a constantly changing environment.

2. THE SOCIALIZATION OF THE YOUNG

Socialization of youth has in the past been a function integrally related to the transmission of knowledge.[12] Young men and women passing from childhood to adulthood gained by their association with teachers and fellow students in the residential college a broader view of the contemporary world. They were introduced to a diversity of viewpoints

---

[12] For a thoughtful and stimulating analysis of the interrelation of these processes see Talcott Parsons and Gerald M. Platt, "General Education and Studentry Socialization: The Undergraduate College," *The American University* (Cambridge, Mass.: Harvard University Press, 1973), chap. 4, pp. 163–224.

and a world of art, music, and culture beyond the parameters of the family in which they spent their childhood. In many instances the paternalism of the small residential college prolonged the period of adolescence, but the colleges and the universities were (and are) expected to aid the student to assume the responsibilities of adulthood, to deal with adults as equals, and to formulate ethical, religious, and political values of their own to replace those impressed upon them by parents.[13]

The growth of enrollments has brought into the institutions of higher education many, and (if, or as long as, enrollments continue to grow) will bring more, young people from a wide variety of backgrounds. The sheer numbers being educated, the more limited association the institution has with a substantial proportion of all who are enrolled, and the greater maturity of many students, particularly those in the graduate and professional schools, limits the extent to which the institution can contribute to the socialization of each student. Moreover in an urban society, those who enroll have been exposed during their adolescent years to a variety of forces—television, the big-city high school, travel, the racial and labor movements, and even the shopping center—that have given them a view of a society outside the home and acquainted them with adults outside the family circle.

Proposals to limit the size of the individual institution (e.g., to no more than 5,000 students) and to establish "cluster colleges" within the large institution constitute efforts to retain the communal character that formerly enabled the college or university to contribute to the socialization of the young. But the clear prospect is that many institutions, particularly the larger urban institutions of higher education, will not in the future perform effectively this much needed socialization function for those who attend classes on their campuses and will not attempt to perform this function for those served in their places of work and elsewhere. The more the pity, for the other socializing institutions of our society—the family, the church, and the community—are less able to perform this function than in the past.

3. THE CERTIFICATION OF GRADUATES

Certification has long been a prime function of the college or university. In the dim past, this function was limited to the equipment of young

---

13 Arthur W. Chickering identifies seven "vectors of development" for the young adult and identifies seven elements of the college and university making a difference to student development in an illuminating discussion of the socialization process (*Education and Identity*, San Francisco: Jossey-Bass, Inc., Publishers, 1969).

people for those professions (teaching, law, medicine, and the ministry) and business activities (e.g., the sale of securities) in which privileged members of the society earned their living. As enrollments have grown, first knowledge and then employment have become increasingly specialized, and institutions have been pressed to certify that their graduates are equipped for employment in fields ranging from accounting to zoology.

Much criticism has been voiced of the continual striving by students and the reliance by employers and the public on degrees, and increasingly on degrees purporting to evidence the grasp of specialized areas of knowledge, e.g., the bachelor of science in medical technology, the bachelor of science in accounting, the bachelor of science in physical education. The assumption that completion of specified courses equips the individual for the performance of a profession or paraprofession misleads both the student and the prospective employer. The emphasis on specialization equips some individuals for professions and paraprofessions the demand for which is diminishing or will disappear, and, worse, it limits the development of a broadly "educated" individual.

Yet the institution of higher education will likely be expected to place greater rather than less emphasis on this certification function than in the past. The persistent growth and subdivision of knowledge will create new areas of specialization. New professions and paraprofessions will emerge. Each will, as the older professions have in the past, strive to raise the standards for entrance and will look to the institution of higher education to collaborate in fixing these higher standards and to tend the entry gates to the profession. Moreover, increasing concern with the protection of the consumer (e.g., the patient treated by the physical therapist) will reinforce the demands of the professions that these institutions certify the qualifications of individuals to serve the public or employers in many fields.

4. THE CONDUCT OF RESEARCH

The persistent effort to discover new knowledge and to integrate what is discovered into the whole body of accumulated knowledge is fundamental to higher education, for education is more than the transmission of what is known; it is the inculcation of a process of learning, the development of intellectual curiosity. Second, research (at least in the sense of scholarship) is essential in order that faculty members may continue to learn and grow.[14] Third, in modern societies the key institu-

---

[14] Dael Wolfle, *The Home of Science* (New York: McGraw-Hill Book Company, 1972), p. 134.

tions and "the powers that be"—in business enterprises, in the colleges and universities, in most major metropolitan areas, and in the society at large—"are increasingly dependent upon intellectuals, particularly those in universities, research institutes, and the cultural apparatus generally."[15] Fourth, research not only is an educational activity, it also provides an essential source of income to support itself and, importantly, to support graduate education.

These four reasons for the maintenance of research as a function integral to higher education apply with differing force to each of the four-year colleges and universities. Research, in terms of scholarship, i.e., the continual study that enables the teacher to "keep up" and that enriches teaching, is not pursued by a substantial proportion of all teachers in the four-year colleges or in the less prestigious universities.[16] Research in terms of the search for new knowledge (aided by grants from foundations such as the National Institutes of Health, the National Science Foundation, the Atomic Energy Commission, or other agencies) is carried on by an even smaller number of scholars predominantly in (approximately one hundred) more prestigious universities. Research into the application of knowledge to the solution of problems (under contract by the Department of Defense, the National Aeronautics and Space Administration, and other agencies and business enterprises) utilizes the services of a larger but small proportion of all faculty members in the major universities, often in relatively separate institutes or laboratories, and has little impact on the instruction of other than a few graduate students.

In the future, research that is an extension of scholarship, the reading and inquiring that the true scholar inevitably does to deepen his understanding, will be encouraged as in the past. The truly basic research that produces new knowledge will be continued, but predominantly in those universities with the ablest faculties and the best facilities.

On the other hand, there is a growing "conviction that universities are not the place to obtain effective interdisciplinary research on societal problems."[17] (See the discussion Chapter 7.) This conviction is coupled with a substantial body of opinion which holds that the resources of

---

15 Ibid., p. 137.

16 Arnold Toynbee has argued that it now "seems . . . beyond human capacity for faculties to practice on 'traditional lines' both teaching and research." He bases this view on the reasoning that "the pace of change has become so rapid that the quantum of change that a human being now has to digest within a lifetime has become almost too great for human nature to cope with it" (cited in *The Future of the University*, a report to the people by the Executive Planning Committee of the University of Oklahoma, 1969, p. xxii).

17 Wolfle, op. cit., p. 137.

universities should not be used to pursue military objectives. These convictions forecast that interdisciplinary research focused on solving applied problems and, at the least, those problems posed by this country's military establishment will be abandoned. The divorce of its major laboratories by the Massachusetts Institute of Technology is a step that likely will be followed by other institutions. Generally, there will be an effort to limit research within the university to that which has some clear value to the instruction carried on within the institution.[18]

5. THE PROVISION OF SERVICES

Provision of services has been defined as the application of special knowledge to the solution of problems in the larger society. The variety of services now provided by universities and some colleges gives a broad interpretation to this definition.[19]

Many university faculties include especially qualified individuals who possess scarce talent and knowledge that are useful and often needed in resolving urgent problems and in providing services such as those that have been identified.[20] Yet many observers of university operations contend that universities should limit their activities to the discovery and transmission of knowledge and should accept no obligation for the application of knowledge to the solution of social issues.[21] They argue, and others have argued for decades in the past, that the assumption of obligations for the provision of services limits the objectivity of faculty members as well as the interest and attention they devote to teaching. On the other hand, some contend that: "The universities are called

---

[18] "Report of the President's Committee on the Future of the University of Massachusetts," December 1971, pp. S9 and 79–82.

[19] A typical state university may assist (a) local communities with the study and solution of current problems (e.g., the revision of tax systems or the overcoming of air pollution), (b) the state government in identifying and solving similar problems, (c) the poor (e.g., by providing legal services, designing special educatonal programs), (d) the professons in maintaining and developing their skills (e.g., by retraining physicians and by training paramedical personnel), (e) the public schools with the refinement of curricula and instructional methods, (f) farmers in improving breeds of cattle and planting and fertilization, and (g) business firms in maximizing their profitability. This statement of the variety of services provided is adapted from a prescription of the public services that could be provided by the University of Massachusetts (ibid., pp. 97–106).

[20] For a development of this line of reasoning see John J. Corson, "Public Service and Higher Education: Compatibility or Conflict?" in Dobbins and Lee, eds., *Whose Goals for American Higher Education?* (Washington: American Council on Education, 1969), pp. 83–90.

[21] See, e.g., Robert Nisbet, *The Degradation of the Academic Dogma* (San Francisco: Jossey-Bass, Inc., Publishers, 1971).

upon not to stop serving society, but to take direct and vigorous steps to broaden the nature of the clientele they serve, so as to include more than the Establishment."[22] And, since an increasing proportion of those institutions that provide public services are publicly supported, it is unlikely that those institutions will reject the calls made upon them by state and local governments, by the poor, the professions, the farmers, or by important tax-paying businesses throughout the state.

6. THE OBSERVATION AND APPRAISAL OF SOCIETY

The growth during the 1960s of the range of services provided has tended to create a mistaken notion of its function at the very time when the institution of higher education has become visible to a much larger proportion of the citizenry. This notion is that these institutions exist to (*a*) "train" large numbers of persons (a function that has been magnified in the public eye by the expanding demand for specialized manpower and by the spread of community colleges), (*b*) aid by applying knowledge to a wide variety of problems, and (*c*) supply qualified members of the faculty to serve in government and elsewhere.

This is a sterile concept of a college or university. If learning—by students and by faculty—is to be vital, it involves continual questioning of the status quo. The search for new knowledge, the quest for truth necessarily involves, in teaching as well as in research, the evaluation of existing institutions and the prevailing culture. If the institution of higher eductaion is dedicated to learning (in a dynamic rather than a rote fashion), it inevitably serves as the critic of society.

In the last quarter of the twentieth century, the question will be recurrently raised as to whether faculty members of the college or university shall be free to criticize the society and particularly the government upon which these institutions are dependent for support. The intimacy of the "compact society" and the pervasiveness of the means of communication illumine challenging questions and criticisms that in decades past would have gone unnoticed.

Higher education cannot be responsible for developing inquiring minds, for proposing change, and for producing new knowledge without "stepping on toes." A persisting tension between the institutions of higher education and the society has been normal. The maintenance of an environment within which rational, objective inquiry and examination can go on, and simultaneously the maintenance of the right to

---

22 David Easton, "The Political Obligations of the University," *AGB Reports*, vol. 14, no. 6, March 1972, p. 5.

affect the course of the society that supports it, is an essential—although less assured—function for the future.[23]

PROSPECTIVE STRUCTURE

During the 1950s and 1960s, as the number of institutions of higher education grew rapidly, the structure of this country's higher education industry was altered markedly. New institutions, particularly community colleges, appeared. Many institutions changed their roles: some two-year colleges became four-year colleges; branches of universities attained independence as colleges; the "state teachers colleges" became first liberal arts colleges and then some became regional universities offering graduate and professional education.

Functions once performed almost exclusively by the four-year college and university were claimed by other institutions. The community college provided instruction for a growing proportion of all undergraduates. Profit-making proprietary colleges and schools gained a stronger foothold and an improved image in the field of postsecondary education, particularly in the provision of technical training.[24] With the community colleges the proprietary institutions assumed a large responsibility for certifying many young people who enter occupations requiring technical skills. The "think tanks" emerged to do research for governmental agencies and business firms. Private business firms contracted with government to perform research in the "hard sciences" and to solve problems requiring applied research and development and, in some instances, to operate proprietary schools. Some professional associations (e.g., the American Society of Clinical Pathologists) undertook the training of paraprofessionals, and others took on responsibility for formulating curricula the colleges would use in their respective fields.

---

[23] For a fuller discussion of the relation of the institution and society, see Eldon Johnson, "Confrontation: University and Public," *From Riot to Reason* (Urbana: University of Illinois Press, 1972), chap. 2, pp. 30–51. According to Johnson, this essential institutional-social relationship requires that: (1) the public's view of the institution as an objective searcher of truth should be maintained; (2) "a distinction between corporate and individual views and acts" should also be maintained; (3) "the university must be free to do whatever it takes to keep relevant in its age," e.g., the university must be involved; (4) "the university must not lose its 'critical capacity'—the critical competence which inheres in the specialists and the custodians of knowledge who make up the faculty"; (6) "in its external relations the university must not seek power—intellectual power, the power of knowledge, yes; but not legal power or the capacity to coerce"; and (7) it "must not deny its accountability."

[24] Provisions in a succession of acts of Congress during the 1960s, which enabled students to use monies made available for the financing of postsecondary education to pay the charges of the profit-making proprietary institutions, materially altered the status of these institutions.

A leveling off of enrollments and the scarcity of resources prompted in the early 1970s a reassessment of the complex of activities carried on by the various institutions of postsecondary education. That reassessment continues. Meanwhile, the unmanageability of some large institutions, the increasing difficulty of financing many private colleges and universities, and a growing desire to shorten the period of years the individual devotes to education make patent that a substantial distribution of responsibilities and a significant restructuring of the existing nonsystem of more than 2,900 institutions is being brought about by the forces that are at work. That restructuring will affect in varying ways each of the several categories of existing institutions—public and private institutions; the research universities, other doctoral-granting universities, the comprehensive universities, and the liberal arts colleges; the independent, church-related, black, and other colleges; and the specialized institutions.[25] The restructuring is prompted by the forces that are redetermining what the society will expect of those institutions and is being conditioned for each institution by such factors as these:

- Public policies relative to the provision of support (e.g., the diminution of federal aid for graduate education and the increase of aid for "developing" institutions serving black and Spanish-surname students)

- The relative liberality of financial support provided for higher education by the state

- The assignment of functions and roles to public institutions by state coordinating agencies or departments of higher education

- The geographical location (e.g., urban versus rural), the economic and population growth of the area served, and especially the number of institutions competing within the area for available students

- The accumulated resources of the institution, not only in terms of invested endowment, land, and buildings, but as well in terms of a large and attached alumni and ongoing associations with corporate and individual donors

---

25 In visualizing the probable nature of this redistribution, I have studied particularly Carl Kaysen, "Higher Education for Whom, At Whose Cost?" a talk at the Invitational Conference on Testing Problems, sponsored by the Educational Testing Service, Oct. 31, 1970; several volumes in the series of publications issued by the Carnegie Commission on Higher Education, and particularly the essay previously cited, by James A. Perkins, op. cit.; John D. Millett, *Reconstruction of the University*, a brochure published by the University of Cincinnati, October 1968; and Eric Ashby, *The Structure of Higher Education: A World View*, occasional paper no. 6, International Council for Educational Development, 1973.

- The institution's status in the academic community (e.g., its recognition and reputation among the counselors in secondary schools)

That restructuring is destined to alter significantly the structure of the "higher education industry" by 1980. The following table offers *not* a prediction but a suggestion as to what the altered mix of colleges and universities may be by 1980.

CHANGED FUNCTIONS

The forces and factors that have been identified will not only alter the number of each type of institution and the distribution of enrollment among them but, as well, the functions they will perform. Prediction, again, is impossible, but evaluation of the forms of governance required in the future necessitates considered speculation as to what activities will be governed. Such speculation suggests the following.

1. *The doctoral-granting institutions* will tend to decrease the emphasis and resources devoted to undergraduate education. That tendency will be impelled by the enrollment of an increasing proportion of all first-time enrollees in community colleges. But this lessened emphasis on undergraduate education will be postponed, particularly in the private universities, as total enrollments tend to level off. The aggregate of the doctoral-granting universities will "shuck off" much of all applied

	No. of Institutions				Enrollments			
	Percent of Total		Percent Public		Percent of Total		Percent Public	
Type of Institutions*	1970	1980	1970	1980	1970	1980	1970	1980
Doctoral-granting universities	6.2	6.3	62.4	64.7	31.5	30.6	75.0	78.0
Comprehensive universities and colleges	16.0	16.9	68.0	71.5	29.4	28.5	79.0	82.0
Liberal arts colleges	25.4	21.5	3.9	5.2	8.1	4.0	6.0	10.0
Two-year institutions	37.5	40.1	75.9	83.5	27.6	33.4	94.0	97.0
Specialized institutions	14.9	15.2	15.2	17.1	3.4	3.5	37.0	40.0
TOTAL	100.0	100.0	46.4	52.0	100.0	100.0	75.0	86.0

* The typology utilized is a condensation of the classification developed by the Carnegie Commission on Higher Education, *A Classification of Institutions of Higher Education,* 1973. The suggestions as to the likely "mix" in 1980 is the result of analyses of changes affecting each type of institution.

research now being performed under contract and will divest themselves of many affiliated laboratories and institutes.

These doctoral-granting institutions will concentrate, to a greater degree, (*a*) on the task of training those scientists and scholars needed for their own several faculties, and for the professions, particularly law and medicine, and (*b*) on the development of that small minority of young men and women of exceptional capacity who will be needed "to provide new ideas, new techniques, and the statesmanlike treatment of complex social and political problems" without whom "a nation can drop to mediocrity in a generation."[26] This will involve "intellectual interchange between able, highly motivated students and more experienced scholars in an institution heavily engaged in graduate education and research." The great importance to the society of these educational activities will result in more explicit recognition and support of the 50 to 90 preeminent "research universities" that form the intellectual core of this country's higher education industry.[27]

2. *The "comprehensive universities and colleges"* are those institutions that now concentrate predominantly on undergraduate education in the liberal arts as well as in such career-oriented areas as teaching, nursing, engineering, and business administration, while offering master's degrees and in a few instances doctor's degrees in a limited number of fields. These institutions, and particularly those among them located in large urban centers, are, and will increasingly be, the "work horses" of undergraduate education. Their undergraduate programs will likely be increased in number and variety to fill the demand for specialized manpower while their desires to expand graduate programs will be thwarted by limited financial resources. These institutions will produce a rising proportion of the teachers; social workers; health workers; librarians; foresters; engineers; business and public administrators; restaurant, hotel, and food-service professionals; and such other professionals and paraprofessionals as are determined (by their professional associa-

---

26 Sir Eric Ashby, *Any Person, Any Study: An Essay on Higher Education in the United States* (New York: McGraw-Hill Book Company, 1971), p. 101; see also T. R. McConnell, "Can the Elite University Survive?" *The Research Reporter,* University of California, Berkeley, vol. 8, no. 2, 1973, p. 7.

27 For a supporting view see Kenneth Roose, "Fifty Top Rated Institutions: Their Role in Graduate Education," *The Research Reporter,* University of California, Berkeley, no. 1, 1971; for a contrary view as to the desirability of identifying and supporting a group of universities as "national universities," see William E. Petrowski, Evan L. Brown, and John A. Duffy, " 'National Universities' and the ACE Ratings," *Journal of Higher Education,* October 1973, pp. 495–513.

tions or the educational institutions) to require a baccalaureate degree.[28]

Among these institutions there will be less and less diversity of educational programs. They will likely concentrate, to a greater degree than in the past, on the provision of programs that are increasingly standardized (a chilling concept) within each state by the impact of state coordinating agencies and accrediting associations and, more generally, by the influence of professional associations. In the face of these impacting pressures there will be a continuing effort to broaden curricula and to raise the level of accomplishment attained by a diverse body of students who seek the baccalaureate degree.

The admission standards of these institutions are not exacting and will not likely be raised as enrollments level off or decline. Faculties will be made up predominantly of individuals who concentrate on teaching and do not profess simultaneously to be researchers.

3. *The liberal arts colleges* are destined to decline in number and in enrollments. That decline will result from the likely closing, or absorption by other institutions, particularly of public and small private institutions with enrollments in 1970 of less than 750 students, many of which are church-related. Enrollments in those private liberal arts colleges will be reduced by the persisting competition of lower tuition in public institutions, particularly the community colleges.

The more selective and relatively prestigious private liberal arts colleges (approximately one-fifth of the total of all liberal arts colleges, and including the "Tiffanys" of American higher education) will persist in offering luxury-like, diverse, residential programs for the relatively few students whose parents can afford, and will pay for, this type of educational experience. The price of survival for these institutions will include a gradual lowering of admission standards and conversion to coeducation by those that have served a single sex. The curricula of these erstwhile elite liberal arts colleges will tend increasingly to parallel those of competing public institutions unless those who lead these institutions will imaginatively combine the essence of the liberal arts curriculum with such vocationally oriented courses, work experiences, and exposure to practitioners as will give a new vitality and realism to the educational offering.[29] Such diversity as they maintain (and this diversity may be

---

28 For a fuller consideration of the prospective role of the regional state universities see Fred F. Harcleroad, H. Bradley Sagen, C. Theodore Moler, *The Developing State Colleges and Universities,* American College Testing Program, 1969, pp. 102–114.

29 See the comment by Landrum Bolling, then president of Earlham College, in *The Earlhamite,* Winter 1973; and Lewis Mayhew, "Academic and Social Goals and Values," *Journal of Higher Education,* March 1972, p. 184.

the *sine qua non* of survival!) will rest increasingly on the physical and social environment established in the past and the extent to which the earlier accumulation of endowments, physical facilities, and loyal alumni permit them to continue in the ways of their past.

Their faculties will be made up, in principal part, of those individuals now serving on their staffs and the graduates of major research universities who are not recruited by those institutions and who choose not to accept assignments in the larger, urban, more production-like comprehensive colleges and universities.

The decline in number of institutions and in enrollment will be experienced by the greater number of less selective and less prestigious liberal arts colleges. These institutions will bear the brunt of the competition of lower tuition public institutions and from the trends toward commuting and part-time attendance. To survive many will modify their educational programs, incorporating an increasing variety of career-oriented programs and programs designed to attract transfer students from the community colleges and part-time students. Admission standards have been lowered in many instances and will continue to be less selective than prior to 1970. The retrenchment that will force the reduction in number of faculty members will make recruitment of qualified replacements increasingly difficult.

4. *The community colleges* will become increasingly the vestibule for those going on beyond the high school. They will in effect serve as the "lower division" of many neighboring four-year institutions. These institutions will resist efforts by competing private and public colleges and universities to force them to abandon university parallel-college transfer programs, which during the early 1970s attracted an increasing proportion of all secondary school graduates in many states. They will strive to maintain lower tuition rates (or no tuition) and, in succeeding, will likely attract a growing proportion of all first-time enrollees (perhaps 60 percent by 1980).

The community colleges serve, and will increasingly serve, the broader function of community service. This involves the provision of a wide range of opportunities for vocational and adult education. But it includes as well serving as the hub of a network of institutions and community agencies—the high schools, industry, the church, voluntary agencies, youth groups, the prisons, and still other agencies in making available developmental opportunities for all who can be induced to participate.

Those functions are gaining such general acceptance in a "knowledge society" as to ensure that the number of institutions that has grown rapidly will increase and that the enrollment in community colleges will approximate one-third of the aggregate enrolled in institutions of higher education.

5. *The specialized institutions* include a miscellany of educational enterprises not affiliated with other colleges and universities. This considerable number of institutions includes theological seminaries; medical schools and medical centers; other separate health professional schools; independent schools of engineering and technology; schools of business management; schools of art, music, and design; law schools; teachers colleges; maritime academies; the military academies; and a small number of other specialized institutions.

The prospects for these institutions vary by type and by source of financing. Some among the smaller theological seminaries (all private, of course) will disappear in the early future. The number of public medical schools and the enrollments in both public and private institutions will grow. The teachers colleges will face a declining demand and their numbers and enrollments will likely shrink. The three military academies, the enrollments of which make up nearly 40 percent of the aggregate enrollment of all specialized institutions faced with unprecedented difficulties in recruitment and a large attrition among enrollees, can be expected to survive; but these academies face the need for some redefinition of mission.

STEPS TOWARD BETTER GOVERNANCE

Greater restructuring than has been described would be required if the existing 2,900 institutions were to be made into "an efficient, economic national system of higher education." But there is little evidence that an efficient, economic national system of higher education would serve this nation well. There is need for a constructive effort to overcome the diseconomies and the mediocrity of much that has been offered by overly ambitious institutions that have strived to be "all things to all men" and by the smallest institutions with inadequate resources. There is a still more urgent need for strength in the individual institutions, for free enterprise sufficient to enable each (or many at the least) to develop individual and distinctive programs while the prospective restructuring that is impelled by the forces at work in the American society goes on.

The building of that internal strength has to be accomplished despite the struggle among constituencies that has been going on in many institutions, despite the undermining of leadership that has tended to make headless many institutions, and despite the strains that growth in size and proliferation of activities have placed on organizational structures ill adapted to the academic function.

The Distribution of
Authority for Governance

*The distribution of authority and responsibility among the
various members of the university is now in question as it
has not been for generations.*   McGeorge Bundy[1]

12 The one change that had taken place in their institutions in the
recent past that college and university presidents regarded as
"most significant," when asked in 1969, was change in the
distribution of "internal authority."[2] More specifically they referred to
"increases in faculty authority" and "increases in student authority."
This judgment was voiced by presidents of both public and private institutions, large and small institutions, institutions granting only undergraduate degrees, and doctoral-granting institutions.

The diffusion of responsibility for making decisions in a college or
university makes essential both clear understanding by all participants
of the responsibility of each and mechanisms for enlisting and integrating the energies, initiative, and zeal of the large number among whom
responsibility for decision making is shared. The administration of colleges and universities is a continuum in which trustees, presidents,
deans, department chairpersons, faculty members, and students within
and the alumni, professional groups, and governmental authorities without have interrelated and mutually responsible parts to play.[3]

To allow the educational and student development programs of a college or university to be shaped solely by students' choices of courses
and programs and the formal demands they make through an articulate
minority is essentially an abdication by academic administrators and the
faculty of their responsibility for educational guidance. To allow the
educational and student-development programs to be shaped solely by
the faculty is to risk the framing of discipline-oriented programs little
related to the knowledge needs students will face upon graduation. To

---

1 From a speech made at the inauguration of President Malcolm Moos of the
University of Minnesota entitled "The Faculty and the President," May 8,
1968.

2 Harold L. Hodgkinson, *Institutions in Transition* (New York: McGraw-Hill
Book Company, 1971), p. 219.

3 See the 1966 "Statement on Government of Colleges and Universities" of the
American Association of University Professors for a supporting view.

let these programs be shaped by the pressures from articulate and powerful professional groups in the community (e.g., accountants, nurses, policemen, real estate salesmen, and teachers) is to risk making the institution a credential mill rather than an educational institution. For academic administrators to acquiesce without vigorous rebuttal to many of the decisions of state authorities is to stultify innovation and to undermine faculty morale. For trustees to rubber stamp program proposals made by faculty members and academic administrators is to fail in their responsibility to bring to bear on such proposals understanding of the needs and will of citizens and taxpayers.

The two constituencies whose parts have been magnified by developments over the past decade are, as the presidents pointed out, faculty members and students. That magnification has altered the arrangements for governance in many institutions. Hence, this chapter analyzes the part being played in institutional governance by each of these constituencies, the logic on which their participation is founded, and the parts each will likely play in the future.

THE FACULTY'S ROLE IN GOVERNANCE

BASES OF FACULTY PARTICIPATION

The logic of faculty participation in governance (as of student participation) rests in part on two fundamental ideas. One is the democratic belief that those affected by governing decisions have a right to be heard by those making the decisions. The second is that the zeal of individuals within an enterprise will be more fully mobilized if those individuals are granted a voice in determining what shall be done and how. But, as Morris Keeton has written, "The primary justification is that faculty alone have the minds and degree of qualification essential to the task of the college or university."[4] That "qualification" for a part in the interdependent process of governance is rooted in three facts:

1. Faculty members are experts. They bring to the institution (in varying measures, of course) expertise in their subject-matter fields. They possess the basic stock-in-trade that students seek when enrolling in a college or university.

2. Faculty members are intellectuals—that is, a substantial proportion are. They are learning people, committed to the pursuit of knowl-

---

[4] *Shared Authority on Campus* (Washington, D.C.: American Association for Higher Education, 1971), p. 11.

edge, and thus equipped to develop inquiring, reasoning minds. Men and women with a true intellectual bent must be allowed freedom to explore, to voice their findings, and to have them heard.

3. Faculty members are professionals. The hallmark of professionalism is the right of self-direction. For the administration to tell a talented and trained individual *how* he shall do what he has been trained and experienced to do is both foolhardy and wasteful. The professional anthropologist or zoologist must be given freedom to influence substantially those decisions as to courses, programs, and modes of teaching that are involved in the governance of a college or university.

CONCEPTS OF DECISION MAKING

To understand the part of the faculty (or of students) in the interrelated processes by which decisions are made in a college or university, two concepts must be understood: the concepts of primal and communal authority.

Mary Parker Follett, perhaps the first American woman to write about problems of organization and management, pictured realistically the nature of organizational decision making.[5] She made it clear that the process includes the formulation of a proposal, the consideration of the proposal by affected and informed parties, consultation among the parties, and finally the articulation of a decision by the individual or body with formal authority to decide. She emphasized that decision making is a process, not an act that takes place at a moment in time. The essential decision is one that reflects "communal authority" when the process is carried out in such a way as to assure a consensus among the parties affected. But in each decision that party or individual possessing particular understanding of the issue or being especially affected may be granted what is described as "primal authority," i.e., the right to formulate the proposal that shall be considered.

As colleges and universities attract increasingly well-qualified faculty members, many trained at the more prestigious universities, and as institutions grow in size, pressures for expansion of the faculty's authority are advanced. These pressures generate conflict and the prospects for conflict between the faculty and those who hold hierarchical power

---

5 *Dynamic Administration* (New York: Harper & Bros., 1940), pp. 146–150.

are increased as the institution grows in size and the number of faculties and the diversity among faculty members are increased.[6]

DECISION-MAKING AREAS

The areas of decision making in which the faculty—as individuals, as groups (committees or departments), or as a whole—is granted an opportunity to participate vary from institution to institution, as tradition, the aggressiveness of the faculty, and the nature and attitudes of the president and trustees dictate. The role of the faculty is most limited in those institutions that have recently emerged from community college or normal school teachers' college status. It is larger in the longer-established universities. It tends to be largest in the prestigious liberal arts colleges (e.g., Antioch, Amherst, Wesleyan, and Williams) and in the national research universities (e.g., Harvard, Stanford, Michigan, and California). Generally the faculty participates, with varying degrees of primal authority, in seven areas of decision making.

The faculty is usually granted a substantial responsibility for making decisions as to *academic policy.* Such decisions include those dealing with the organization of academic departments, the framing of educational programs, degree requirements, the content of courses, assignment of teachers to courses, and patterns of student education. In summary, the faculty shapes decisions as to what shall be taught, who shall teach it, what shall be required of students, and the freedom students shall have to frame their own programs. Viewed in relation to the purpose of a college or university, these several decisions go far toward determining the character of the institution.

If administrators or trustees differ with decisions as to matters of academic policy (or of research, the provision of services, or personnel actions) the bases for their objections should be openly stated and the faculty's reconsideration requested. The substitution of the president's or the trustees' judgment for a faculty proposal in these areas should be infrequent.

A second and closely related area in which the authority of the faculty, and particularly the individual faculty member, is great is that of *research.* As an intellectual he is logically authorized to apply his energies and much of his time where his interests and capabilities direct

---

[6] See J. Victor Baldridge, "College Size and Professional Freedom," *Change,* May 1973, pp. 11–12, 63–64. In this article Baldridge reports the results of a study of "decision making and power" in 300 colleges, universities, and community colleges.

him. This freedom has been circumscribed by the right of academic administrators to determine what resources—time, funds, space, equipment—can be made available. More recently, it has been circumscribed by decisions of the whole faculty and/or of administrators and trustees that members of the faculty would not be supported in types of research deemed socially undesirable—e.g., "classified" research, research related to the waging of war.

Faculty members, as individuals, are granted substantial, but not uninfluenced, authority to decide what *services* they will provide to claimants or clients outside of the institution. Their personal decisions will be guided by interest and the prospect of financial compensation. Those decisions may be influenced by pressure from administrators, particularly in the public institutions, who would encourage faculty to undertake services for groups whose support will benefit the institution and in activities that enhance its image.

Personnel decisions, i.e., those with respect to hiring, promotion, the granting of tenure, retirement and dismissal of faculty members are, and should be, usually entrusted to the faculty. That authority is effectively delegated to the departments. It is delegated on the reasoning that as professionals, faculty members alone are qualified to pass judgment on the capabilities of individuals who will be expected to teach, perform research, or render services requiring expertise in a particular discipline.

Such decisions normally are made by the departmental chairperson or departmental faculty, subject to budgeted limits as to the number of posts. Recommendations as to *who* shall be promoted are similarly made by the individual's colleagues when funds are made available by the president or the dean of a school.

The president and trustees bear responsibility for the overall quality of the institution's faculty. That involves ensuring that the selection processes followed by the faculty are adequate, for ensuring that only faculty members adjudged by their peers to be fully qualified attain professorial rank and tenure, as well as for ensuring that the total annual payroll is within the institution's resources.

Personnel decisions that often cause conflict originate when a departmental faculty is obviously unbalanced, i.e., is made up of individuals voicing a particular ideology or school of thought, or is clearly less competent than the standard prevailing in other departments of the institution. In such instances, the president and trustees have an obligation to act. They can do this by convening an ad hoc committee of peers serving in the same subject-matter field in other institutions (the more prestigious the better) to review the operations of the faltering department and to recommend action to be taken by the president and trustees.

Authority to make *decisions as to the composition of the student body*, and as to those aspects of student life that will affect the educational process (other than in the professional schools), is sometimes claimed by faculties. Generally, however, the faculties of the undergraduate schools in universities with enrollments of 5,000 or more students exhibit no substantial concern with either area of decision making.

Their disinterest results in the flow of authority for decisions in these areas to those members of the president's staff who carry the administrative responsibility for these activities, particularly the director of admissions and the dean of students. Yet if the faculty is concerned with the development of young men and women, rather than merely with the conduct of courses and research in subject-matter fields, it should manifest a continuing interest in admissions and in the impact of the whole institution on the individual. That broader concern will ideally be manifested in the day-to-day relationship of teachers and students. It should also be manifested in the functioning of faculty committees that work with and oversee the admissions and student personnel activities.

A voice in *financial decisions* as to the acquisition of revenues through fund raising, tuitions, appropriations and the management of endowments, and the allocation of revenues among various areas of expenditure was asserted by faculties with increasing vigor as the relative plentitude of resources enjoyed during the 1960s evaporated in the early 1970s. Faculty members have a natural, personal interest in the whole range of such financial decisions, and at times the faculty as a body will be deeply concerned with particular budgetary decisions. Their dependence upon the financial well being of the institution entitles them to full information about such decisions and an opportunity to voice such views as they wish to be considered. Their part in financial decision making, however, is generally limited to the formulation of recommendations as to the annual budget. The faculties of an increasing proportion of all four-year colleges and universities have gained an influential role in the formulation of the annual budget. Particular weight is logically accorded their recommendations as to expenditures needed for the broad educational program. But it is their views as to faculty compensation, a major element in the total annual budget, that are pressed with especial vigor. Assurance that such views will receive earnest consideration is increased by the advent of collective bargaining on some campuses, the growth of the faculty's voice on others, and the threat of faculty organization on many others.

Faculties generally claim a part in and are usually invited to participate in *the selection of academic administrators*—the president, members of his staff (e.g., vice president for academic affairs, director of admissions, dean of students), and particularly the deans and department chairpersons. They are dependent on department chairpersons and deans to represent them in aspects of governance critical to their interests. In the longer run, their educational objectives and their personal welfare are substantially dependent upon the caliber and philosophy of those individuals who serve as president and upon the president's staff. Hence, equity dictates that these several academic administrators should not be selected without full information being given the whole faculty and prospective selectees being discussed with the appropriate faculty committee or its ad hoc representatives.

To add perspective to this depiction of faculty decision making three areas in which faculties are often adjudged to be unqualified must be identified. Faculties are usually deemed to be little qualified to assist in the resolution of questions of administrative feasibility. They are regarded as equally unqualified to contribute to the making of decisions having to do with public relations. And, most important, faculties are sometimes deemed to be little qualified to cope with such broad socio-educational issues as the inclusion of ROTC courses in the institution's educational program.

ORGANIZATION FOR DECISION MAKING

Most institutions of higher education have three levels of organization to formulate the faculty's views on the foregoing types of decisions. The basic unit through which a faculty makes most decisions for which it has primal authority is the department made up of the faculty members of a particular discipline (philosophy) or disciplines (behavioral sciences). Decisions as to the content of individual courses, the substance of research to be carried on, and methods of instruction (to the extent that they are influenced by other than the individual professor) are arrived at by the department.[7] Decisions as to the hiring, promotion, retirement, and dismissal of individual members of the faculty are usually made by the department. The faculty's views as to the makeup of the student body, the processes of admission, the allocation of resources among all activities of the institution (rather than the allocation to the individual department and school) proposed in the annual budget are

---

[7] For a description of the role of the department see Marven W. Peterson, *The Organization of Departments*, Research Report No. 2, American Association for Higher Education, Dec. 1, 1970; Stanley Ikenberry and Renee C. Friedman, *Beyond Academic Departments* (San Francisco: Jossey-Bass, Inc., Publishers, 1972), pp. 101–102; and Paul Dressel, F. Craig Johnson, and Philip M. Marcus, *The Confidence Crisis* (San Francisco: Jossey-Bass, Inc., Publishers, 1970).

usually shaped and expressed through faculty committees, standing committees on academic affairs and financial affairs, or ad hoc committees created to formulate opinions on particular problems as they arise. Finally, and importantly, the faculty senate in most institutions represents and legislates for the entire teaching body, and oftentimes includes in its membership representatives of the library, computer center, and student personnel staffs. The faculty senate is, in many instances, a large and unwieldy body that attracts to its regular meetings, usually held monthly, only a minority of its members. Yet it is through this mechanism that decisions entrusted to the whole faculty are made.

THE ROLE OF STUDENTS IN GOVERNANCE

LOGIC OF STUDENT ROLE

That student participation in the governance of a college or university is consistent with our democratic values was recognized and advocated early in this country's history when Thomas Jefferson proposed that a student senate be made part of the governing machinery of the University of Virginia.[8] That early effort to grant students a role in the governance of the institutions they attended, however, had little influence on the patterns of internal governance that developed during subsequent decades. Paternalistic attitudes that viewed students as wards limited their part in governance to student social and recreational affairs on most campuses, and often subject to the close supervision of faculty members.

These attitudes and the patterns of governance that prevailed until the 1960s were subjected to severe attack. The extent of student unrest and their demonstration of power during the years 1964–1972 forced reconsideration of their role in governance. Their manifestation of grievances against the institutions and the society illuminated the illogic of the arrangements that existed and the need for institutionalizing new forms of student participation. Four arrangements for a larger role rapidly gained acceptance.

Some observers argued, as Thomas Jefferson had suggested more than a century earlier, that American beliefs in democracy justified the granting of a voice in institutional governance to students. Others contended that since higher education had become relatively essential for a substantial proportion of all young men and women, their dependence on

---

[8] Gary Knock, "Institutionalization of Student Part in the Academic Community," *Journal of the National Association of Women Deans and Counsellors*, Summer 1971.

the educational institution warranted their being given a voice in the governance of the institution. Recognition that students are more mature and more sophisicated than those of earlier generations and the underwriting of this fact by the legal recognition of individuals eighteen years of age as adults constituted a third, and influential, argument. Finally, the fourth argument advanced was that participation in governance offered substantial educative values.

On the other hand, there were those who contended that students lack the experience and knowledge needed to enable them to participate in policy making. Students, it was emphasized, are transient members of the academic community. And it was argued that students must give primary attention to academic responsibilities, and, hence, have little time to devote to governance.

Influential in resolving these counterarguments was the demonstration of student power manifested on many campuses. That demonstration of power was made during a period in which other previously submerged groups—the urban poor, blacks, organized workers, and even some younger members of the hierarchy of the Catholic church—were demanding a larger voice in decisions that affected their work and their lives. The result was a marked expansion of the authority accorded students in the processes of institutional decision making.

AUTHORITY OF STUDENTS

As with the faculty, the role accorded students in governance varies as among types of institutions and from campus to campus. The significance of the generally apparent expansion of their role is clear when viewed in terms of separate areas of decision making.

STUDENT LIFE Generally students have been granted primal authority for decisions as to social and other extracurricular activities of the student body. These activities include student publications, student organizations, operation of the student center, and such services as bookstores, travel bureaus, placement agencies, residential facilities, and others which exist to serve students. In addition, students are authorized to propose rules of conduct and to consult with institutional administrators, usually the dean of students, as to the formulation of such rules as are to be issued. These rules include regulations as to living in dormitories and fraternity houses, the use and parking of automobiles, association among male and female students, and conduct in public places. And students have been granted on many campuses the right to participate with institutional administrators in framing standards for disciplinary action and procedures for enforcement.

FINANCIAL AND BUSINESS AFFAIRS   Academic administrators and trustees less often accept as valid students' claims for a part in decision making as to the institution's financial affairs. Students have an obvious interest in and contribution to make to decisions as to the raising of tuition and fees and charges for room and food service, and they have asserted a right to voice their views on these issues to whatever official or body makes the decisions—financial vice president, president, trustees, the state board of higher education, or the state legislature. Students have sought and usually gained authority to voice their views as to the institution's annual budget (e.g., the proportions allocated to various auxiliary services), the management of endowments (e.g., the extent of investments in corporations producing war materiel or those operating in South Africa) and capital expenditures (e.g., the relative need for a library versus a dormitory, classroom building, or student center).

Students have also claimed a part in decisions as to a widening range of operational policies. Such decisions include those fixing the hours during which the library and dining rooms are open. Decisions as to the procedures followed by police on the campus have engendered more conflict but the greater influence of students is apparent. And students have usually been granted the opportunity to participate in decisions as to regulations concerning vehicle parking.

Students bring less understanding and little experience to the consideration of issues arising in several of these areas of governance. If listened to, they can provide pertinent views and some counterforce to the pressures of dominant interests. Yet while permitted and encouraged to express themselves on this range of issues, their views are often given relatively little weight by financial and business officers, presidents, and trustees.

The authority of students in financial and operational decisions in the future will be related to the immediacy of the impact of each type of decision. If a larger portion of institutional costs are to be borne from tuition income, students will claim and be granted a substantial voice in the determination of these charges and in budgetary decisions as to the use of such revenues. Similarly, if the unionization of faculties spreads, students will gain the right to participate in decisions that might force increased tuitions, might interrupt their educations by the calling of a strike, or might diminish their role in governance.

ACADEMIC AFFAIRS Students have long exercised consider-able power over decisions as to educational programs. Their power derived from their demand for the institution's services: They chose courses and professors; they chose the extracurricular activities in which they would participate. Some dropped out of school. Faculty and admin-istrative decision making, hence, has long been more responsive to such manifestations of demand than has often been admitted. This fact is demonstrated by the elimination of foreign language requirements from many curricula in response to pressure from students.

During the early 1970s, students gained on a considerable number of campuses more formal authority in decision making as to a wide range of academic issues. These include admissions standards; the reten-tion of students; decisions as to curricula, the offering of courses, methods of grading, and processes of appeal on grades; a myriad of logistical questions that condition the academic environment; and the evaluation of professors and courses.

The trend in 1974 clearly was toward granting students an even greater part in making decisions as to each of the foregoing matters. That trend is most apparent in the acceptance of student evaluations of courses and of instructors as a useful means of improving the educa-tional program. It is also apparent in the consultation with students as to such matters as the scheduling of courses, library policies, and meth-ods of grading. And it is apparent on a minority of all campuses, in the provision of opportunities for student participation in establishing admission policies and in the planning and conduct of efforts to increase enrollments.[9] Kingman Brewster explained and interpreted this trend when he wrote that "in a world in which ideas, and policies and institu-tions have a high rate of obsolescence, the young are more perceptive if you will than their elders."[10]

On a small but growing number of campuses this participative role of students in decision making for academic affairs is institutionalized by including students on departmental committees composed of faculty members and students, or by creating student advisory committees for

[9] Earl J. McGrath has suggested that there is "a serious question of whether such a socially significant decision as to who shall be admitted to college, and under what criteria and circumstances, can properly be left to a single social group, the faculty. Both students and the general public have a deep interest in admissions policies. If their concern is to be reflected in the needed reas-sessment of existing admissions standards, they ought to be represented in such a review" ("Who Should Have the Power?" in Harold Hodgkinson and L. Richard Meeth, eds., *Power and Authority*, San Francisco: Jossey-Bass, Inc., Publishers, 1971, chap. 12, p. 203).

[10] A booklet issued by Yale University, October 1969, including two statements by its president, Kingman Brewster, p. 20.

departments. In other institutions students serve as members of faculty-wide curricula planning committees or on faculty-administration committees concerned with academic programs and academic practices. The area of academic decision making in which students are least often granted a part is that concerned with the hiring, promotion, and compensation of faculty members; this is an area of decision making in which students have manifested an interest, but one for which faculty members resist student involvement.

EXPERIENCE WITH STUDENT PARTICIPATION

Trial and error with student participation in governance during the period 1964–1974 provided the basis for three conclusions. First, the greater maturity of the majority of all students, coupled with their recently gained legal status as adults, warrant their being given the pre-eminent voice in decisions as to student life on the campus. Second, the student viewpoint on financial, operational, and academic issues needs continually to be sought, listened to, and sincerely considered. Third, mechanisms that will select student representatives capable of reflecting the views of most students and that will maintain more sustained interest and participation of students need to be developed.

No authoritative study has examined the extent to which the greater authority granted students has benefited the institution, contributed to the development of the individual student, or created a greater awareness in students and in trustees, presidents, and others of the rights and obligations of students as citizens of the academic community. Available evidence, however, suggests that while students have been granted greater opportunities to participate in governance, their views, particularly with respect to academic and financial affairs, have not been influential. This may be attributable, in part at least, to the fact that students, having won the right to voice their views in decision-making forums, have failed, in many instances, to exercise the authority granted. Their attendance at committee meetings has been notably limited. Their representatives have often been little prepared to discuss scheduled issues. And a small proportion of all students (usually 30 percent or less) have participated in elections on most campuses.

QUESTIONS POSED BUT UNANSWERED

The increase in authority of both faculty and students poses three significant and related questions. Are these constituencies destined to claim still greater power over the governance of colleges and universities? Are faculty and students destined to confront each other as the power of each grows? Will the further extension of faculty and student power negate leadership on the campus?

The prospects for the further extension of faculty and student power are manifest in proposals (and in a few institutions by approval of such proposals) that faculty members and students be added to the governing boards. The prospect is implied by the suggestion that the president and chief administrative officers will be elected or selected by faculty and student representatives.[11] Yet the prospective decline in future enrollments, the increase in the proportion of part-time, less-attached students, and the weakened economic status of the professoriate that will accompany these developments raise doubts as to further extension of the power of either group.

Much of the additional authority that students have won has been at the expense of the faculty, e.g., the right to evaluate professors and courses. While a portion of the faculty has supported this extension of the student voice, a substantial majority of all faculty members resists "control" or "voting power on committees" by students over the content of courses, degree requirements, admissions policy, and faculty appointments and promotions.[12] As the average age of faculty members increases, as it is destined to increase between 1975 and 1985, this resistance is likely to be stiffened.

Finally, as faculties and students have gained power, those responsible for leadership—the department chairperson, dean, or academic vice president, and particularly the president and trustees—have lost power. In the Catholic colleges, the black colleges, and in many comprehensive colleges and universities, in most of which the presidents had occupied a position of substantial power, the reduction of administrative authority was especially apparent. The broadening of participation in decision making at a time when the growth in size and in range of activities made leadership and forceful decision making more rather than less essential, highlighted the simple question: "How do you get everybody into the act and still get some action?"[13] It is this question to which we address the next chapter.

---

11 James A. Perkins, op. cit., pp. 259–260.

12 Carnegie Commission on Higher Education, "Tables from the Carnegie Commission Surveys on Student and Faculty Attitudes," *Governance of Higher Education* (New York: McGraw-Hill Book Company, 1973), app. A, pp. 104–105.

13 Aptly put by Harlan Cleveland in an address before the Asian–United States Educators Conference at Chiang-Mai, Thailand, July 15–20, 1973.

Leadership in the
College or University

People have innumerable reasons for wanting, needing and enjoying vigorous leadership.

... one of the great functions of leaders is to help a society achieve the best that is in it. John W. Gardner[1]

13 Those who make up the college or university have basically identical reasons for "wanting and needing" leadership as do those people who make up other organizations—a corporation, a government department, a military regiment, or a church. These can be simply stated though their nature is difficult to communicate. They are to assist members of the organization in formulating objectives and to relate those objectives to the context in which the organization functions; to assemble needed resources; to maximize the interest and enjoyment of members in their several roles, even to build a sense of superiority in the group as a whole; to monitor and appraise performance; and to represent the enterprise and its members to the external world.

The character of leadership "wanted and needed" varies markedly by type of organization. Contrast for example the kind of leadership that "fits" a large, prestigious law firm; an automated, unionized automobile assembly plant; and a company of marines. Styles of leadership vary among individuals, largely in the degree to which the leader chooses (and is able) to concentrate authority in his own hands or to delegate authority among those he is obligated to lead.

Leadership, in the American society and in its organizations, has been under attack. Previously submerged groups—youth, blacks, women, and the poor—in their struggle for enhanced status, have limited the authority of those now in leadership positions in industry, government, the church, and academia. Specialists have increasingly challenged the ability of generalists to lead. And persisting pressures toward centralization have diminished the authority of leaders at lower levels in many enterprises.

In the college and university these forces have created a dilemma. The growth in enrollments, in aggregate expenditures, in the number

---

[1] *Excellence: Can We Be Equal and Excellent, Too?* (New York: Harper & Brothers, 1961), pp. 23, 126.

of subsidiary units—departments, institutes, schools, centers, and services—and in the size of the faculty have heightened the need for leadership. The expanding involvement of faculty members and many segments of the institution with the off-campus world has created a further demand for integrating and decisive leadership. The growth in power of state coordinating councils and governing boards has made apparent to all within the institution the lessened authority of those formerly believed to be responsible. In summary, when the need for strong, decisive governance is great, the authority of those responsible for leadership—the departmental chairperson, the dean or academic vice president, the president, and the trustees—has been limited.

DEPARTMENTAL CHAIRPERSON

NATURE OF THE DEPARTMENT

The role of departmental chairpersons varies as the departments they are expected to lead vary. Departments vary in number of faculty members as the size of the college or university varies (from as few as 3 or 5 members in the liberal arts college to as many as 75 to 85 members in the large university); they vary in orientation as the stature of the institution varies;[2] they vary in the extent to which they "service" other departments and schools as do the English, mathematics, history, and chemistry departments or focus on the "production" of majors in their discipline or in such professional fields as business administration, nursing, social work. They vary in the extent to which they serve both undergraduate and graduate students. And departments vary with respect to the objectives of their members—undergraduate teaching, graduate teaching-research-publication.

Yet the department, regardless of these variations, is the basic organizational building block of a college or university. The work for which the institution exists is carried out in principal part through the departments. It exerts a major influence on decisions that determine the character of the institution, i.e., such decisions as determine the content of courses, who shall teach them, requirements for majors, the compensation and status of each faculty member, and what students shall be admitted to graduate programs.

---

2 Paul L. Dressel, F. Craig Johnson, and Philip M. Marcus, *The Confidence Crisis* (San Francisco: Jossey-Bass, Inc., Publishers, 1970), pp. 215–219.

THE CHAIRPERSON: ORIGIN AND FUNCTION

To preside over the department a member of the discipline is either selected by the dean, academic vice president, or president, or is elected by members of the department. In most institutions the tenure of the chairperson is indefinite, but usually limited to a few years, e.g., three to five. The selection is usually based more on the teaching ability and seniority of the individual as seen by his colleagues than on any demonstrated capacity for administrative leadership.

Yet effective leadership of a department requires recurring initiation of such activities as these: "budget formulation; selection, promotion and retention of academic staff; faculty salaries; sabbatical leaves; interdepartmental relationships; research grants, educational development, and innovation; university committee membership; discipline representation; professional growth; advice to dean on departmental matters; administration to faculty relationships; new faculty orientation; departmental meetings; adequate nonacademic help; student administration; student advising; class scheduling; student personnel records; faculty load; graduate student application approval, grading standards and practices; and curriculum changes." In addition, effective leadership of a department requires "knowledge of the administrative routine of the college; institutional legislative organization; government grant procedures; policies relating to graduate students; and scholarly productivity of department faculty."[3]

The static department chairperson sees to it that such activities are taken care of; the leader-like chairperson, striving to enhance the reputation of the department, does more. He strives to stimulate his colleagues to enrich course offerings. He encourages innovation in teaching method, prods his colleagues to recruit the most promising graduate students, and strives to seek out able young instructors and occasionally, as opportunities occur, prestigious scholars for ranking posts on the departmental faculty. He helps his colleagues obtain grants to support their research and to provide aid for graduate students. In addition, and importantly, the departmental chairperson represents his colleagues in discussions with the dean and other administrative officers. Simultaneously he or she represents the administration of the institution. He or she has the dual obligation of interpreting to the administration the needs and wishes of the department and of communicating to his or her colleagues the bases for decisions made by the dean, the president, the trustees, or the more remote state coordinating agency.

---

[3] Ibid., p. 13.

CONSTRAINTS

Most departmental chairpersons are expected to discharge these leadership responsibilities while subject to a variety of handicapping constraints. Since his or her professional reputation is based on competence as a teacher and researcher, the departmental chairperson strives "to keep his hand in," to discharge the responsibilities of the chairpersonship while teaching a course and, in the more prestigious institutions, continuing his researches. He is given little staff assistance to handle the correspondence, reports, questionnaires, and other routines associated with departmental operations. He has at hand little organized information as to courses, students, faculty members, or comparative costs.

Each senior member of the department is usually expected to serve as chairperson for a time, but the academic value system in many institutions deprecates those individuals who would strive to hold the position of chairperson for more than a limited period. The chairperson is constrained by the fact that many departments' bylaws stipulate that most decisions are made by a faculty executive committee, by the whole faculty, or by the chairperson only after he has consulted with key members of the department. The chairperson is, as the supervisor in industry or government, an intermediary; he carries out his responsibilities between two factions often at loggerheads: the departmental faculty and the institution's administrators.

STRENGTHENING LEADERSHIP

What is required to strengthen the leadership of departments can be gleaned from the functioning of well-administered and respected departments found on many campuses. The chairpersons have in most instances been selected by a positive dean (or president) who after analyzing the department's needs and its membership "sold" his choice of a chairperson to the department's faculty. They have as well been counseled by the dean as to the institution's objectives and as to what the administration expects of each chairperson in achieving those objectives. As the chairperson demonstrates his ability to lead his colleagues, he is delegated increasing freedom in the making of decisions as to staffing, and supplemental resources are made available to support his proposals whenever feasible. Continually he is brought together with other departmental chairpersons to discuss the institution's problems (e.g., its relations with the state coordinating agency) and plans, and to exchange views with his peers on the tasks and techniques of the departmental chairperson. As his stature with the administration grows and his ability to "represent" his departmental colleagues well becomes apparent, they, too, tend to grant a greater freedom to lead.

THE DEANS

PROGRAM LEADERSHIP

A wide variety of offices bear the title of dean. They include: (1) those with responsibilities for the whole institution, titled dean of faculty, dean of academic affairs, or provost; (2) dean of students or deans of men and deans of women; (3) deans of arts and sciences colleges—in the liberal arts college *the* dean, in the university one among perhaps eight or twelve deans; (4) deans of professional schools and colleges; (5) deans of graduate studies, and sometimes research; and (6) deans of continuing education, of "general studies," and of "nontraditional education."

The position of dean in American higher education originally came into existence to provide aid for the president to take over principally educational functions when the burden of his responsibilities no longer permitted him to handle these activities. It is this original function, that of providing leadership for the educational program, on which we focus in this section. Hence, we exclude from this discussion the first two categories of deans listed above. They assist the president with essential activities, but are not centrally concerned wtih shaping educational programs. The remaining four categories of deans bear responsibility for educational programs, even though (like the presidents) some among them become so consumed with finance, business, and public relations that educational affairs claim a minor portion of their time and energy.

The role of the remaining four categories of deans varies, and particularly in terms of the nature of the educational programming task (e.g., the college of arts and sciences versus the recently emerging colleges of nontraditional studies) and the time the dean can concentrate on that task. Moreover, the role of the dean varies from the small institution to the large: as the institution grows in size, greater responsibilities are assumed and more authority is delegated by the president; as the institution grows in stature the faculty tends to claim from the dean increasing authority for educational programming. Hence, assessing the role of the dean is akin to that of drawing a bead on a moving target, but meaningful generalizations can be drawn for three distinguishable groupings.

DEANS OF ARTS AND SCIENCES

The deans of arts and sciences colleges—in the small liberal arts colleges (less than 1,500 enrollees) or in the larger universities—generally bear little responsibility for financing, the acquisition of physical facilities, or the alumni or public relations of their colleges. The dean may be called upon to talk with prospective donors; to aid in campaigning for a new library, dormitories, or a classroom building; or to meet with alumni or public groups. But usually he or she is not held responsible for formulating fund raising, building or public relations programs, or the accomplishment of such programs.

In the smaller institutions, the dean devotes much time to student affairs, to counseling students on academic, financial, and personal affairs, to counseling with parents by mail, by telephone, and in person, and to maintaining a variety of student records. With respect to the selection, promotion, and fixing of compensation of faculty members, the dean serves as assistant to the president, playing such part as the president delegates to him. The most effective deans earn a substantial role in assessing the capabilities of the faculty, department by department (there are few departments of more than four or eight members in the small college), and in searching for able instructors to bring in as vacancies permit. The more effective deans also lead their faculties in the continuing reexamination of curricula and the adaptation of courses to keep pace with the changing requirements of the society into which students will be graduated. The responsibilities of many deans for leadership in educational programming is limited by the president's concentration on the activity—education—that consumes the predominant part of the budget.

In the larger institutions, the dean of students takes over most of the dean's responsibilities for student affairs—counseling, contacts with parents and with employers,[4] and the registrar assumes the record-keeping tasks. The director (sometimes dean) of admissions takes over the nettlesome problems of selection, if indeed the decline in enrollments or the social emphasis on open access has not dissipated such problems. In the larger college these officers—dean of students, registrar, and dean

---

4 The role of the dean of students in the university and the relation of student personnel work to the institution's goals are eloquently and perceptively discussed by T. R. McConnell in "The Relation of Institutional Goals and Organization to the Administration of Student Personnel Work," in Martin L. Snoke, ed., *Approaches to the Study of Administration in Student Personnel Work,* Minnesota Studies in Student Personnel Work, no. 9 (Minneapolis: University of Minnesota Press, 1960), pp. 19–35.

of admissions—may report to the dean, but in the smaller institution they will likely be a part of the president's office.

The status of the dean tends to grow as the institution grows larger. His influence grows as he is delegated, by an overburdened president, larger responsibilities for control of the budget and its allocation among the several departments, and for the promotion and selection of faculty members. The "strong" dean will vigorously encourage his departmental faculties to search extensively for the best of talent to fill vacancies on the faculty, and will insist that the departments demonstrate that their nominees are better qualified than individuals available from other sources. His influence over budget and personnel is primarily dependent on his powers of persuasion. He must persuade faculty committees that his budget is appropriate and stimulate other faculty committees to be discriminating in judgments on all new appointments and promotions to tenure rank. In few institutions does the president any longer insist upon personally meeting each nominee for a faculty post, as once was the case.

The measures of the dean's accomplishments are found in the growth in reputation of the school's faculty and in the evolution of the school's educational program. Usually the dean's ability progressively to build the faculty is limited by the lack of effective methods for appraising the individual teacher's performance (see the discussion in Chapter 10), and by the protective views of departmental faculties. His ability to stimulate the departmental faculties recurrently to appraise course offerings and to explore opportunities for interdepartmental teaching and research is often circumscribed by the drive of departmental chairpersons for provincial autonomy.

DEANS OF PROFESSIONAL SCHOOLS

The professional school dean has either a simpler or a more complex and a different array of responsibilities than does the dean of the college of arts and sciences in the same institution. His role is simpler in that he usually deals with a smaller faculty which has fewer if any powerful departments to challenge his leadership. He can often claim a more comprehensive understanding of the several disciplines represented in the faculty. The school over which he presides has a greater unity than the undergraduate college consisting of twenty or more separate, discipline-oriented departments. With smaller faculties and more closely knit organizations, the dean of the professional school (except in the very largest schools) functions simultaneously as dean and department head.

When departments do exist in professional schools, they usually lack the narrow orientation characteristic of departments in the humanities, social sciences, and natural sciences. Professional deans can make (or at the least participate in) decisions affecting the school's educational program with greater acceptance than their fellow deans of the liberal arts. Many professional schools, having been organized more recently, allow the dean to claim much of the status and many of the prerogatives of the departmental chairperson. Most professional school faculty members hold the same professional allegiances (as in law, engineering, medicine, pharmacy, forestry, or library science) as does the dean. This contributes to the relatively close-knit relationship that enables the dean to exercise a greater leadership in educational programming and faculty selection.

His role is more complex and more difficult (than that of his counterpart in the arts and sciences) because of the demands made upon him by outside forces, particularly the profession, and by his obligation to raise a greater portion of the funds that support the school he heads. These deans must cultivate the professions they serve, derive financial support from them, and maintain an independence from them. The dean's faculty measures his accomplishments in terms of the stature he builds with the organized profession (e.g., the business school dean's corporate directorships, the social work school's dean's status in the hierarchy of the National Conference of Social Work and his relationships with the relevant governmental agencies) and especially in terms of the resources he acquires for buildings, for faculty salaries, and for scholarships.

DEANS WITHOUT FACULTIES

The deans of graduate schools of continuing education, of general studies, and of the recently emerged schools of nontraditional learning have a common problem: that of developing and coordinating special educational areas without the aid of faculties serving these areas exclusively. Those men and women who teach in the graduate school are often physically and intellectually affiliated with the department of their disciplines—anthropology to zoology—and not with the graduate school. So it is with those who offer courses in continuing education, in the extension centers of the "school of general studies," or who prepare materials and supervise students in nontraditional learning. Members of the evening school faculty are predominantly part-time "adjunct professors" who devote only a few hours each week to their teaching duties. Consequently the roles of these deans differ markedly from those of the deans of arts and sciences or of professional schools.

The graduate dean benefits from the greater prestige and status accorded graduate study. The individual chosen is usually a senior and respected scholar. He serves as chairperson of a "committee on graduate study" or of a graduate faculty. While those who teach graduate courses hold primary allegiance to their respective departments, they value the opportunity to be recognized as members of the graduate faculty. Yet, since he must develop the graduate program through departmental chairpersons over whom he has only indirect influence, the graduate dean finds it difficult to give substance to the concept of a graduate school. The graduate students are admitted by the subject-matter departments, and the departmental faculties regard the advanced students and the graduate courses they offer as "theirs."

The graduate dean's accomplishment is measured in terms of admission standards, of degree requirements, and of the caliber of the faculty. Yet he has little direct influence over any one of these factors. Standards of admission and degree requirements are established by decisions of graduate faculties as a body or in committees; and the faculty is chosen in principal part by the department. His is the opportunity to build a great graduate school that will bring esteem to the institution, but the task is a difficult one requiring skill in interpersonal relations, tact, and tenacity.

The deans of continuing education (in any of its forms) perform a promotional as well as an administrative task. They must seek out opportunities to make the institution's teaching services available off the campus, finance the provision of those services through tuition and supplementary sources (e.g., contributions of employers or of a community), and draw on the university's departments for instructors and for the approval of the courses and programs offered. The time and energies of these deans are consumed by the problems of attracting students, scheduling classes, managing registration, budgeting the division's finances, and arranging for needed physical facilities (e.g., classrooms), books, and equipment. They have little time and frequently little zeal for educational programming and for the stimulation of instructors.

Despite the substantially different roles that the several deans perform, their ability to lead is constrained by a common force—the myopic interests of and the strength within the college or university of the discipline-oriented department. The dean, charged with responsibility for a part of the institution's very reason for being—the planning and carrying out of an educational program cannot exercise overt leadership. He is a leader of equals. He must shape, head, and carry out his program by the manipulation, as Harlan Cleveland has written, of what is essentially a legislative process,[5] and by dint of persistent persuasion.

THE PRESIDENT

The more ardent advocates of faculty control argue that there is no need for administrative leadership,[6] yet the functions of the college or the university cannot be accomplished by an unintegrated mass of faculty members segregated into discipline-oriented departments and schools. Effective governance requires also leadership that possesses an understanding of and concern with the functioning of the whole institution, and is capable of making boldly, promptly, and conclusively those decisions which are required to effectuate the goals of the whole institution.

ROLE OF THE PRESIDENT

That need for leadership derives from three sources. An institution that spends from $2 million to $500 million annually on activities from the operation of the dining room and power of the small college to the operation of vast medical centers, research laboratories, and the sixty or more separate campuses of a large state university, requires central planning, direction, and administration of such logistical operations. The faculties rely on the institution's leadership to support their activities, to mediate differences among their members and with other constituencies and occasionally the public, and for representation to sources of support and to the public.[7] And the institution, made up of constituencies that are often in conflict, requires a positive force to press for agreement on educational objectives, to assess progress regularly, and to suggest new goals and next steps.

---

5 "The Dean's Dilemma: Leadership of Equals," *Public Administration Review,* Winter 1960, pp. 22–27.

6 Peter J. Caws has written: "I should myself wish to restrict membership in the university to students and faculty, who would then hire the administration. The administration would be a service, not quite on the level of the janitors but having rather similar relationship to the body itself" (*Daedalus,* Winter 1970, p. 99).

7 Douglas McGregor after several years as president of Antioch College during which, as he subsequently wrote, he strove "to operate . . . as a kind of adviser" to the faculty and staff "to avoid being 'boss'" concluded that ". . . a leader cannot avoid responsibility for what happens to his organization."

The provision of leadership is not solely the task of the president. Faculty leaders and student leaders as well as departmental chairpersons, deans, and trustees have leadership roles to perform. But the leadership required of the president is central and distinctive. It differs in scope or in character from that of colleagues within the institution. It is dissimilar from the leadership of the business executive, the political official, or the military officer. It comprehends (as does the leadership required of other executives) the ability to listen to, to amass and assess information for,[8] to consult with, to persuade, and to communicate to audiences which are transient (students, alumni, faculty members, trustees, state officials, and legislators) and which have limited concerns. Those constituencies proscribe different goals for the institution, insist upon different ways of achieving desired ends, and claim the right, even obligation, to differ with and to criticize the president in a fashion unmatched in the business firm, governmental agency, or military unit.

PRESIDENTIAL METHODOLOGY

Conventional wisdom suggests that college and university presidents are, simultaneously, administrators, mediators, and political leaders.[9] That distillation of the experiences of presidents and of the judgments of observers is confirmed by the methods successful presidents use. In leading their faculties, they search for, recognize, and encourage promising curricular, instructional and research ideas, and aspirations. They may plant ideas in the minds of faculty members, but seldom will they overtly press for their own ideas and plans.

Successful presidents generally make a continuing effort to build their identities with the students and to intensify loyalty to the institution. They do this by supporting those activities and projects which appeal to students, e.g., athletics, the building of a student union, or the relaxation of parietal rules, and which are consistent with the values acceptable to other constituencies. And presidents strive to create in students' minds an image of an aspiring institution that is and intends to be something

---

[8] "Leadership in the 1970s and 1980s will depend in substantial degree upon a comprehensive management information system . . . structured on a program basis . . . [that supplies] accurate data about the outputs and the cost of each . . . program" (John D. Millett, in a privately circulated paper entitled "Governance, Management, and Leadership in Higher Education," August 1973).

[9] A dissenting (and stimulating) view is voiced by Michael Cohen and James G. March in *Leadership and Ambiguity: The American College President* (New York: McGraw-Hill Book Company, 1974), p. 40.

larger than classrooms, laboratories, dormitories, and athletic arenas. They strive simultaneously and continually to communicate a similar image to alumni, and thus to kindle the loyalty established during student days.

In relation to their support staffs, successful presidents, chameleon-like, present another front. Their leadership with these staffs involves the joint formulation of goals for accomplishment and the establishment of yardsticks of cost and efficiency. They regularly review accomplishments, and persistently assess the causes of crises (e.g., what to do about student "streaking" or dissatisfaction with the food service, or how to overcome rising maintenance costs) and to prescribe remedies.

Successful presidents also work at making trustees effective. This involves (a) informing them about and involving them in the real problems of the institution; (b) spending time with individual members on social as well as official occasions and using these opportunities to share with them the problems being coped with; (c) frankly revealing mistakes and failures rather than surfeiting them with little and sometimes exaggerated successes; (d) bridging the gaps that tend to separate trustees from the institution—the "generation gap," the "faculty-trustee gap," the "business world–academia gap"; (e) subtly claiming a part in determining the membership of the board—this requires persuasion, but the president's interests are identical with those of the governor, the board chairperson, or the nominating committee that strives to build a strong board; and (f) demonstrating a constant flexibility of mind, a willingness to accept ideas—the president is in relation to the trustees, a teacher whose task it is to help trustees learn about the process of education that they may contribute from their diverse experiences; he loses his following among trustees (and others) if he suggests that education is an arcane science about which he and his faculty are profoundly informed and trustees cannot be expected to know much.

Finally successful presidents manifest a capacity for leadership outside the institution. The public institution's president spends half his time seeking the support of the state's executive and legislative officials, of powerful professional and business interests, and of the alumni who can relate him to each of the foregoing forces in the off-campus world. The private institution's president seeks the support of these same forces, in differing proportions. Both public and private institutions' presidents must cultivate the confidence of those community leaders who can support the institutions, and must manifest the capacity to deal with these leaders as informed, respected equals.

Some observers doubt that the rank and file of all presidents can provide such leadership. If such pessimism is well founded, the college and university will suffer. Thus, it is important to consider how the president can achieve the power to lead. Certainly he must gain great facility in the use of his time, for he must be in frequent touch with many within and without the institution. And, the president of a college or university must possess those qualities which inspire trust in his several constituencies. These include the capacity to reason with the politicians, to talk like a businessman with the trustees, to be recognized as a scholar by his faculty, to be approachable by and intelligible to students, and to create visions for the alumni. In addition the president must, in the eyes of each of these constituencies and the general public, be recognized as a broadly educated, cultivated, and reasoning person who envisions large and understandable goals and accomplishes what he sets out to do.[10]

POWER AND CONSTRAINTS

The president has means he can use to build his power. Simultaneously he suffers from substantial constraints on the exercise of that power. The position of president endows the incumbent with the means of continually informing himself as to the operations of the whole enterprise; in that information lies power. Much of the power he has within the institution flows out of the opportunity he has to use that information in shaping the annual budget; in raising funds for particular projects (e.g., a new educational program for elderly persons); in assessing major faculty and administrative appointments; and in controlling judiciously such support activities as the provision of space, major items of equipment, and other needed facilities. Those sources of power will not give force to his leadership for long unless he takes advantage of both his obligation to frame (in collaboration with his faculty and trustees) and to communicate inspiring and considered long-range plans for the institution. Nor will they maintain his power unless the president demonstrates ability to utilize the many opportunities he can claim to interpret and to illuminate, through public statements for the public and the academic community—the purpose, problems, accomplishments and needs of the institution, and the contribution it can make to the society.

The constraints that make difficult the exercise of leadership by the president are threefold. First, his responsibilities for the handling of (*a*) financial matters, particularly the raising of funds, (*b*) public and

---

[10] Cohen and March, op. cit., in a chapter entitled "Leadership in an Organized Anarchy," offer a contrasting picture of the leadership problems and tactics of a college president, and particularly a stimulating challenge to existing theories of managerial decision making.

alumni relations, and (c) problems of facilities consume (for most presidents) two-thirds or more of his time. Hence, his efforts to give direction and stimulation to the institutions' educational programming are in most instances drastically limited by these competing demands on his time. Second, his attempts to offer new ideas are discouraged or rejected by a faculty that regards this area as its province. Third, the efforts of the public university president to plan for the future, and gain acceptance within the university for such planning, are hindered by his colleagues' knowledge that increasingly such plans are subject to approval by a superior agency of the state government. The faculty's reaction not infrequently is: Why don't we deal directly with the state board?

FREEING PRESIDENTIAL LEADERSHIP

The nature of the president's responsibilities, particularly his responsibilities for financial, business, and public affairs, and for the resolution of conflicts, is such that his ability to act promptly and decisively must not be stultified by a time-consuming requirement that he consult with one or more constituencies.[11] Consultation should be a continuing part of the process of governance on a campus, and the machinery for such consultation, i.e., a communitywide council, a broadly based senate, a body representative of the students and a network of committees that interrelates these several mechanisms for consultation, should be kept well oiled. But the president, as the chief executive officer, subject to the policies set by the trustees and the advice offered by these advisory bodies, should be free at all times to act.

Two processes can ensure that the president's actions will be guided by and responsive to the consensus of the community. The first is regular review by that agency which most broadly represents the several constituencies of the community (e.g., such a body as the Princeton Community Council). That review should comprehend matters the president submits for review (e.g., the budget, long-range educational plans) and those matters that any one of the constituencies asks the agency to review. The agency in this way can continually offer advice; and, in instances of especial disagreement, its recourse is to inform the

---

11 For a confirming viewpoint see Howard R. Bowen, "Governance and Educational Reform," in G. Kerry Smith, ed., *Agony and Promise*, American Association for Higher Education (San Francisco: Jossey-Bass, Inc., Publishers, 1969), pp. 173–186.

trustees of its disagreement with an action or actions of the president.[12]

The second process would formalize a system of executive accountability as the *quid pro quo* for the freedom of the president to act boldly, promptly, and decisively. Kingman Brewster proposed in 1969[13] that the president be appointed for a fixed term (e.g., five or seven years) with the proviso that his performance would be reviewed by his several constituencies prior to his reappointment by the board of trustees at the end of that term. This process would induce the president to consult continually during his tenure with each of the several constituencies. It suggests the desirability of an annual published report by the president setting forth the institution's accomplishments under his leadership, the rationale underlying significant actions taken during the year, and plans for the forthcoming year.

In summary this second process would give "the top administrators some assurance that they will have a reasonable period of time to move their institutions forward," and simultaneously would provide "a counterbalancing assurance among all the constituencies directly affected ... that they will have an opportunity to assess and judge the quality of their leadership, and either endorse it or replace it."[14]

THE GOVERNING BOARD

The term "board of trustees" (or board of regents, board of overseers, board of visitors) historically was used to refer to the group of lay persons who were vested with the ultimate authority for governance of a

---

[12] An alternative process is described by David Schimmel in an article entitled "Conditional Decision-making: An Alternative to the Committee Octopus," *Journal of Higher Education*, February 1972, pp. 85–96. The Schimmel "conditional decision-making process" proposes the delay of a presidential decision by ten days so that a relevant committee of the community's constituencies may react to a proposed decision submitted for review. While such a process might be suitable for the consideration of some decisions, particularly in the field of educational programming or admissions policies, it does not allow the president sufficient freedom for executive action in other areas of institutional administration

[13] In "The Politics of Academia," an address to the Yale Political Union, September 1969. Alvin C. Eurich seconded Brewster's proposal and suggested that the president submit an annual report ("Plan or Perish," *College and University Journals*, Summer 1970).

In 1972 the board of trustees of the State University of New York adopted a policy providing that all presidents of institutions within that system shall be appointed for five-year terms and their performance intensively evaluated before reelection for a subsequent five-year term.

[14] Ernest L. Boyer, "Managing Tomorrow's Education," an essay in a volume entitled *Challenge to Leadership*, The Board, 1973, pp. 176–177.

college or university. Since 1960, the number of boards of public colleges and universities has been markedly reduced, while the number of institutions has grown. Many state colleges and universities have been consolidated into multicampus systems or been placed under a single board governing all four-year colleges and universities within a state.[15] Indeed, by 1974 nearly half of the states had established statewide or systemwide boards to govern their four-year colleges and universities, and the federal government had enacted legislation proposing the requirement that certain federally financed activities would be subject to the review of a state commission.[16]

In theory, the governing board, be it a statewide governing board, a board controlling a multicampus system, or the board of a single institution (as is the case for most private colleges and universities) is endowed, either by the state constitution, by statute, or by a publicly issued charter with authority to make or approve all decisions involved in the governance of the institutions for which they are responsible. Few observers would contend in the mid-1970s that the existing boards exercise such comprehensive authority. Rather, at this point in their evolution, governing boards of the several categories are beset by criticism of the capabilities of the individuals who serve, of methods of selection, and particularly of their tendency to interfere with and inability to contribute to the basic educational functions of the institutions they govern.[17]

CRITICISMS OF GOVERNING BOARDS

The conflict that was experienced on a number of campuses between 1967 and 1972 illuminated the deficiencies that have attracted criticism. Generally trustees had not concerned themselves with those aspects of college and university functioning which determine the character and

---

15 For further information as to this trend see S. V. Martorana and E. V. Hollis, *State Boards Responsible for Higher Education* (Washington: U. S. Office of Education, 1960); and J. L. Zwingle, "Governing Boards," in A. S. Knowles, ed., *Handbook of College and University Administration* (New York: McGraw-Hill Book Company, 1970). See for further commentary F. F. Harcleroad, H. Bradley Sagen, and C. Theodore Molen, Jr., *The Developing State Colleges and Universities* (American College Testing Programs, 1969), pp. 71–84.

16 Federal Higher Education Act of 1972, Section 1202.

17 "At the very pinnacle of the academic establishment, and therefore attracting a good many of the lightning bolts, stand the trustees of colleges and universities. Hitherto secure in the most absolute sense, trustees are now not only criticized for their alleged attitudes and activities, but their very existence is being challenged" Samuel B. Gould, "Trustees and the University Community," in James A. Perkins, ed., *The University as an Organization* (New York: McGraw-Hill Book Company, 1973), p. 215.

quality of these institutions. They had devoted too little time to the affairs of these institutions to obtain a real understanding of the problems that might be dealt with. As individuals the board members are only partially equipped to cope with the kind of problems peculiar to the functioning of an educational institution. And they are denied any real authority (to fulfill the responsibilities they are charged with) by a tradition that delegates comprehensive authority to the faculty. As a consequence, numerous critics proposed either that their membership be strengthened and broadened, that their functions be modified, or that these boards be abandoned.[18]

Such criticisms of the governing boards are supported by analyses of the functioning of boards and the composition of their memberships. Generally boards devote about a fourth of their time and attention to such central socioeducational matters as admissions, curricula, and the quality and ideological balance of the faculty as a whole.[19] They devote much of their time and attention to:

- Financial matters—in the private institutions particularly to fund raising and investments and in the public institutions to the budget and budget transfers, the approval of purchase orders, the acceptance of gifts and bequests, and the fixing of tuition and fees

- The physical plant—consideration of the master plan for the campus, the awarding of contracts for the construction and renovation of buildings, approval of the capital budget, and approval of a substantial number of incidental matters arising out of the foregoing

- Personnel matters—primarily the approval of recommended appointments, and in addition the fixing of salaries, conditions of employment, staff benefits, and tenure promotions and appointments

[18] Professor Henry G. Manne (*AGB Reports*, October 1972, pp. 2–13) contended that trustees have no real interest in, and little or no influence over, the central issues that confront colleges or universities (e.g., admissions, curricula, and faculty composition) and proposed that boards be abandoned. J. K. Galbraith (*The New Industrial State*, pp. 370–378) charged that the influence of boards made up of industrialists, bankers, and lawyers was pernicious when effective, and he argued for the abandonment of lay boards. T. R. McConnell ("Faculty Government," an essay published as Chap. 7 in Harold L. Hodgkinson and Richard L. Meeth, *Power and Authority*, San Francisco, Jossey-Bass, Inc., Publishers, 1970, pp. 98–125) shared Professor Manne's view of the limited worth of boards but proposed that they be reconstituted to include faculty members and students rather than be junked.

[19] That trustees should concern themselves with such "balance" was proposed by Lewis F. Powell, Jr., in a memorandum prepared at the request of the U.S. Chamber of Commerce, Dec. 23, 1971, prior to his becoming a justice of the U.S. Supreme Court.

- External affairs—relations with the alumni, potential donors, the legislature, the governor, and the press

In dealing with these matters, they consider a large number of individual items, ranging from 350 to 500 items in the course of a year, most of which involve *pro forma* actions on long lists of detailed operational matters.[20] The members of these boards (the number of members may range from as few as seven to more than a hundred) devote to their duties as trustees from forty to eighty hours a year; this approximation includes the time devoted to as few as two or as many as ten meetings of the full board, to committee meetings, to soliciting contributions or consulting with legislators, and to all other institution-related activities.[21]

Few members bring to the boards on which they serve familiarity with problems of higher education or the processes of a college or university. Most are selected by governors or legislatures (or in a few states elected) for extraneous political reasons, by church bodies for religious reasons, by alumni because of a popularity derived from various activities, or by self-perpetuating boards for financial reasons. Moreover, boards of trustees are made up predominantly of white Protestant males, fifty years of age and over, drawn largely from among industrialists, bankers, lawyers, merchants, and the public service.[22]

During the years 1969–1973, a number of younger men and women, blacks, faculty members, and students were added to a limited number of boards. Still, the aggregate membership of boards had not been materially altered by the close of 1973. Hence, they were frequently criticized as not being able to understand the problems of the substantial and growing proportion of blacks, Puerto Ricans, Chicanos, and young people from low-income families that seek the opportunity offered by higher education.

Selected for various reasons unrelated to their understanding of higher education, or of the structure and functioning of a college or university,

---

[20] This summary description of trustees' activities is founded on the author's own early observations, as reported in *The Governance of Colleges and Universities* (New York: McGraw-Hill Book Company, 1960, pp. 49–58), in a score of institutions where he served as a consultant between 1960 and 1973, and on the surveys by Morton A. Rauh, "The Trustees of Higher Education: A Survey Report," *AGB Reports,* January 1969, pp. 3–25; R. T. Hartnett, "College and University Trustees, Their Back-Service," 1969, pp. 45–46; and *College and University Trustees and Trusteeship,* recommendations and a report of a survey (Albany, N.Y.: New York State Regents Advisory Committee on Educational Leadership, 1966, pp. 43–45); and J. G. Partridge, Julie Hurst, A. Morgan, *Boards of Trustees: Their Decision Patterns,* Center for Research and Development in Higher Education (Berkeley: University of California, 1973), pp. 14–54.

[21] See the three surveys cited in footnote 20: Rauh, p. 19; Hartnett, p. 67; and New York State Regents Advisory Committee, pp. 38–39.

[22] Ibid.

or of the aspirations of the "new students," many (not all) bring to the institutions illustrious names, but little capacity to contribute to the socioeducational decisions central to their funcioning. Lacking familiarity with the substance of the educational process and with the needs and aspirations of those for whom programs are being adapted, many trustees are hobbled by a fear of involving themselves in matters they simply do not understand.[23] The result is unquestioning approval of many determinations formulated by the faculty or by busy administrators.[24]

THE REASONS WHY

Prevailing criticisms of governing boards must be attributed to three pragmatic forces—capabilities, tradition, and a misinterpretation of logic.

First, the choice of individuals to serve for reasons extraneous to the central needs of the institutions they serve has made them vulnerable to criticism.

Second, they have been made doubly vulnerable by the delegation by previous generations of trustees to their presidents, and by presidents to the faculties, of authority to act on most of what counts in a college or university. Such delegation has obtained for so long that administrators and faculty members contend that powers once delegated are now theirs by right.[25] Delegation and decentralization are good, but they do not relieve the delegators of responsibility for what is done. In business and in government the directors and the chief executive maintain processes of review; few governing boards do.

Third, governing boards are generally vulnerable to prevailing criticisms because they misinterpret the logic of the dictum that they should confine their attention to policy matters. The prime policies of a college or university are those that determine who may attend, what shall be taught, and who shall teach; in this area boards commonly exercise little influence. In other areas in which they feel more comfortable—finance, physical plant, and public relations—many boards involve themselves "with excessive amounts of operational detail," i.e., "implementation of previously approved programs, the setting forth of detailed operational procedures where no interpretation of policy was involved, appoint-

---

[23] Ibid., p. 189.

[24] Partridge et al., op. cit., p. 29.

[25] Martin Trow, "Elite and Popular Functions in American Higher Education," in W. R. Niblett, ed., *Higher Education: Demand and Response* (San Francisco: Jossey-Bass, Inc., Publishers, 1970), chap. 9

ments of personnel or awards of contracts or purchases of materials within established policy guidelines."[26] Their innate curiosity should dictate that they keep their "noses in," i.e., that they should insist upon being continually informed, that, being assured as to what is going on, they may keep their "fingers out."

WHAT THE INSTITUTION NEEDS OF THE BOARD

Although the governing board is endowed with the legal power to make decisions on all matters, the conventional wisdom holds that the board should (1) select the president and approve selection of other key officers, (2) define the objectives of the institutions and ensure consistent pursuit of those objectives, (3) oversee the financing of the institution—approving the annual budget, plans for obtaining needed resources, and the investment of endowments, (4) preserve and develop needed physical facilities, and (5) represent the institution to the public and to sources of funds.[27]

But if it be granted that a prime objective of the governance of higher education is the maximization of the vitality and the quality of the educational performance of the individual college or university, a greater, different, and more positive contribution is needed from its trustees— be they members of an institutional, a system, or a statewide board.

First and foremost, interest in and understanding of educational issues is needed. Trustees' decisions on nonacademic matters depend for their validity on the trustees' understanding of educational objectives and processes. Decisions as to budgets and buildings should be founded on an understanding of the activities being financed and housed. Decisions as to when to support the president or defend the faculty, when public criticisms are voiced, are usually more persuasive when based on an obvious understanding of educational values.

This understanding of educational issues is needed because decisions as to who shall be educated, what programs shall be offered, and who shall teach are of too great importance to the society to be made by faculties, and in major part by departmental faculties alone (see Chapter 12, pp. 239–240). Faculty members are only partially equipped to make such decisions. Chosen as subject-matter specialists, most professors see their futures as historians, chemists, or authors. They are interested in

---

26 Partridge et al., op. cit., p. v.

27 Algo Henderson, "The Role of the Governing Board," *AGB Reports*, October 1967, pp. 3–31.

the caliber of the students who enroll in their courses, but generally not in the economic, ethnic, or work status of the student body. Few pretend to have much interest in curriculum planning. Personally concerned with the hiring, promotion, and compensation of faculty members, they have difficulty in viewing such issues objectively. Without the backing of a board, of which at least some members have the time and interest to inform themselves as to educational issues, deans and presidents will not withstand the persisting pressure of an aggressive faculty.

Second, trustees must provide the institution with a bridge to the society.[28] Institutional trustees are not solely advocates for the individual college or university they serve. They are agents of society, deriving their authority from a public grant. The decisions they make as to admissions determine the reality of the state's guarantees of educational opportunity. The decisions they make or countenance as to curricula constitute their diagnosis of the educational needs of the society being served.[29] The decisions as to faculty in the institutions for which they are responsible markedly influence the quality of the education offered. Their decisions are *social* as well as educational and financial. Through such decisions they contribute viewpoints needed to supplement those of faculty and administrators.

Third, trustees, even while serving as an agent of the society, must be expected to aid the institution in repelling the mounting forces of bureaucratization. Members of the statewide governing board cannot be counted on to aid when "the outside insistence on 'accountability' meets the academy's insistence on 'campus independence' "; their concern is with accountability, and their emphasis is persistently a negative one.

Private and public institutions are both units within a system for which policies are set in increasing measure by the federal government (e.g., Section 1202, Educational Amendments of 1972), and for public institutions particularly by the state governments. If trustees fail to discharge their responsibility as as an agent of the society *and* fail to see to it that their institution's objectives are clearly defined and vigorously

---

[28] James A. Perkins, "Conflicting Responsibilities of Governing Boards," in James A. Perkins, ed., *The University as an Organization* (New York: McGraw-Hill Book Company, 1973), chap. 11, pp. 207–209.

[29] For example, statutes establishing some of the regional public universities provide that the institution's program shall "be attuned to the needs" of the area to be served. This statutory language would seem to fix on the trustees of such institutions the obligation of seeing to it that curricular, faculty-selection, and admission policies proposed by faculty and administrators effectively meet the particular needs of the region they represent.

pursued, authority tends to flow from the institution to these governmental bodies.[30]

Fourth, trustees can and should provide continuing objective appraisal of internal operations. To provide this needed service, the statewide or even the multicampus system board tends to be too far removed. No management (that of a corporation or that of a university) has the capacity for impersonal and objective self-appraisal.[31] For institutional trustees, the task involves no more than the conscientious study of each matter they are asked to decide upon and the asking of considered and revealing questions.

The asking of such questions in any enterprise—business or academic —has real and substantial therapeutic value. In the college or university it stimulates faculty and administrators to establish effective processes for the making of basic determinations within the institution. Preferably, it leads to the trustees' asking that a proposal be reconsidered rather than their substituting a decision they formulate at the moment. Finally, the asking of such questions lends greater reality to the theory that they, the trustees, are responsible for the quality of the institution.

FUTURE OF THE INSTITUTIONAL BOARD

In the mid-1970s the prospect seems clear that the boards of individual public institutions will either be eliminated or their functions delimited and their status lowered in the years ahead. Only the private institutions will likely have boards of trustees by the year 2000.

That trend seems unfortunate. The lay board of trustees for the individual institution should neither be abandoned nor decimated.[32] Rather, both public and private institutions can be the stronger if they have governing boards that fulfill the responsibility they are now charged with either in charter or in statute.

This will mean that, as Beardsley Ruml urged in 1959,[33] boards will reclaim from their faculties powers that had been entrusted to the

---

[30] Allan W. Ostar in an address before the Education Commission of the States, June 28, 1973, said: "In watching the lay boards yield their power to agencies of the state, I believe we are watching the colleges recede from their role as vital contributors to the progress and improvement of society."

[31] E. Everett Smith provides a relevant analysis of the role of the corporate board in "The Goldberg Dilemma: Directorships," *Wall Street Journal*, Feb. 7, 1973.

[32] Perkins, op. cit., p. 259.

[33] *Memo to a College Trustee* (New York: McGraw-Hill Book Company, 1959), p. 13. See also Earl J. McGrath, *Should Students Share the Power?* (Philadelphia: Temple University Press, 1970), pp. 51–60.

boards and for the exercise of which they are responsible. Such reclaiming of authority for decision making on academic matters does *not* mean trustee involvement in day-to-day operations. It need *not* mean interference in the activities of the president, the deans, or the faculty. It will mean more extensive *monitoring* of all aspects of institutional functioning. A board of trustees cannot and should not *run* the institution. The board's role (as in the case of the corporate board of directors) is direction, not management; the distinction is vital. That role can be fulfilled by question asking.

With respect to admissions, trustees logically should not confine themselves to questions as to the number of enrollees and the yield of tuition rates. They should also ask for and examine data as to the makeup of admittees by ethnic group, by ability groupings, by financial status of families, and by work status, i.e., whether they are simultaneously carrying a job.

With respect to faculty hiring and promotion, trustees should be informed, in connection with each appointment to the rank of full professor, of the names and qualifications of *other* candidates who were considered and passed over, as to what processes were used for the evaluation of professors and with what results, and as to the proportion of the faculty members at each rank who have been granted tenure. They should also ask for, at least six months in advance, evaluations of those individuals to be recommended for tenure. The detail involved in these several personnel activities may make it desirable for review by a committee of trustees rather than the board as a whole; the essential is that the trustees be informed and the faculty know that it is informed.

With respect to courses and programs, trustees should seek information that will enable them to understand how each proposed program or course is related to the specific objectives of the institution, as well as information that will reveal the increase in the relative number of courses being offered by each department.

Boards will also likely find it necessary in the future to ask for evidence as to the quality of the institution's output. Few measures of output are available,[34] but trustees are confronted with the irksome fact

---

[34] In 1973, data provided by the Graduate Record Examinations and the examinations for admission to the medical, law, and graduate business administration schools provide some evidence of the caliber of an institution's performance. The development and widespread acceptance of the *National Assessment*, a nationwide effort to determine what children learn in this country's elementary and secondary schools, suggests the need for a like measure of the educational accomplishments in higher education. Clearly the diversity in student bodies and among institutions makes the development of such measures exceedingly difficult.

that many parents and citizens are now questioning the value of a college degree—its value in terms of mental conditioning, in terms of qualification for employment, and in terms of the greater income it will produce. This means that colleges and universities will be called upon more frequently to demonstrate what they really are accomplishing.

Three further changes seem essential. Individuals from more heterogeneous backgrounds, who have a deep-rooted curiosity as to the processes of educational administration and have the time to inform themselves, need to be appointed to boards in larger proportions.

During the years 1970–1973 many contended that faculty members and students should be included as members of governing boards. This contention was advanced on the grounds that such members would bring to the board's discussion first-hand familiarity with the views of these constituencies. But the board should not be made a forum in which spokespersons for various constituencies "bargain out" the policies that shall prevail. The role of the board is responsible overseeing in the public interest. The objective, dispassionate, and positive surveillance expected of the board will be done better by boards made up of members not representing any constituency.[35] Can an adequate number of capable men and women with requisite time and curiosity be found? It is only these three qualities—intelligence, time, and curiosity—that are needed.

Second, if individuals with these qualifications are to be appointed in greater number, both public and private institutions need to adopt new bases and methods of selection. Governors may well utilize distinguished nonpartisan individuals serving on nominating commissions. Such commissions have been used for the selection of judges in some states and this approach has been proposed for the nomination of trustees in California.[36] Such commissions would establish criteria for

---

[35] Howard R. Bowen wrote in "Governance and Educational Reform," an essay included in G. Kerry Smith, ed., *Agony and Promise*: "A lay governing board composed of distinguished citizens is needed to insulate the university from improper pressures of the public, politicians, and donors, and to represent the public interest in a way that no combination of administrators, faculty, students or employees could do" (p. 181).

[36] The California state legislature's Joint Committee on the Master Plan for Higher Education proposed in 1972 èstablishment of a "blue ribbon nomination commission" to be responsible for nominating trustees. The governor would be limited to choosing individuals nominated in making appointments to the boards of the University of California, California State University and Colleges, and California Community Colleges. The Carnegie Commission on Higher Education in its report entitled *Governance of Higher Education* recommends: "Members of governing boards of public institutions (where the governor makes the appointments) should be subject to appropriate mechanisms for nominating and screening individuals before appointment by the governor to assure consideration of properly qualified individuals, or to subsequent legislative confirmation to reduce the likelihood of purely politically partisan appointments, or both" (New York: McGraw-Hill Book Company, 1973, p. 35).

membership on any state college or university board and would nominate individuals meeting such criteria for the governor's appointment. In private institutions the need is for aiding nominating committees find a greater number of potential nominees and to accept the desirability of including as trustees men and women with experience and views that differ from their own.

The operating practices used by most boards to acquaint themselves with the viewpoints of the institution's constituencies, particularly of the faculty members and students, also require change. Most boards talk to and hear from only, or principally, the president and his immediate staff. Additional channels of information must be utilized if the board is to play a positive role in the governance of the institution. This need is met in a number of institutions by the scheduling of regular meetings of the board, or of its committees, with representatives of the faculty and of students, and/or the inclusion of faculty members and students as members of trustee committees.[37] The president should be privileged to participate in all such meetings or to be represented by members of his staff.

---

[37] Samuel Gould, "Updating the University Trustee's Job," in a series of *Conversations* published by the ARA-Slater School and College Services, no. 6, 1969.

Restructuring the College or University

For too long, colleges and universities have borrowed their governance models from business and public administration. Neither is appropriate for most functions of academic institutions.[1]

Assembly on University Goals and Governance

14 The organization of colleges and universities, as described in their bylaws and illustrated by charts, is misleadingly simple. It depicts a hierarchy of units, suggests relationships, and uses titles (executive vice president, vice president, director, manager, and comptroller) borrowed in principal part from the corporate organization form. But the organization implied by the chart does not exist in fact because unlike the corporation, in which power to govern flows substantially from the stockholders through the directors to the president and the staff, the capacity to make decisions in the college and university does not flow in equal measure from the top.[2]

ELEMENTS OF RESTRUCTURING

The power to make decisions of significant consequence to the college or university flows from multiple sources. Four internal constituencies—the trustees, administrators, faculty, and students, three of which are relatively independent of the institution—possess power. In some institutions, the administrators of the university's research laboratories, spokespersons for the professions (e.g., the organized scientists, physicians and lawyers, and, although less likely in the future, the alumni) form additional sources of power. In most public institutions, the power to make a broadening array of decisions on matters of internal operation

---

[1] Assembly on University Goals and Governance, *A First Report* (Cambridge, Mass.: American Academy of Arts and Sciences, February 1971). This statement is contained in the forty-ninth of eighty-five theses promulgated by the Assembly.

[2] There are signs that this distinction is diminishing. As corporations include in their staffs more highly skilled professional workers, the capacity of directors and chief executives to make many decisions tends to gravitate to those with the knowledge required. See John Kenneth Galbraith, *The New Industrial State* (Boston: Houghton Mifflin Company, 1967), chap. 6, "The Technostructure," and chap. 7, "The Corporation," pp. 60–85.

(e.g., teaching loads, and even visitation hours in the dormitories) reside in agencies of the state government. Not only does power flow from each of these sources, but that power may be exercised in diverse directions.

The flow of power from these multiple sources, rather than from a single superordinate source, is but one of four fundamental differences the college or university must cope with in developing more appropriate organizational structure. It differs, also, in the degree to which it can define its goals and objectives in clear, operational terms, in the extent to which authority over the operations which turn input into final output is widely diffused, and in the greater proportion of professional personnel in its total staff.[3]

These differences have obtained and promise to continue. But the functions of the college, and more the university, have changed (as was pointed out in Chapter 11) and are expected to undergo further change. The "shucking off" of some research and public service activities, the prospective development of new technologies (TV, cassettes), the extension of the campus to include learners in their homes and workplaces, and the further professionalization of faculty members foreshadow the need for organizational evolution.[4] That evolution will involve modification of structural forms and the devising of new approaches to relating the efforts of increasingly diverse professional staffs, for an organization is both a complex of subunits and a chain of understanding among the men and women who make it up.

STRUCTURAL PROBLEMS

Three organizational problems stemming from changes in the functions of institutions and the transference of functions among classes of institutions may be typified as structural problems. They are the bifurcation, lower-division, and vertical-elongation problems.

THE BIFURCATION PROBLEM

The bifurcation problem evolved from an earlier problem observable in colleges and universities for a half century. These institutions were divided in two clearly distinguishable and little-related parts. On one

---

[3] This statement summarily reiterates reasoning presented in Chapter 4. This reasoning is affirmed by Stanley O. Ikenberry in his essay "The Organizational Dilemma," *Journal of Higher Education*, January 1972.

[4] James A. Perkins, op. cit., "Missions and Organization: A Redefinition," pp. 259–260.

side there was the academic organization, on the other side, the business and operational organization. The academic organization consisted of departments, schools, institutes and centers reporting to deans and academic vice presidents, a complex of faculty committees heading up to a faculty senate, and, perhaps, an executive committee of the faculty. The business-operational organization was made up of offices providing an increasing array of supporting services. Among others, accounting and budgeting, building maintenance, duplication, food service, purchasing.

These historical parts of the college and the university performed clearly differentiated functions. But they were separated as well by the different backgrounds, skills, and values of the individuals employed in each. Traditionally members of the academic organization have regarded members of the business-operational organization as inferior and have not cultivated relationships with its members. As institutions have grown larger the business-operational organization assumed responsibilities for the assembly of information as to the functioning of the academic organization and for the exercise of controls. This development, along with power that the business-operational organization acquired through its responsibility for interpreting the rules and regulations of state budgetary, purchasing, personnel, and other agencies, worsened rather than bettered the relationships between these two parts.

During recent decades other parts emerged and became, in varying degrees, similarly separate. The student personnel organization grew from simple beginnings in the office of the academic dean. It expanded to include separate units concerned with admissions, counseling, health, housing, recreational, religious, and other related activities. In many of the larger universities a research and service structure was established. Its makeup, perforce, varied from institution to institution but often included independent laboratories, a computing center, a university press, and perhaps the division of continuing education. Associated with the latter in some instances, and separate in others, a radio and television station was found on some campuses.

The persisting problem is how to better relate these several parts in day-to-day operations. Differing hierarchical structures are utilized on most campuses, tailored to cope with the relative emphasis placed on the activity, the personnel involved, and the circumstances (e.g., available physical facilities) indigenous to the particular institution. So it should be. Resolution of the problem is dependent more upon the development of a revealing management information system, the facilitation of communication throughout the institution, and the subtle forcing of more frequent association and interchange among the individuals who make up each of the several parts.

THE LOWER-DIVISION PROBLEM

The lower-division problem derives from the large and prospectively increasing proportion of all first-time enrollees who are admitted to the community colleges as distinguished from the four-year colleges and universities. This recent trend in enrollments reduces the revenue derived from large (and relatively profitable) first- and second-year classes. It forces institutions, subtly or overtly, to reconsider the roles of departments that provide "services" (e.g., English, mathematics, statistics, history, and chemistry) and those that produce a considerable number of majors and are involved in graduate instruction (e.g., economics, physics and the more applied "departments" such as business administration and social welfare). When coupled with a shift in demand from courses emphasized in the liberal arts and reduction of the number of required courses, the contraction of enrollment in the lower division necessitates the reallocation of resources (faculty positions as well as dollars) of harrowing proportions.

In addition, for doctoral-granting institutions the reduction of lower-division enrollments poses a particular problem. It reduces the opportunity to finance graduate students who are now supported by compensation earned teaching first- and second-year courses.

In the long run, the organizational change likely to result is the elimination of lower-division instruction in a number of comprehensive universities and colleges and doctoral-granting universities. This solution is an unpalatable one for many educators but will likely be induced by the continuation of low tuition fees and the proximity of community colleges. In the shorter run, the reallocation of resources will take place.

THE PROBLEM OF VERTICAL ELONGATION

The problem of vertical elongation is a consequence of the growth in enrollments, the proliferation of activities, and the centralization of increasing authority in state governing or coordinating boards.[5] As these forces have combined to increase the number and the complexity of decisions made in governing a college or university, additional staff frequently has been added. That staff has often formed an additional echelon or echelons between the president and the faculty.

---

[5] Jonathan A. Gallant and John W. Prothero identify seven dsyfunctions that have attended university growth: (1) "diffusion," (2) "absence of community," (3) "dead and overspecialization," (4) "administrative complexity," (5) "bureaucracy," (6) "alienation," and (7) "the striving for status as an end in itself" ("Weight Watching at the University: Consequences of Growth," *Science*, vol. 175, pp. 381–388).

The significance of this trend is reflected by a statement found in a self-study report prepared by the faculty of a southern state university. "It is a recognized management principle," the report states, "that in an organization where members are intelligent and given to independent thought and creativity that the structure must be far more horizontal than vertical in character."[6] Yet the action taken by the president to meet problems cited by that self-study report was to add six provosts between the deans of the university's several schools and the executive vice president, the chief academic officer being below the president. Doubtless additional executive staff was needed, but the effect of this vertical elongation of the university's organizational structure violated the principle stated.

The validity of the principle is illustrated by the steps involved in the handling of actions of critical importance to individual faculty members—an increase in compensation, the promotion of a faculty member to a tenured position, the approval of a departmental proposal for the introduction of a new degree program. The increase in compensation will often be a blanket action taken with little regard to the performance of an individual. Recommendations for the two other actions must be formulated and agreed upon by a departmental faculty, forwarded to and approved by the dean of the relevant school, forwarded to and approved by the relevant provost, and at this point reviewed by and approved by a universitywide faculty committee. Upon approval by such a committee, the recommendation is forwarded to the executive vice president and president; if approved by them, it is forwarded to the chancellor of the state university system for final decision by the state board of regents.

"Intelligent" individuals "given to thought and creativity" expect, in whatever organization they serve, a substantial right of self-direction. Traditionally in the college or university, faculty members have been granted substantial freedom in the determination of what teaching and research they would do and how they would do it. When their personally determined course of action had to be modified or decisions affecting them as individuals were made by others, it was by their peers—men and women who held their respect as fellow professionals and whom faculty members often faced when such decisions were made.

In the elongated hierarchy, decisions are more often made by faceless officials removed by four or five echelons, and perhaps by the distance to the state capital. The result is, in many instances, frustration or resentment among those who innovated and developed ideas that expired

---

6 *Agenda for the Next Decade*, summary report of the Steering Committee of the Florida State University Self-Study, vol. II, p. 18.

in the course of bureaucratic review. In some instances such impersonal review has been cited as a cause contributing to the success of unionization; in other instances it contributes to the alienation of faculty members.

In some measure there is no discernible solution to this problem. The growth in the size of institutions imposes such organization and such processes. But size does not dictate the number and kind of decisions that must be made at the topmost echelons. A regular and earnest effort to decentralize decision making—to ensure that no decision is made above the level of th dean of a school and the faculty of that school, or above a universitywide faculty committee and the provost when it could be made below—is the basic antidote for the problem.

THE SPECIALIZATION PROBLEM

The specialization problem focuses on the department, the module of which colleges and universities are made. This makes for a logical association of individuals with common interests and some related activities; it constitutes a logical unit for the performance of essential activities—the design of courses; the assignment of courses among individuals; the framing of elements of the educational program, particularly the major; and the recruitment, development, and promotion of teaching personnel. Yet the department suffers, simultaneously, as an organizational unit, from insulation and isolation induced by excessive specialization.

Moreover, as an institution grows from the status of a college to that of a university and acquires greater prestige—by virtue of the accomplishments of departments—the disabilities of the department as a functioning organizational unit tend to increase. This is made apparent by the revealing categorization of departments developed by Dressel, Johnson, and Marcus in their work *The Confidence Crisis*. They identify three types of departments and relate each to the stage of development of the institution in which each is found.

- *The university-oriented department*, usually found in a university of moderate size with strong undergraduate emphasis, is dependent wholly or in principal part on general funds. Its activities are limited to teaching and the interests of its members are focused on the priorities of the institution of which the department is a unit.

- *The department-oriented department* is found in a larger and more complex university. This department is more specialized and includes senior members aware of their obligations to the institution and to undergraduate education as well as younger members who recognize that reputations and promotions are attained more rapidly by research and publication. As a whole the department is increasingly concerned with its national reputation in research and graduate work.

The discipline-oriented department has attained a national reputation for its research and the production of doctorates. It includes members with reputations by virtue of which they have obtained research funds which enable them to operate fiefdoms within the department. The chairmanship, a position of eminence in other types of departments, is in this department a chore that threatens the individual's own scholarship, and is endowed with little influence. Undergraduate education tends to be neglected and the priorities of the university honored in the breach.

Dressel et al. have suggested that "departmental organization based upon disciplines is perhaps too simplistic a concept for university organization." Such a conclusion is underwritten by those undergraduate deans who have struggled to provide broad liberal education, those graduate deans who have strived to bring together faculty from a number of departments for research and interdisciplinary graduate teaching programs, and by those directors of continuing education who have been repeatedly rebuffed when appealing to departments for assistance in conferences and training programs designed to serve particular groups and which, hence, overlapped disciplinary boundaries.

The organizational problem is how to grant the departments enough autonomy that they may perform their functions well and then bring them under enough control by a central administration that the whole institution may remain viable. This problem is exemplified by the efforts of departments to offer courses duplicating what should be provided by the "service" departments (e.g., the offering of a course in statistics by the sociology department). It is exemplified by the resistance of departments to efforts in formulating programs to meet new demands which require the integration of specialties (e.g., the integration of knowledge from economics, history, political science, and sociology in a program to train men and women for the public service). It is exemplified by resistance to proposals for the development of broadly permissive programs for undergraduates. It is exemplified by the difficulties encountered when it is proposed that the institution undertake research and service activities to meet social needs (e.g., urban redevelopment, environmental pollution).

A variety of organizational solutions to cope with such problems engendered by specialization has been tried. The formation of institutes—of governmental research, labor relations, international affairs, and population research—to bring specialists from relevant departments together is a common one.[7] The setting up of "task-oriented" programs (in industry the analogous development is commonly called "project management") is a second effort; the most common illustration of this approach is the graduate program in which a graduate dean with a committee representing various departments sets standards of admission, the nature of graduate work, and the degrees to be offered, and encourages interdisciplinary approaches; in some universities heavily oriented toward graduate work the same approach is used when a dean of undergraduate studies is established. A third approach is the establishment of "divisions" within which departments with common interests (which may be the emphasis on graduate work more than the interrelatedness of their disciplines) are grouped together.

The limited success achieved by these solutions makes patent one distressing conclusion. The problem of the department will not be met until there is "further understanding of the department as a type of organization," until "a theory of department" has been developed.[8]

REESTABLISHING COMMUNITY

The societal change to which the college and university were exposed during the 1950s and 1960s wrought a grievous loss—the sense of community that tended to weld the institution into an effective organization.[9] The essentiality of a sense of community is not unique to the college or university.[10] It is an ingredient essential to the effectiveness of the corporate, the religious, the military, and the professional organi-

---

[7] Ikenberry, op. cit.

[8] William H. Faricy, "Grouping Departments," *Journal of Higher Education,* February 1974, p. 110.

[9] Warren Bennis spelled out this loss ("The University Leader," *Saturday Review—Education,* January 1973, p. 44) in these words: "Today, the faculty, once unified by a common definition of the nature and purposes of scholarship, is fragmented into competing professional citadels. Many have shifted their concern from the intellectual and moral content of education to privilege and ritual.

"Students in the multiversity find very little real personal contact or summoning call of the spirit. . . . Alumni, too, are estranged; many of the older are outraged by the weird sea changes of the campus they remember, while the younger feel no affectionate bond for the institution. And the greatest loss of community, the greatest estrangement, is among the general public—the citizens and parents and their mirror images in legislatures and Congress—on whom the very life of public institutions depends and who are no longer at all sure it is life worth saving."

[10] See, for example, the discussion by Chester Barnard in *The Functions of the Executive* (Cambridge, Mass.: Harvard University Press, 1950), pp. 89–91, of the large and central importance of communication in enabling an organization to achieve a common purpose.

zation.[11] It is the social cement that holds disparate groups together in striving to achieve a common purpose.

If one considers the assertion made earlier in Chapter 12 that "the administration of colleges and universities should be viewed as a continuum in which trustees and professors, presidents, deans, and department chairpersons, students, and alumni have interrelated and mutually responsible parts to play," the especial difficulties of maintaining a sense of community become apparent. The "efficiency of an organization," i.e., its effectiveness in carrying out the function for which it was created, is directly related to its effectiveness in securing the complementary personal contributions of all those who make up the organization. In the college and the university those whose contributions are required have various degrees of attachment to the institution (i.e., for the trustees and alumni, a "part-time" or relatively remote attachment; the students, a transitory attachment; the administrative staffs, a relatively permanent and substantial attachment; and the faculty, an attachment that is in continuing competition with their attachment to their individual disciplines). (See discussion in Chapter 4.) Those who are truly central to the functioning of the institution, the members of the faculty, in addition demand a large degree of "self-determination": the right and opportunity "to spend one's time and energy and mind upon whatever seems to him most intriguing and exciting; not to be directed by what some client or customer may request, or by what some absentee bureaucrat is willing to support."[12] In this, faculty members have long claimed a right that a growing number of professionally trained employees of business enterprises and governmental agencies are asserting with increasing frequency.

A number of colleges and universities, forced by events on their campuses during recent years to recognize the obvious loss of a sense of community, have been establishing mechanisms that would interrelate and regain the allegiance of their various constituencies, build fuller agreement on function and values,[13] and bring about acceptance

---

11 Irwin T. Sanders, "The University as a Community," in James A. Perkins, ed., *The University as an Organization,* (New York: McGraw-Hill Book Company, 1973), chap. 4, pp. 57–78.

12 Inaugural address of Kingman Brewster, as president of Yale University in 1964.

13 Robert Nisbet has enumerated six elements integral to the existence of a sense of community within an organization: (1) a function to be achieved, (2) a transcending agreement as to values, (3) the recognition of authority founded in consensus, (4) an apparent functioning hierarchy, (5) a sense of solidarity, and (6) "a striking sense of not merely distance from the surrounding world, but of superiority to it" (*The Degradation of the Academic Dogma,* pp. 43–45).

of authority. Students have been named to committees to sit with faculty members, administrators, and others in formulating decisions on a broad variety of questions. Faculty members have been invited to serve on a variety of administrative and trustee committees. In a few institutions (e.g., the universities of Minnesota, New Hampshire, Pennsylvania State, Columbia, and Princeton) new councils, senates, or assemblies have been established to bring together regularly representatives of the constituencies that share power in the university to discuss issues requiring decision, to confront each other with their respective views, and to offer the trustees and president advice.[14]

Underlying establishment of such forums is recognition that the college or university is a "political community," i.e., it is made up of competing constituencies, each of which possesses parochial views and the power to advance or to disrupt the institution's operations,[15] and as a whole it lacks central and unchallenged authority. Decisions that will stick (i.e., that will harness the individual's zeal or at least gain his acceptance) can only be made through a process in which the several constituencies are consulted and given an opportunity to voice their opinions and exercise an influence commensurate with the competence or concern they bring to each particular decision.[16]

Such mechanisms have proved beneficial. They are helpful when they take out of the president's office the interaction between students and faculty, between faculty and administration, and between students and administration. But such mechanisms remain to be polished and perfected. Answers must be hammered out to such questions as these:

---

[14] A useful summary of the powers, composition, members, and methods of operation of such councils in a number of universities is presented as appendix C in the report of the Carnegie Commission on Higher Education, *Governance of Higher Education* (New York: McGraw-Hill Book Company, April 1973), pp. 133–200. See also David D. Dill, *Case Studies in University Governance* (Washington: National Association of State Universities and Land Grant Colleges, 1971), pp. 147–154.

[15] Daniel Bell put this thought in other terms when he wrote ("Quo Warranto," in *Power and Authority*, p. 71): "Clearly the university must become, more formally, a political community. The making of policy decisions must be open, subject to debate, and to some form of confirmation by the relevant constituencies in the university. There are, it seems to me, three major areas which require exploration: (1) The structure of representation, . . . (2) The relevant constituencies, . . . (3) The division of powers." Charles E. Lindblom provides a fascinating description of functioning in "Yale as a Political System," *Yale Alumni Journal*, 1972.

[16] Robert E. Helsabeck (*The Compound System*, Center for Research and Development in Higher Education, University of California, Berkeley, 1973) offers a theoretical analysis of participation in institutional decision making and identifies three dimensions of participation. See especially chap. 3, "Summary Propositions."

1. Who shall be represented on such a council, senate, or assembly? Shall the librarians or the teaching assistants, for example, serve on the executive committee? Logic dictates that all who have a significant impact on the educational functioning of the institution, all whose continuing allegiance is needed, should be represented.

2. How and in what proportion shall each faction be represented?[17] A decision on this point must reflect the relative numbers, status, and power of the various factions within the institution. It is consensus among all members of the community that is sought. Representation must be designed to provide the prospect of consensus.

3. What authority shall the council, senate, or assembly have? That is, what range of issues will it be authorized to consider and what weight will its decisions have? Decision making for the institution of higher education must involve widespread consultation, but in addition, the president and trustees must be free to act promptly as circumstances require. These considerations dictate that the council, senate, or assembly consider a broad range of academic, financial, and other questions of concern to the whole community, and particularly should consider the annual budget and whatever institutional plans are formulated. The council should have access to full information. It should be expected to formulate conclusions regularly, and it should be clear that such conclusions are *not* governing decisions but are developed as advice for the president and trustees.

A SUMMARY

The eventual test of the system of governance that obtains in our colleges and universities lies in its capacity progressively to adapt and develop educational programs as knowledge accumulates, as student bodies expand and change, and as the needs of the society change, while eliciting the participation of its several constituencies and maintaining a climate of rationality. The system of governance's organizational ar-

---

[17] The Yale Commission that considered the reorganization of governance procedures rejected the idea of an all-university representative assembly because ". . . an assembly of even as many as two hundred members which is as large as hopes for sustained discussion permit, is so small relative to the number of faculty, students, and staff it is designed to represent, that its members would be at a loss to know the opinions of constituents . . ." (Yale University Study Commission on Governance, *Final Report*, New Haven, Yale University, 1971, pp. 21–22).

rangements—structure and processes—inherited by our institutions of higher education have been proved unequal to the effectuation of educational advance when the institution is taxed by student unrest, the growing professionalism and independence of faculties, the pressure of minorities for equal educational opportunity, less abundant financial resources, and enveloping governmental controls.

No clear theory of governance has yet been propounded that specifies the structure suitable for all four-year colleges and universities. No pattern has been shaped that can be fitted to large and small institutions alike, to the unitary college and the multischool university, to the relatively independent private institution, and to the public institution that is a unit within a state system. But seven distinctive characteristics of the institution of higher education (each of which has been specified in preceding pages)[18] make patent certain directions in which the modernization of the structure and the distribution of authority to govern should proceed in all or most institutions.

1. The functions of the college, and particularly of the university, need to be narrowed and clarified.

These institutions have been called upon to assume responsibility for a variety of activities as the social importance of knowledge has become increasingly apparent. The need now is for (a) the "shucking off" by all institutions of those research and development activities and those services that are not integral to the learning process so that the core activity of higher education may be better performed and (b) the redefinition of the relative roles to be performed respectively by community colleges, liberal arts colleges, the comprehensive universities and colleges, and the doctoral-granting universities.

2. The independence of the individual institution—its intellectual and administrative independence—needs be reaffirmed.

Higher education has become too important and too integral to the functioning of the society to make possible the reestablishment of a much-treasured autonomy that probably existed more in fiction than in fact. But it is essential that broad-gauged political leadership that understands the distinctive nature of a college or university be devel-

---

[18] (1) The central position of the institution within the society, (2) its increasing subjection to governmental controls, (3) its unique relationship to the teachers who constitute its stock-in-trade, (4) its transitory and increasingly casual relationship with the students it enrolls, (5) the consequent diffusion of authority to govern, (6) the limited power that can (because of the characteristics cited) be granted to a president, and (7) the tenuous and limited involvement of most trustees in the affairs of the institution.

oped to effectively modify the forms and degree of intervention by both federal and state agencies. Particularly needed are guidelines to govern the activities of state coordinating boards of higher education that emphasize their responsibility for maximizing the vitality and the initiative of the individual institution.

3. Mechanisms for reestablishing a sense of community need be developed.

The common values that bound the small college of an earlier generation into a body of scholars cannot be duplicated in the much larger, multischool university. But mechanisms, commonly called "community councils" or "broadly based senates" are being created to permit the disparate constituencies—particularly the faculties, students, staffs, and administrators—to exchange views and to seek a consensus for the advice of the president and trustees. No ideal mechanism has yet been designed, but prototypes exist in sufficient number to offer promise that the structure will be found that can continually produce some of the social cement needed to hold the college or university together.

4. The concepts of primary and communal (or institutional) authority need be established.

No constituency can be granted exclusive and final authority for aspects of the institution's functioning. The college, and even more the university, is a community of professionals in which each individual and each constituency collaborates with other professionals in providing an inextricably interrelated service. The end objective is neither the conduct of a particular course, the provision of a major in a subject-matter area, the maintenance of a collection of books, or the formulation of the annual budget. It is the development of graduates who are informed and are capable of reading, communicating, and reasoning, and who possess values.

Each constituency can and should be given "primary authority" to formulate those policies and to take those actions for which its members have especial competence. Each constituency simultaneously has the right to voice its views as to any policy or any action which affects it and in which the constituency, or a member of the constituency, has a substantial concern. Responsibility for the exercise of "communal authority," i.e., for the review and final approval of policies which affect the society that supports the institution or which provoke conflicting views among its constituencies, rests with the institution's president and trustees. The exercise of communal authority by the president and trustees must be as final as the circumstances of the moment demand, but should result more often in a request for reconsideration of a controversial proposal rather than outright disapproval or the substitution of an alternative decision by the president or trustees.

Efficient management of a body of professionals—in a large law office, a business enterprise, or a university—involves more than the timeliness of action and the economy of expenditure. It involves as well the maintenance of the willingness of the group to collaborate.

> 5. *The primary authority of the faculty to formulate policies and to take actions with respect to "such fundamental areas as curricula, subject matter and methods of instruction, research, faculty status, and those aspects of student life which relate to the educational process"*[19] *needs be reaffirmed.*

That reaffirmation must specify the simultaneous responsibility of the president and trustees for the review of faculty proposals and for ensuring their relation to the basic objectives of the institution. The machinery for the exercise of faculty authority needs to be improved in many institutions, and particularly the understanding by trustees, administrators, and students of the rationale for the metes and bounds of faculty authority needs to be increased.

> 6. *The primary authority of students to formulate policies as to all social and extracurricular activities of the student body and their rights to a voice in most institutional decisions needs to be clearly established.*

Simultaneously, the ability of students to contribute meaningfully to some decisions relative to financial, operational, and academic affairs and the right to voice views on such matters needs be recognized.

> 7. *The obligation of the president to provide leadership for the college or university needs be more generally recognized. His freedom to act at all times, subject to the policies set by trustees and the advice offered by such mechanisms as exist for the voicing of the consensus of the community, needs to be reaffirmed.*

> 8. *Institutional boards of trustees should be preserved. In turn these boards should make greater and positive efforts to inform themselves as to each aspect of the functioning of the college or university for which they are responsible if they are to fulfill the responsibilities placed upon them by charter or by statute.*

---

[19] As stated in the *Statement on Government of Colleges and Universities* promulgated by the American Association of University Professors, 1966.

The responsibility of trustees is direction. This involves continual and comprehensive monitoring and surveillance of all activities of the college or university for which they have accepted responsibility. They should not involve themselves in the operations of the institution—as individuals or through committees or a board—but they must see to it that they have a sufficiently full and comprehensive flow of information that they may influence the character and the quality of the institution.

Progress in these directions will shape a system of governance adapted to the distinctive characteristics of the college or university that exists in the late 1970s. The resulting system of governance can be expected to mobilize the efforts of the vast variety of individuals—trustees, administrators, faculty, and students—that have enrolled in a collaborative effort to learn and advance learning.

Index